CONTEMPORARY GERMAN WRITERS

CHRISTOPH HEIN

Series Editor

Rhys W. Williams has been Professor of German and Head of the German Department at University of Wales Swansea since 1984. He has published extensively on the literature of German Expressionism and on the post-war novel. He is Director of the Centre for Contemporary German Literature at University of Wales Swansea.

CONTEMPORARY GERMAN WRITERS

Series Editor: Rhys W. Williams

CHRISTOPH HEIN

edited by

Bill Niven
and
David Clarke

CARDIFF
UNIVERSITY OF WALES PRESS
2000

© The Contributors, 2000

British Library Cataloguing-in-Publication Data
A catalogue record for this book is available from the British Library.

ISBN   0-7083-1614-X paperback
        0-7083-1650-6 hardback

All rights reserved. No part of this book may be reproduced, stored in a retrieval system, or transmitted, in any form or by any means, electronic, mechanical, photocopying, recording or otherwise, without clearance from the University of Wales Press, 6 Gwennyth Street, Cardiff, CF24 4YD, www.wales.ac.uk/press.

Cover design by Olwen Fowler.
Printed in Great Britain by Dinefwr Press, Llandybïe.

Contents

	page
List of contributors	vii
Preface	ix
Abbreviations	xi

1 Von den unabdingbaren Voraussetzungen beim Kleist-Lesen
  Christoph Hein 1

2 Christoph Hein: Outline Biography
  David Clarke 9

3 »Ich arbeite nicht in der Abteilung Prophet«: Gespräch mit Christoph Hein am 4. März 1998
  Bill Niven und David Clarke 14

4 Unvollständige Rekonstruktion: Über das Lektorat des Buches *Von allem Anfang an* von Christoph Hein
  Angela Drescher 25

5 Die versteinerten Verhältnisse zum Tanzen bringen? Der Autor Christoph Hein auf der Bühne
  Klaus Hammer 41

6 'Die Vergewaltigung [. . .] ist nicht das Thema meiner Erzählung': Rape and Female Identity in the Work of Christoph Hein
  Beth Linklater 62

7 'Spiele aus Notwehr': Re-reading Christoph Hein's Critique of the West in *Das Napoleon-Spiel*
  David Clarke 83

8 On Private Utopia and the Possessive Mentality: Christoph Hein's *Randow*
  Bill Niven 100

9 'Mehr Freiheit zur Wahrheit': The Fictionalization of Adolescent
   Experience in Christoph Hein's *Von allem Anfang an*
   Dennis Tate   117

10 Bibliography
   David Clarke and Bill Niven   135

Index   165

List of Contributors

David Clarke studied at the Universities of Leeds, London (University College) and Wales (Swansea), where he recently completed a Ph.D. on the prose fiction of Christoph Hein.

Angela Drescher has been a *Lektorin* at Aufbau-Verlag since 1974, where she has worked with numerous contemporary German writers, including Christoph Hein, Christa Wolf and Klaus Schlesinger. She has also edited volumes on Christa Wolf, Christa Wolf's correspondence with Franz Fühmann and Brigitte Reimann, as well as Brigitte Reimann's diaries.

Klaus Hammer is Professor of German literature at the *Technische Universität Dresden*. He has published widely on aspects of German literature of the eighteenth, nineteenth and twentieth centuries, and is also editor of *Chronist ohne Botschaft. Christoph Hein. Ein Arbeitsbuch* (1992).

Beth Linklater is Lecturer in German at the University of Wales Swansea. Her study *'Und immer zügelloser wird die Lust'. Constructions of Sexuality in East German Literatures. With Special Reference to Irmtraud Morgner and Gabriele Stötzer-Kachold* was published in 1998. Her recent research has focused on the reception of GDR literature in the academic community.

Bill Niven is Reader in German at The Nottingham Trent University, and is the author of a book on the reception of Friedrich Hebbel in Nazi Germany. In addition, he has published a range of articles on Christoph Hein, as well as on other aspects of twentieth-century German literature. He is currently writing a book on post-1990 representations of National Socialism in Germany.

Dennis Tate is Reader in German Studies at the University of Bath. He has published extensively on East German literature, including a monograph on Franz Fühmann (1995) and edited volumes on Günter de Bruyn (1999) and Heiner Müller (forthcoming 2000). He is now working on a study of autobiographical writing by GDR authors before and after unification.

Preface

Contemporary German Writers

Each volume of the Contemporary German Writers series is devoted to an author who has spent a period as Visiting Writer at the Centre for Contemporary German Literature in the Department of German at the University of Wales Swansea. The first chapter in each volume contains an original, previously unpublished piece by the writer concerned; the second consists of a biographical sketch, outlining the main events of the author's life and setting the works in context, particularly for the non-specialist or general reader. A third chapter will, in each case, contain an interview with the author, normally conducted during the writer's stay in Swansea. Subsequent chapters will contain contributions by invited British and German academics and critics on aspects of the writer's *œuvre*. While each volume will seek to provide both an overview of the author and some detailed analysis of individual works, the nature of that critical engagement will inevitably depend on the relative importance of the author concerned and on the amount of critical material which his or her work has previously inspired. Each volume includes an extensive bibliography designed to fill any gaps or remedy deficiencies in existing bibliographies. The intention is to produce in each case a book which will serve both as an introduction to the writer concerned and as a resource for specialists in contemporary German literature.

Christoph Hein

The current volume begins with the text of a speech given by Christoph Hein in the Kleist Theatre in Frankfurt (Oder) in November 1998. The speech demonstrates Hein's long-standing interest in the social and political reception of literature. In a thought-provoking analysis of the impact of Kleist's *Michael Kohlhaas*, Hein points out that this work is a standard school text in

Germany, yet could be understood as providing a negative role model in the rebellious figure of Kohlhaas (by contrast, Martin Walser, in his controversial speech in Frankfurt am Main in October 1998, had seen in another of Kleist's rebellious figures, the Prince of Homburg, a *positive* role model). Hein's speech is followed by a biographical sketch and an interview with Hein addressing both literary and political issues. There then follows a piece by his *Lektorin* at the Aufbau Verlag, Angela Drescher, who assisted Hein in preparing his most recent novel *Von allem Anfang an* for publication. Drescher's insights will prove invaluable for scholars interested in the genesis of the work. In Chapter Five, Klaus Hammer provides a comprehensive overview of Hein's literary oeuvre, focusing especially on his dramatic output. The remaining four articles by British Germanists concentrate on Hein's recent works, on which, to date, little has been written. But they also seek to place these works within the wider context of Hein's literary production and of works by other writers. Beth Linklater sheds new light on Hein's treatment of the theme of rape in the story *Die Vergewaltigung* (1990), and in earlier works such as the novella *Der fremde Freund* (1982). After examining Hein's play *Passage* (1986) and novel *Der Tangospieler* (1989), David Clarke argues that the much-criticized novel *Das Napoleon-Spiel* (1995) should be read as a fundamental critique of capitalism's lack of common values. Bill Niven contends that Hein's play *Randow* (1994) can also be understood as a comment on the divisiveness of capitalism, and in a sense as a sequel to *Die Ritter der Tafelrunde* (1990). Bringing the volume up-to-date, Dennis Tate explores the legitimacy of autobiographical readings of Hein's novel *Von allem Anfang an* (1997), which he sets in relation not just to the novel *Horns Ende* (1985), but also to a wide range of post-1990 autobiographical writing by a number of German authors. As in previous volumes, the final chapter comprises a detailed bibliography.

Editors' Note

The German contributions to this volume have been edited according to the rules of the 1996 German spelling reform. Quotations from, and references to, sources that predate the reform preserve the old spellings.

Abbreviations

Throughout the current volume, the quotations from primary texts by Christoph Hein, unless otherwise indicated, will be followed by one of the abbreviations listed below and the relevant page number(s) in parentheses. The editions referred to are those most widely available. In some cases these are the first editions, but where this is not so, the current Aufbau Taschenbuch versions of Hein's texts are used.

AK   *Als Kind habe ich Stalin gesehen* (Berlin, Aufbau, 1990)

Cr   *Cromwell und andere Stücke* (Berlin, Aufbau, 1981)

EK   *Exekution eines Kalbes und andere Erzählungen* (Berlin, Aufbau Taschenbuch, 1996)

fF   *Der fremde Freund. Novelle* (Berlin, Aufbau Taschenbuch, 1993)

HE   *Horns Ende. Roman* (Berlin, Aufbau Taschenbuch, 1994)

MJ   *Die Mauern von Jerichow. Essais und Reden* (Berlin, Aufbau Taschenbuch, 1996)

NfM   *Nachtfahrt und früher Morgen. Prosa* (Berlin, Aufbau Taschenbuch, 1994)

NS   *Das Napoleon-Spiel. Ein Roman* (Berlin, Aufbau Taschenbuch, 1995)

Öa   *Öffentlich arbeiten. Essais und Gespräche* (Berlin, Aufbau, 1987)

Rw   *Randow. Eine Komödie* (Berlin, Aufbau, 1994)

RT   *Die Ritter der Tafelrunde und andere Stücke* (Berlin, Aufbau, 1990)

Ts *Der Tangospieler. Erzählung* (Berlin, Aufbau Taschenbuch, 1995)

VA *Von allem Anfang an* (Berlin, Aufbau, 1997)

WK *Das Wildpferd unterm Kachelofen. Ein schönes dickes Buch von Jakob Borg und seinen Freunden*, illust. by Susanne Rotraut Berner (Weinheim, Beltz & Gelberg, 1990)

The following commonly cited volumes of secondary literature will also be referred to by abbreviations as listed below.

CB *Chronist ohne Botschaft. Christoph Hein. Ein Arbeitsbuch. Materialien, Auskünfte, Bibliographie*, ed. by Klaus Hammer (Berlin, Aufbau, 1992)

TDB *Christoph Hein. Texte, Daten, Bilder*, ed. by Lothar Baier (Frankfurt/M., Luchterhand, 1990)

TuK *Text und Kritik*, 111 (1991)

1

Von den unabdingbaren Voraussetzungen beim Kleist-Lesen

CHRISTOPH HEIN

Vor 25 Jahren reiste ich von Berlin nach Warschau, um dort eine Aufführung des *Prinzen von Homburg* zu sehen. Es war keine polnische, keine warschauer Inszenierung des Kleistschen Stücks, sondern das Gastspiel eines berliner Theaters. Den Zeitumständen war es geschuldet, dass ich, im Ostteil Berlins wohnend, diese Aufführung eines Theaters des westlichen Stadtteils nur sehen konnte, wenn sich jenes Theater und ich auf eine längere Reise begaben, länger als die berliner Stadtbahn dafür vorsieht. Es war den Zeitumständen geschuldet, sagte ich, und ich ahne, dass ich bereits in wenigen Jahren einiges mehr zu erklären hätte, denn diese Umstände waren so aussergewöhnlich, dass bereits die nächste Generation diesen Umstand ungläubig bestaunen und für nicht glaubhaft ansehen wird. So wie Mitte der 80er Jahre in dem geteilten Land und der geteilten Stadt eine Generation in Ost und West heranwuchs, der nicht mehr vorstellbar war, dass Land und Stadt anders geordnet und denkbar sein könnten als eben geteilt durch eine unüberwindliche, unveränderbare Grenze. Die gebrechliche Einrichtung der Welt ist nur erträglich, weil wir rasch vergessen und vergessen können, und weil es an Fantasie gebricht, uns eine andere Einrichtung vorzustellen als jene, in der wir leben, eine andere, die freilich ebenso fragil und fragwürdig wäre.

Ich fuhr nach Warschau, um den *Prinzen von Homburg* der gastspielenden westberliner Schaubühne zu sehen. Am Abend zuvor wurde das *Fegefeuer in Ingolstadt* der Marieluise Fleißer gegeben, und das warschauer Theaterpublikum feierte das Ensemble, begeistert von der Inszenierung, aber auch von dem Stück, das eine deutsche Kleinstadt auf die Bühne stellt, eine Kleinstadt mit der Freizügigkeit und geistigen Grösse einer Klosterschule, gezeichnet von der Disziplin, der Zucht und den Zwängen des Katholizismus und des Kleinbürgertums. Die Theatergänger des katholischen Warschaus waren fasziniert der Aufführung gefolgt.

Am folgenden Abend stand der *Prinz von Homburg* auf der Bühne, um sein Vergehen eines voreiligen und nicht befehlsgerechten Angriffs zu verteidigen und schliesslich willig zu akzeptieren, dass selbst ein Sieg nicht eine Disziplinlosigkeit entschuldigen oder gar aufheben könne. An diesem Abend fiel der Beifall knapp aus, das Publikum reagierte kühl, was umso auffälliger war, da diese Kleist-Aufführung keinesfalls der Inszenierung des Fleißer-Stückes nachstand und in den deutschen Zeitungen allerhöchstes Lob erhalten hatte.

Als ich mit meinen polnischen Freunden das Theater verliess, erkundigte ich mich nach dem Grund für die mir nicht erklärliche Reserviertheit des Publikums. Man sagte mir, das Stück sei in Polen kaum bekannt, werde nicht aufgeführt und gehöre daher auch nicht und anders als in Deutschland zum Repertoire des Theaters. Ich fragte weiter, da für mich die vorgebrachten Gründe selbst erklärungsbedürftig schienen, und einer der polnischen Bekannten, ein Professor der warschauer Universität und ein Sprachen- und Schriftgelehrter, sagte zu mir: Ach, weisst du, mein Freund, das Problem deines deutschen Homburgs, das hätten wir bei einem Gläschen Wodka geklärt.

Ist der *Prinz von Homburg* ein bizarr deutsches Stück, und Kleist offenkundig ein ausnehmend deutscher Autor? Von den Deutschen bewundert und geliebt, aber doch so deutsch, dass sie sich hinter der Grenze nur schwer Aufmerksamkeit verschaffen können? Immerhin, Kleists Kohlhaas hat sich weltweit einen Namen verschafft, und rüstige und originäre Nachkommen des Kohlhaas haben sich nicht nur im Mecklenburgischen gezeigt.

Goethe freilich tadelte Kleist und seinen Kohlhaas. Ihm missfiel, so jedenfalls wurde es uns überliefert, die nordische Schärfe des Hypochonders. »Es gehöre ein großer Geist des Widerspruches dazu, um einen so einzelnen Fall mit so durchgeführter, gründlicher Hypochondrie im Weltlaufe geltend zu machen«, habe Goethe zu der Novelle angemerkt. Er hätte die heiteren italienischen Novellen dagegengesetzt und in Erinnerung gebracht, »daß die heitersten jener Erzählungen ebenfalls einem trüben Zeitraume, wo die Pest regierte, ihr Dasein verdankten.«

Goethes Urteil mag korrekt überliefert sein, der Hypochonder und der Geist des Widerspruchs sind nicht zu leugnen wie auch nicht der Gegensatz zum heiteren Italien.

Dessenungeachtet bleibt Kleist uns nah und teuer, seine Stücke und die Prosa zählen wir zu den Meisterwerken deutscher Dichtkunst, trotz aller unbestreitbaren Hypochondrie. Vielleicht aber kennzeichnet Goethes Urteil weniger oder nur vermittelt die Kleistsche Dichtung als vielmehr den Charakter und die Mentalität der Deutschen, denen das Unschöne in der Natur, das Beängstigende, der Widerspruchsgeist, die nordische Schärfe des Hypochonders in seinen Werken darum so nah und lieb sind, weil sie sich in ihnen erkennen, sich in ihnen erfasst und gespiegelt sehen. Dann erklärt sich die Vorliebe der Deutschen für diesen Schriftsteller. Dann erscheint sein Selbstmord den Deutschen weniger schrecklich und ist ihnen letztlich nicht völlig unbegreifbar, sondern wird ein abschliessender, ein alles umfassender, vollendender Schluss dieser Dichtung und dieses Lebens.

»Vor kurzem habe ich auch den 'Kohlhaas' von Heinrich von Kleist gelesen«, schrieb der junge Heinrich Heine an einen Freund, »bin voller Bewundrung für den Verfasser, kann nicht genug bedauern, daß er sich totgeschossen, kann aber sehr gut begreifen, warum er es getan.«

Und dieses Urteil zu Kleist bleibt gültig, mit dieser Lesart wird der Dichter, werden seine Arbeiten künftig gelesen. Der Autor der Berliner Romantik wird nun zum klassischen Erbe der Deutschen gezählt, es werden Kleist-Kolloquien und -Festtage veranstaltet und Stätten des Gedenkens und der Forschungen zu Kleist eingerichtet. Kohlhaas und Homburg, sie sind uns nahe, sind uns wesensverwandt. Die Texte sind daher Schullektüre, denn sie scheinen uns geeignet, der Jugend etwas von der Eigenart der Deutschen zu vermitteln, von jenen Werten, die uns Deutschen wichtig sind.

»Die Schilderung der äußerlichen wie der innerlichen Vorgänge interessiert uns aufs höchste; wir stehen ganz auf Kohlhaas' Seite und freuen uns der Rache, die er nimmt. Sein Mut, sein Geschick, sein Verstand entzücken uns, seine Liebe zu Frau und Kind rührt uns, sein Rechtsgefühl und sein frommer Sinn erfüllen uns mit Bewunderung. Wie wir an Tell und dem Schweizer-Aufstand unsre Herzensfreude haben, so auch an diesem Kohlhaas [...] Kohlhaas bleibt Kohlhaas bis zuletzt, mutig, frei, hochherzig, ein Mann aus einem Guß.« So urteilte Theodor Fontane, und mögen wir Nachgeborenen auch dieses oder jenes Wort auswechseln, um die emphatische Wendung eines vergangenen Jahrhunderts heute kühler zu formulieren, sein Urteil entspricht unserem, ist geradezu gültige Auffassung. Noch immer und unverändert bewundern wir sein Rechtsgefühl, erfreuen uns an seiner Rache und bemühen uns, die Bewunderung für den Selbsthelfer unseren Kindern zu vermitteln. Dabei hatte Kleist unübersehbar und bereits in den ersten Zeilen der Novelle ein Urteil über seinen Helden gefällt, das – ungeachtet aller Zuneigung und Sympathie des Autors für seine Figur – bis zum bitteren Schluss der Geschichte Gültigkeit behält. »Das Rechtsgefühl aber«, schreibt Kleist, »machte ihn zum Räuber und Mörder.«

Rührt und entzückt uns ein Mörder? Begeistert uns die blutige, masslose Rache eines Räubers? Schätzen wir das Rechtsgefühl und bewundern wir den frommen Sinn eines Verbrechers? Ist uns ein Krimineller Vorbild, prägend für unsere Rechtsauffassung, für unsere Auffassung von Gerechtigkeit, Rechtsstaatlichkeit, von Recht und Unrecht?

Das alles wäre noch erklärlich, wenn sich der Mann in einem Unrechtsstaat sein Recht verschaffen müsste. Dann wäre es für uns eine Lektion in Sachen Mannesmut vor Königsthronen und Tyrannenmord. Aber diesen Gefallen erweist Kleist uns nicht. Seine Novelle spielt, wie das Ende ausweist, in einem Rechtsstaat, in dem schlussendlich alles Unrecht gesühnt wird und der betrogene Kohlhaas seine Pferde rechtsstaatlich zurückerhält, die zuvor – wie das rechtsstaatliche Gesetz es verlangt – dickgefüttert und ehrlich gemacht werden mussten. Ihm wurde schliesslich sein Recht, sogar doppeltes Recht. Er bekam, was ihm zustand: seine Pferde mussten zuvor ihm übergeben werden, danach sein Kopf dem Scharfrichter. Der uns als Vorbild gerühmte Räuber und Mörder mordete und raubte in einem Rechtsstaat. Er mordete und raubte, weil ihm in diesem Rechtsstaat von einem Junker ein Unrecht zugefügt wurde. Aber davor ist kein Staat, kein Gemeinwesen gefeit, auch kein Rechtsstaat. Auch in einem Rechtsstaat geschieht Unrecht, der Rechtsstaat zeichnet sich nur dadurch aus, dass er *post festum* das geschehene Unrecht zu sühnen sucht.

Gewiss, Kohlhaas kommt erst zu seinem Recht, nachdem er mit dem von ihm verübten Unrecht, mit Brandstiftung und Mord, die Rechtssprechung erzwingt. Aber auch in jedem Rechtsstaat wird nicht jedem Individuum Recht gesprochen, und schon gar nicht sein Recht. Nicht jedes Unrecht ist zu sühnen und zu tilgen, das Recht bleibt stets ein – verschiedentlich nicht einlösbares – Ideal. Ein Ziel, aufs innigste zu wünschen, aber nicht immer realisierbar.

Wäre es da nicht angebrachter, dem Goetheschen Verdikt über diesen Kleistschen Helden zu folgen und nicht noch dessen Geist der Hypochondrie und des Widerspruchs der Jugend als Vorbild hinzustellen? Wäre es für den Frieden der Gesellschaft und für den Landfrieden nicht förderlicher, dem historischen Luther zu folgen, der den historischen Kohlhase zum Nachgeben zu überreden suchte, zum Aufgeben?

Es wäre besser gewesen, schrieb Luther an Kohlhase, »die Rache nicht furzunehmen, dieweil dieselbe ohne Beschwerung des Gewissens nicht furgenommen werden mag [...] könnt Ihr das Recht nicht erlangen, so ist kein ander Rat da, denn Unrecht leiden [...] so rate ich, nehmet Friede an, wo er Euch werden kann, und leidet lieber an Gut und Ehre Schaden [...] Dazu helfe Euch Christus, unser Herr, Lehrer und Exempel aller Geduld und Helfer in Not. Amen.«

Ist nicht diese Aufforderung zu christlicher Geduld und Demut unserem Gemeinwesen und unserem Rechtsstaat förderlicher als das Beispiel Kohlhaas? Wenn wir in der Schule nicht allein für die Schule, sondern für das Leben etwas lernen, was für ein Beispiel wird uns mit dem Räuber und Mörder gegeben?

Aber die Deutschen setzten nicht nur unerschrocken auf dieses Exempel, sie schritten furchtlos weiter und schmückten geradezu tollkühn eine der höchsten Auszeichnungen, die in der Bundesrepublik vergeben werden, mit dem Namen jenes Mannes, nach dem seinerzeit als Mitglied einer kriminellen Vereinigung in Deutschland gefahndet wurde. Er war sogar ein führendes Mitglied, ein Meinungsmacher dieser kriminellen Vereinigung, die nicht nur aufrührerische Reden führte und ebensolche Flugblätter druckte und verbreitete, sondern sich auch mit Waffen versorgte. Jener Büchner, heute ein Heiliger der Literaturseminare und des deutschen Theaters, war Mitglied einer Vereinigung, die sich nach heutigem Sprachgebrauch als Armeefraktion bezeichnen würde.

Noch haben wir in dieser Welt keinen Rechtsstaat, der völlig frei ist von unauflösbaren Widersprüchen, die sich für das Individuum im Einzelfall als Unrecht konkretisieren. Die Demokratie, die Meinungsfreiheit, der Pluralismus, die Gleichheit, auch die Gleichheit der Rechte und Pflichten, alles findet Einschränkungen und Grenzen, die das Eigentum setzt. Wo ein Ding ist, kann ein anderes nicht sein, oder das eine muss das andere verdrangen.

Davon ausgenommen sind allein unsere Pflichten, denn diese sind kategorische Imperative, die sich in den Sphären der reinen und vernünftigen Vernunft nicht aneinander reiben müssen: sie haben dort genügend Platz, sich zu behaupten. Sind es jedoch tatsächlich uns zwingende und für uns unumgängliche Pflichten, werden wir, um keinen zu behindern, unserem Nächsten den Vortritt lassen und die Erfüllung unserer Pflicht aufschieben.

Aber unsere Rechte, da steckt der Teufel im Detail; in jenem Detail, das den Streit und den Juristen auf diese Welt brachten, und den Krieg und den Soldaten. Unser Recht trifft immerzu auf das Recht eines anderen, stösst sich an ihm und wird gestossen und holt sich blutige Beulen. Und wer so aus der Gemeinschaft gestossen wird oder nur vermeint, gestossen zu sein, wird – von einem Kohlhaas belehrt – wie ein Kohlhaas sagen: wer mir den Schutz der Gemeinschaft und der Gesetze versagt,»der stösst mich zu dem Wilden der Einöde hinaus; er gibt mir [...] die Keule, die mich selbst schützt, in die Hand.«

Was Medizin nicht heilt, wissen diese Selbsthelfer, heilt Eisen; was Eisen nicht heilt, heilt Feuer.

Mit diesen Texten, diesen Helden, diesen Leidenschaften füttern wir unsere Kinder und sind verwundert, wenn Samenkörner dieser Saat in ihnen aufgehen.

Jene Gruppe von Räubern und Mördern, die sich selbst Armeefraktion nannte und die Bundesrepublik bis aufs Blut reizte und sie bis zur Aufgabe rechtsstaatlicher Grundsätze herausforderte, sie waren ohne Zweifel Staatsfeinde. Für das, was sie für Recht hielten, waren sie wie Kohlhaas bereit, jene mit Mord und Feuer zu überziehen, die sie für schuldig hielten. Sie waren im Unrecht, ganz zweifellos, aber um zwei Pferde zumindest werden auch sie sich betrogen gesehen haben. Und ein Kohlhaas gehörte zu ihrer Sozialisation, zu ihrer Erziehung, zur Bildung ihres rechtsstaatlichen Gefühls und ihrer moralischen Auffassungen.»Wir stehen ganz auf Kohlhaas' Seite und freuen uns der Rache, die er nimmt«, schrieb Fontane. In diesem Stolz, mit dieser Freude und Bewunderung für sein Rechtsgefühl wurden wir erzogen. Spricht es da für oder gegen unsere Pädagogen, wenn sich bislang nur wenige der so Erzogenen an dem Selbsthelfer Kohlhaas ein Beispiel nahmen und Unrecht mit Mord und Brand auszulöschen suchten?

Hat eins mit dem anderen nichts zu tun? Wäre nicht in den Terroristenprozessen die Kleist-Lektüre, die Unterrichtung in der Bewunderung für das Kohlhaassche Rechtsgefühl, strafmindernd zu veranschlagen?

Von den unabdingbaren Voraussetzungen 7

Noch in der Klage der Eltern von Wolfgang Grams, der als Terrorist gesucht wurde und in Bad Kleinen ums Leben kam, ist ein Echo auf diesen Kohlhaas auszumachen. Sie verklagten den Staat auf Erstattung der Bestattungskosten, weil sie rechtlich keine andere Möglichkeit hatten, die Wahrheit über den Tod ihres Sohnes zu ermitteln und gerichtlich feststellen zu lassen. Aber die verklagte Exekutive, das Bundeskriminalamt, hatte die Beweise nur zum Teil gesammelt und aufbewahrt, andere beiseite gelassen oder vernichtet. Man hatte dem Toten die Hände gewaschen, ein Vorgang, der in einer christlich geprägten Gesellschaft in geradezu obszöner Weise an die Fusswaschung erinnert, der biblischen Geste der Huldigung und Unterwerfung. Aber diese Handwaschung diente lediglich der Spurenbeseitigung. Einen Mord, eine Hinrichtung konnte das Gericht nicht feststellen, da es die Zeugen für nicht glaubhaft ansah. Einen Selbstmord bezweifelte das Gericht freilich ebenso, denn zu tollkühn erschien ihm die Konstruktion, dass der verletzte Grams beim rückwärtigen Sturz auf das Gleis noch die gelassene Sicherheit aufbringt, sich einen Revolver an die Schläfe zu halten und abzudrücken.

Wenige Tage nach der Tötung von Grams auf dem Bahnhof von Bad Kleinen wurde der Generalbundesanwalt entlassen, trat der zuständige Innenminister zurück. Gleichzeitig liess die Exekutive mitteilen, bei dem Vorfall von Bad Kleinen sei nichts vorgefallen, nichts was eine Entlassung, einen Rücktritt erforderlich mache.

Diese Merkwürdigkeiten liessen die rechtsprechende Gewalt zögern. Schliesslich aber sagte das Gericht, die Beweislast dürfe nicht umgekehrt werden. Die Exekutive dürfe nicht genötigt werden, den Selbstmord von Wolfgang Grams zu beweisen, sondern der Nicht-Selbstmord, die Tötung durch Fremdverschulden, die behauptete Hinrichtung müsse von den Klägern, den Eltern, bewiesen werden. Die möglichen Beweise jedoch hatte das Bundeskriminalamt übersehen, nicht gesammelt, hinweggewaschen.

»›Heilloser und entsetzlicher Mann?‹ rief Luther [...] ›wer gab dir das Recht, den Junker von Tronka, in Verfolg eigenmächtiger Rechtsschlüsse, zu überfallen, und da du ihn auf seiner Burg nicht fandst mit Feuer und Schwert die ganze Gemeinschaft heimzusuchen, die ihn beschirmt?‹ Kohlhaas erwiderte: hochwürdiger Herr, niemand.«

Ist uns und unserer Gemeinschaft, unserem Staat dieser Luther nicht angemessener? Sollten die Pädagogen nicht eher Bewunderung für diese Rechtsauffassung der Jugend vermitteln, für

Luthers Vorstellung von Obrigkeit, Rechtsstaatlichkeit und Rechtsgefühl? (»So Ihr meines Rats begehret, wie Ihr schreibet, so rate ich, nehmet Friede an, wo er Euch werden kann, und leidet lieber an Gut und Ehre Schaden [...] Könnt Ihr das Recht nicht erlangen, so ist kein ander Rat da, denn Unrecht leiden.«) Ist sein altväterlicher Rat unserer Zeit nicht angemessener als das Kohlhaas'sche Exempel? Sollten wir nicht besser Luthers Rechtsgefühl bewundern und zu verbreiten suchen?

Sollten wir nicht, statt einem Räuber und Mörder nachzueifern und ihn der Jugend als mutigen, freien und hochherzigen Mann hinzustellen, den Hypochonder wahrnehmen und ihn aus unserer Gesellschaft verweisen, bevor wir solche Texte lesen und sie anderen, der nächsten Generation etwa, in die Hand geben?

Erst wenn unsere Zigarre nicht erlischt und wir keinen Tropfen Wein verschütten bei einem unverstellten Blick auf uns und das, was wir tun, sollten wir Kleist lesen. Um nicht erneut Legislative und Exekutive und schliesslich auch noch die Judikative in unsägliche Verlegenheit zu stürzen. Um des lieben Friedens willen, wie Luther sagte.

Anm. D. Hrsg.: Dieser Beitrag wurde am 16. Oktober 1998 als Eröffnungsrede bei den 8. Kleist-Festtagen (Frankfurter Kleist-Kolloquium) im Kleist-Theater in Frankfurt an der Oder gehalten.

2

Christoph Hein: Outline Biography[1]

DAVID CLARKE

1944   Christoph Hein was born on 8 April in Heinzendorf, Silesia (now Poland), into the family of a Protestant pastor. He was the third of six children.
1945   After the end of the war, Hein's family moved first to Thuringia, then to Saxony. Hein spent his childhood in Bad Düben, near Leipzig.
1958   Unable to study for his *Abitur* in the GDR because of his father's profession, Hein left for West Berlin to attend the *Evangelisches Gymnasium zum Grauen Kloster*.
1960   Hein's family moved to East Berlin.
1961   Hein was in Dresden when the Berlin Wall was built. Returning to East Berlin to discuss the situation with his family, he decided to remain in the GDR, and was thus unable to complete his *Abitur*. He then began an apprenticeship as a bookseller, working in a bookshop on the Alexanderplatz in East Berlin.
1964   Began to attend evening classes to finish his *Abitur*.
1965   Became an unpaid assistant to Benno Besson at the *Deutsches Theater* and wrote short articles for *Sonntag* and *Junge Welt*.
1966   Passed *Abitur*. Marriage to Christiane Zauleck. First son, Georg, born. Enrolled at the *Filmhochschule Potsdam-Babelsberg*, but was prevented from beginning his studies by the authorities. Attempted to begin his course in dramaturgy in Leipzig instead, but was barred by the Ministry of Culture. Worked as a waiter in Leipzig.
1967   Hein took factory work and, in September, was allowed to begin studying for a degree in philosophy at the University of Leipzig. Later changed course to study logic. Whilst a

	student in Leipzig, Hein was asked to co-operate with the Stasi, and was threatened with exmatriculation if he failed to comply. He refused, and told his fellow students about the encounter, but was allowed to continue his studies.
1970	Transferred to the Humboldt University in Berlin.
1971	Birth of second son, Jakob. Employed as a dramaturge under a two-year contract at the *Volksbühne* in Berlin, again working with Benno Besson.
1973	Became a *Hausautor* with a six-year contract at the *Volksbühne*.
1974	Première of two Hein plays, *Schlötel oder Was solls* and the short play for children *Vom hungrigen Hennecke*, as part of the *Volksbühne*'s 'Spektakel II' festival. Hein's translation of Racine's *Brittanicus* was also performed at the *Volksbühne* during the 1974/1975 season.
1976	*Vom hungrigen Hennecke* produced as a puppet play.
1978	Publication of *Cromwell* in the journal *Theater der Zeit*.
1979	Première of Hein's 'revue' *Die Geschäfte des Herrn John D.* in Neustrelitz. Fifteen productions of Hein plays cancelled. Benno Besson and other colleagues resigned from the *Volksbühne* over constant government interference, and Hein was also forced to leave. Hein began to make his living as a freelance writer.
1980	Premières of *Cromwell* in Cottbus, and *Lassalle fragt Herrn Herbert nach Sonja. Die Szene ein Salon* in Düsseldorf. Publication of *Einladung zum Lever Bourgeois* with the GDR's Aufbau-Verlag.
1981	*Cromwell und andere Stücke* published.
1982	Became a member of the *Schriftstellerverband der DDR*. Received the prestigious Heinrich Mann Prize from the *Akademie der Künste der DDR*, with Peter Hacks delivering the laudatio. Première of Hein's adaptation of J. M. R. Lenz's *Der neue Menoza oder Geschichte des Kumbanischen Prinzen Tandi* in Schwerin. Publication of West German version of *Einladung zum Lever Bourgeois*, under the title *Nachtfahrt und früher Morgen*, with Hoffmann & Campe. The novella *Der fremde Freund* published in the GDR.
1983	Première of *Die wahre Geschichte des Ah Q* at the *Deutsches Theater* in Berlin. Publication of *Der fremde Freund* by Luchterhand in West Germany under the title *Drachenblut*.

1984 Hein won the West Berlin *Literaturpreis des Verbandes deutscher Kritiker* for *Drachenblut*. GDR publication of *Das Wildpferd unterm Kachelofen*, a book for children. *Die wahre Geschichte des Ah Q. Stücke und Essays* published in West Germany.

1985 After two years of problems with GDR censors, and following the appearance of the West German edition, Hein's first novel, *Horns Ende*, was published in the GDR, but was largely ignored by the East German press.

1986 *Schlötel oder Was solls. Stücke und Essays* published in West Germany by Luchterhand. *Horns Ende* won the prize 'Der erste Roman' awarded by the *Neue literarische Gesellschaft* in Hamburg. Hein planned a trip to the USA, which was cancelled under pressure from the *Schriftstellerverband*.

1987 Publication of *Öffentlich arbeiten. Essais und Gespräche* by Aufbau. Two-month visit to the United States. Hein delivered his controversial speech attacking censorship in the GDR in one of the discussion groups at the Tenth Writers' Congress of the GDR. Consecutive premières of *Passage* in Essen, Zürich and Dresden.

1988 Publication of *Passage* in West Germany and in the GDR, where it appeared in a Henschel-Verlag volume with *Die wahre Geschichte des Ah Q*. *Passage* adapted as a film for East German television. Hein declared his support for four pupils expelled from the *Ossietzky-Schule* in Berlin because of their protests against militarization in the GDR.

1989 Received the GDR's Lessing Prize for drama. *Der Tangospieler* was published by Aufbau and Luchterhand. In March, at a meeting of the GDR PEN centre, Hein protested against the arrest of Vaclàv Havel in Czechoslovakia. Première of *Die Ritter der Tafelrunde* in Dresden, a play widely interpreted as an attack on the ageing leaders of the SED. This production was rehearsed without official permission, and was only saved from cancellation by the intervention of the Dresden SED chief, Hans Modrow. In October, performances were followed by political discussions between actors and the audience. During the summer, Hein took up a guest lectureship at the *Folkwang-Schule* in Essen. In September, he received the Stefan Andres Prize in Schweich an der Mosel, and criticized the official GDR version of history in a speech to the Berlin branch of the *Schriftstellerverband*. Following police brutality towards anti-government protestors in Berlin between 7 and 9 October, Hein sat as a member of an independent inquiry. During the autumn, Hein gave numerous speeches and interviews calling for democratization in the GDR, including a short address to the famous Alexanderplatz demonstration on 4 November. In December, he delivered a laudatio for Max Frisch on Frisch's receipt of the Heinrich Heine Prize in Düsseldorf.

1990 Publication of *Die Ritter der Tafelrunde und andere Stücke* and *Als Kind habe ich Stalin gesehen* with Aufbau. Luchterhand published a West German version of the latter book as *Die fünfte Grundrechenart* and the play *Ritter der Tafelrunde* as a separate volume. Publication of the story *Bridge freezes before Roadway*. The Dresden production of *Die Ritter der Tafelrunde* televised by ZDF/ORF. Hein received the first Erich Fried Prize in May (laudatio held by Hans Mayer), and (in June and July respectively) was elected to both the West and East Berlin *Akademie der Künste*. In October, a television film version of *Die Ritter der Tafelrunde* was broadcast.

1991 On 13 February, Hein's protest against the Gulf War ('Kein Krieg ist heilig, kein Krieg ist gerecht') was read on almost every stage in Berlin. Première of the film version of *Der Tangospieler* (dir. Roland Graf). Hein received the *Ehrenpreis des Deutschen Kulturpreises* in Dresden. In December, *Der Spiegel* published an essay by Hein attacking racist violence in Germany, and Hein was elected as a member of the newly unified *Berliner Akademie der Künste*.

1992 In March, Hein joined the board of directors at the weekly newspaper *Freitag*, and received one of the Berlin Literature Prizes awarded by the *Stiftung Preußische Seehandlung*. In July, he received the Ludwig Mühlheim Prize for *Die Ritter der Tafelrunde*. He suffered a stroke in Frankfurt, and was forced to enter into a long period of recuperation.

1993 Hein's novel *Das Napoleon-Spiel* published.

1994 Hein published *Exekution eines Kalbes und andere Erzählungen*, a collection of texts written between 1977 and 1990, and gave the opening speech at the Frankfurt Book Fair. In December, *Randow* premièred in Dresden.

1996	Hein became involved in the controversy over the future of the East and West German PEN centres, and called for their speedy unification.
1997	Publication of *Von allem Anfang an*.
1998	In March, Hein visited the Centre for Contemporary German Literature in Swansea. He was awarded the *Peter-Weiss-Preis* in August by the city of Bochum. In October, he was made president of the newly unified German PEN centre.
1999	Première of *Bruch* in Düsseldorf. Première of *In Acht und Bann*, a one-act sequel to *Die Ritter der Tafelrunde*, commissioned as part of a programme under the title 'Deutschland zehn Jahre nach dem Mauerfall' at the *Deutsches Nationaltheater* in Weimar. The radio play *Zaungäste* was broadcast by MDR and received the *Hörspielpreis der Stiftung Kulturpflege und Kulturförderung der Sparkasse Neuss*. Hein publicly criticized the NATO bombing of Serbia.

Notes

[1] Some of the biographical details given here are also to be found in *CB*, 263–7, and Phillip McKnight, *Understanding Christoph Hein* (Columbia, University of South Carolina Press, 1995), xiii–xvi.

3
»Ich arbeite nicht in der Abteilung Prophet«: Gespräch mit Christoph Hein am 4. März 1998

BILL NIVEN UND DAVID CLARKE

DC: Herr Hein, als Sohn eines protestantischen Pfarrers geboren, wurden Sie vom Besuch der Oberschule in der DDR ausgeschlossen. Sie haben die Spannung zwischen zwei Weltsichten, zwischen Christentum und Marxismus-Leninismus, sehr früh erlebt, wie die Hauptfigur Daniel in Ihrem neuen Roman *Von allem Anfang an*. Was für einen Einfluss hat dieses Erlebnis auf ihre frühe intellektuelle und künstlerische Entwicklung gehabt?

CH: Das war damals nicht die Spannung zwischen Weltsichten. Dazu war ich zu jung. Und das begann eigentlich früher, nicht erst mit dreizehn, vierzehn Jahren, sondern schon in den Jahren der Grundschule in Sachsen. Da war ich natürlich auch Sohn dieses Pfarrers und insofern missliebig. Es gab immer dieses Problem, und es stand relativ früh fest, dass ich nicht weiter zur Schule gehen darf. Aber das war für mich, als Zehn-, Zwölf-, Dreizehnjährigen, weniger ein philosophisch-weltanschauliches Problem, als eine Alltagsrealität, die ich sehr viel privater nahm und nicht in diesen politischen Dimensionen wahrgenommen habe.

DC: Das trifft auch für Daniel zu.

CH: Das ist in jeder Geschichte so, die politische Dimensionen hat, dass Kinder sich anders zurechtfinden, ganz gleich in welcher Gesellschaft, in welcher Zeit. Kinder nehmen das anders, auch einfacher, und versuchen sich darin zu bewegen. Sie sind ideologisch nicht verfestigt, sie haben kaum Grundsätze, oder eigentlich keine Grundsätze. Sie versuchen mit ihren Freunden und vielleicht auch mit den Mädchen klarzukommen, und sie versuchen der Gruppe gerecht zu werden, oder sich von ihr abzusetzen. Das ist, glaube ich, viel entscheidender als philosophisch-weltanschauliche Grundsätze, die für die Erwachsenen wichtig sind.

BN: Ist *Von allem Anfang an* stärker autobiographisch als Ihre anderen Romane?

CH: Das ist nicht meine Geschichte, von dem Jungen. Ich habe wie bei jedem Buch meine Biographie genutzt, wie einen Steinbruch, und dann ist alles mögliche dazugekommen, aber letztlich ist es ein Roman, der nur damit spielt, mit Versatzstücken, wie in jeder anderen Geschichte. Es gibt eine große Nähe zur Biographie, aber eine Identität gibt es nicht. Aber es half natürlich, dass man ein bisschen in einer vergleichbaren Situation drinsteckte.

BN: Ist das Buch nicht doch stärker autobiographisch? Sie haben in Zusammenhang damit den Ausdruck »fiktive Autobiographie« benutzt.

CH: Jeder Autor arbeitet mit seiner Biographie, und wenn wir die Gesamtheit seiner Arbeit vorliegen haben, dann haben wir auch ein ziemlich gutes Bild vom Autor. Das einzelne Werk ist nicht identisch mit ihm, es ist nicht Autobiographie, aber wenn ich die Gesamtheit der Schriften von Hemingway oder Franz Kafka kenne, dann kenne ich genau den Burschen auch, der es geschrieben hat. Das ist es, was ich mit fiktiver Autobiographie meinte. *Das Napoleon-Spiel* ist genauso nah. Das schließt sich direkt nach *Von allem Anfang an* an. Ich wurde gefragt, ob ich irgendwann eine Fortsetzung schreibe. Aber die Fortsetzung gibt es schon – das ist *Das Napoleon-Spiel*. Die äußeren Punkte sind wahrscheinlich schwieriger erkennbar, aber von der inneren, fiktiven Autobiographie ist das nicht anders.

DC: Ist das für Sie ein Muss beim Schreiben? Dieses autobiographische Element?

CH: Es hilft. Ich muss dann aufhören zu arbeiten, wenn ich überhaupt keinen Zugang habe. Es gab Stoffe, die mich sehr interessiert haben, zum Beispiel zeitgeschichtliche, wo ich aber in die Figur nicht reinkam. Es gab vor etwa zehn, zwölf Jahren in Sachsen eine Jugendgruppe, die ganz sinnlos Gewalt ausübte. Sie schlug Leute zusammen ohne jede Begründung. Das hatte mich sehr interessiert, weil ich annahm, dass es für diese Gesellschaft und Zeit etwas ausdrückt. Aber ich musste es aufgeben, weil ich merkte, ich kann das nicht zu meiner Geschichte machen, und die Kinder oder Jugendlichen zu verurteilen, dafür ist Literatur nicht da. Es würde mich langweilen. Ich konnte sie nicht zu mir heranziehen; es blieb so eine Distanz, und da konnte ich nicht schreiben. Nach dem *Fremden Freund* gab es relativ viel Erstaunen darüber, dass ein Mann so etwas beschreiben kann. Ich habe versucht, es zu erklären: ich habe das alles beschrieben, soweit ich es auch erleben, erfahren, sehen kann; ich habe versucht, so viel von mir wie möglich in dieser Frau zu sehen und zu entdecken. Und da, wo es nicht weiterging, hörte ich auf. Eine Abtreibung kann ich als Operationserfahrung beschreiben, aber wo es über die Operationserfahrung hinausgehen muss, höre ich auf zu erzählen, spreche nicht weiter.

BN: Bei meinen Studenten merke ich, dass einige mit starker emotioneller Ablehnung auf den *Fremden Freund* reagieren, während andere zum Nachdenken angeregt werden. Sie stellen sogar Ähnlichkeiten zu ihrem eigenen Leben fest.

CH: In Deutschland merkte ich eine Besonderheit – wobei Ost und West ziemlich ähnlich reagierten –, dass diejenigen, die heftig darauf reagierten, dafür oder dagegen, immer jünger wurden. Ich hatte zum Schluss auch Vierzehnjährige, die sagten, »die Frau macht es richtig, genau so muss man es machen« – sie nahmen das geradezu als Anleitung zum Handeln. So muss man sein, also kühl, kalt, Ellbogen ausfahren, Fäuste hoch, keinen ranlassen. Das fand ich doch sehr erschreckend. In meiner Generation waren wir ganz anders mit vierzehn, wir hatten noch sehr viele Illusionen. Diese Vierzehnjährigen dagegen wissen, man braucht sie nicht mehr. Sie werden wahrscheinlich keine Lehrstelle kriegen, studieren ja, aber danach Schluss, nach dem Studium Taxifahrer. Als wir so alt waren, hatten wir eher die Haltung, es ist schwierig, aber ich schaffe es. Das entsprach auch der Situation. Damals wurde ein Großteil noch gebraucht, heute wird eigentlich diese ganze Generation nicht mehr gebraucht.

Vorgestern, bevor ich hierher kam, erzählte mir jemand von einem Großbetrieb, wo eine Position ausgeschrieben wurde. Es gab achthundert Bewerbungen. Er ging mit ihnen zu dem Chef und sagte, es gibt achthundert Bewerbungen, und da antwortete der

Chef,»wir machen die Sache einfach, nehmen Sie mal alle Frauen raus«, und da wurden von den achthundert fünfhundert Karten weggeschmissen. Weil eine Frau schwanger wird, usw. Es blieben nur noch dreihundert Männer. Es ist natürlich verboten, aber wenn er sich beschwert, fliegt er auch. Und das wissen diese Vierzehnjährigen auch, dass sie mit einem Kind sich und ihre Position gefährden. Dann wird diese dicke Haut auf einmal, anders als für mich, eher ein Ideal als ein Schrecken. Wenn ich nicht so bin, habe ich gar keine Chancen. Das ist neu; das habe ich, als ich es geschrieben habe, so nicht gesehen.

DC: Sie haben Ende der 70er Jahre gesagt, die Situation der Dramatiker in der DDR sei »ein Schreibanlass für Prosa«. Seit der Wende aber veröffentlichen Sie vorwiegend Romane und Erzählungen. Ist die Theaterszene im wiedervereinigten Deutschland noch schlechter als in der DDR, oder einfach nicht besser?

CH: Die Theaterszene in der DDR war sehr schwierig. Es gab eindeutig eine verschiedene Aufmerksamkeit der Zensur für die verschiedenen Genres der Literatur. Theater und Film wurden besonders scharf, Videorecorder am wenigsten kontrolliert. Ich glaube, es hing mit der Art der Konsumierung zusammen. Lyrik erreicht einen kleineren Interessentenkreis. Man liest Gedichte einzeln und allein, während es im Kino und Theater eine gewisse »Zusammenrottung« von Menschen gibt, und die Zensur fürchtete dann wahrscheinlich irgendwelche politischen Folgen von Aufführungen irgendwelcher Stücke. Die Zensur war in der DDR beim Film und beim Theater viel durchgreifender als in der Prosa.

Dass ich aber anfing, wegen der Zensur Prosa zu schreiben, das war nur eine Koketterie von mir, das war nicht der Grund. Angefangen hatte ich vollends aus Interesse. Es interessierte mich nebenbei Prosa zu schreiben, und der Wechsel zwischen Dramatik und Prosa war sehr angenehm. Jedes Genre eröffnet ein paar Möglichkeiten (formalistisch, ästhetisch), die sich bei einem anderen Genre verbieten. Wenn ich längere Zeit in einem Genre gearbeitet habe, dann gibt es auch eine Sehnsucht nach dem anderen. Ich sitze jetzt wieder an Dramatik, auch noch für längere Zeit, und nach dieser längeren Zeit werde ich wieder mit Prosa beginnen. Es hat für mich was Anregendes. Ich beneide daher auch die Kollegen, die noch in ganz anderen Künsten arbeiten. Es gibt ja Schriftsteller, die gleichzeitig Maler sind.

DC: In Ihren Theaterstücken aus den 70er und 80er Jahren beschreiben Sie immer wieder das Scheitern der Revolution. Sie bleiben aber eher optimistisch, dass die Menschen eine gerechtere Gesellschaft schaffen werden. Wie sehen Sie den Weg zu dieser Gesellschaft, wenn nicht revolutionär?

CH: Das weiß ich nicht. Sie fragen so, als ob Revolution an sich ein Wert ist. Ich denke eher, dass Revolution nur ein Mittel ist, womit eine Gesellschaft etwas erreichen will, was sie auf einem anderen Weg nicht erreichen kann, etwa durch Evolution, weil evolutionäre Mittel eben einen begrenzten Radius haben. Aber einen Wert für sich haben Revolutionen meines Erachtens nicht. Ich bin nicht sicher, was sie erreichen können. Ich bin kein Gesellschaftstheoretiker, schon gar kein Prognostiker. Ich arbeite nicht in der Abteilung Prophet, sondern eher in dieser anderen Abteilung: Chronisten. Ich beschreibe das, was ist, nicht das, was kommen wird. Davon habe ich keine Ahnung.

Ich nahm mit Erschrecken zur Kenntnis, was passierte, nachdem der Ostblock zusammenbrach, nämlich dass auf einmal der Wettbewerb aufhörte – und der Wettbewerb ist ein sehr befruchtendes Moment für den Kapitalismus. In dem Moment, wo der Wettbewerb wegbricht, hört diese Art von Lebenshilfe für den Kapitalismus auf. Auf einmal wird er etwas faul und träge und dumm. Die Dummheit irritiert etwas. Er hat über die ganzen Jahre, wo es diese Bedrohung durch den Sozialismus gab, sehr schlau und klug gehandelt. Und auf einmal arbeitet er nur noch, als ob Profit das Einzige sei, und opfert sein strategisches Vermögen, das den Kapitalismus zu enormen Leistungen befähigte.

BN: Sie haben 1990 geschrieben, dass mit dem Ende des Sozialismus der Kapitalismus seine bunteren Farben wird ablegen können. Ich habe das damals für eine Übertreibung gehalten, aber im nachhinein glaube ich, dass Sie recht hatten. Sind Sie der Meinung, dass der soziale Teil der Marktwirtschaft zurückgefahren wird?

CH: Ja. Das war besonders deutlich erkennbar in Berlin, einst Schaufenster der freien Welt, Schaufenster der sozialistischen Welt. Ich denke, in beide Teilstaaten Deutschlands haben die jeweiligen Bündnispartner viel reingesteckt. Die beiden Systeme wollten zeigen, wie gut sie sind. Und das brauchte man schlagartig nicht mehr. Die ersten Opfer waren Westdeutschland und Westberlin. Nach 1989 wurden die ganzen Hilfen gestrichen, diese Berlin-Hilfe, Zonenrandhilfe, auch die antikommunistischen Zeitungen und Zeitschriften. Das ging sehr rabiat. Und das Soziale natürlich auch. Das gehörte zum Schaufenster dazu, dass man es eben zeigte, dass selbst bei Arbeitslosigkeit es keine Probleme für die Gesellschaft gibt.

DC: In Ihrem Stück *Randow* haben Sie die Situation im wiedervereinigten Deutschland beschrieben. Die Hauptfigur ist eine Künstlerin, Anna Andress. Sie ist ehemalige DDR-Malerin, war damals politisch engagiert, aber jetzt nach der »Wende« geht es ihr nur um das rein Ästhetische. Können Sie als Schriftsteller diese Position nachvollziehen, dass man sich zurückzieht und sagt, ich kümmere mich nicht um die Politik?

CH: Die Frage kommt für mich ein bisschen überraschend, weil ich sie mir beim Arbeiten nicht gestellt habe. Ich glaube, es gehört mit zum Intellektuellen dazu, in Europa, sich zu äußern. Der Schriftsteller ist unter anderem auch ein Intellektueller, und hat insofern diese Pflicht. Aber es ist, glaube ich, nicht *a priori* eine Pflicht für den Schriftsteller, sich zum Politischen zu äußern. Wir sind alle verschiedene Personen in einer Person, wir sind u. a. auch Intellektuelle mit einem politischen Bewusstsein, die mit wachen Augen die Zeitung lesen, und sich in der Welt umtun. Aber nicht nur. Ich denke, als Intellektueller habe ich, hat jedes *zoon politikon*, die Aufgabepflicht sich zu äußern, nicht unbedingt als Schriftsteller.

BN: Noch eine Frage zu Anna Andress. DC hat gesagt, dass sie sich ins Ästhetische zurückzieht. Könnte es aber auch sein, dass sie versucht, ihr Recht auf das Ästhetische, auf das Privatleben zu verteidigen, und dass dieses Recht ihr im neuen Deutschland genauso wie in der DDR genommen wird? Sehe ich das falsch?

CH: Nein, das denke ich auch.

DC: Ich habe vor allem an diese Szene gedacht, wo sie ein Porträt von dem Jäger Kowalski macht, von diesem brutalen Menschen, aber sie interessiert sich für ihn gar nicht als politische Person oder als gesellschaftliche Person, sondern nur für die Form seines Kopfes.

CH: Das kenne ich von bildenden Künstlern, dieses unheimliche Verliebtsein in irgendwelche Formen. Ich verstehe, dass es dann nebensächlich ist, was er politisch für eine Figur ist – auch wenn er der schlimmste Gewaltverbrecher ist! Als Oppenheimer nach dem Atombomben-Abwurf gefragt wurde, ob er bereit sei, auch an der Wasserstoffbombe mitzuarbeiten, sagte er, es sei »technically sweet«, sie zu bauen. Das muss ein unheimlicher Anreiz gewesen sein, und der Gedanke, ob das böse ist, oder verboten sein sollte, das ist eine andere Ebene. Es ist sehr gefährlich, das nicht zu sehen – gar keine Frage. Aber dass es so etwas gibt, ist auch klar. Es gibt ein Erwachen für jeden von uns. Wir machen eine Sache und erst am Tag danach sehen wir, es gehört eine andere Seite dazu, die wir übersehen haben, weil es »technisch süß« war, sie zu machen.

BN: Bei *Randow* habe ich den Eindruck, Sie wollen auf Kontinuitäten hinweisen. In einem Aufsatz von 1992 haben Sie von einer Mauer aus Geld geschrieben, die die frühere Mauer quasi ersetzt hat, und in *Randow* gibt es so etwas wie eine Mauer gegen die Asylsuchenden. Sehen Sie da gewisse Kontinuitäten in der deutschen Geschichte?

CH: Ja, die Kontinuität ist da, nicht bei mir, ich reagiere nur darauf. Inwieweit sie nur auf die Deutschen beschränkt ist, weiß ich nicht genau. Es gibt ein heftiges Bestreben, diese Mauern wieder aufzurichten. Z. Z. wird Polen dafür bezahlt, eine Mauer zu errichten. Die Polen sind dafür zuständig, dass aus Asien nichts hereinkommt. Das, was an der deutsch-polnischen Grenze passiert, soll verlagert werden in Richtung Polen. Nach dem Schengener Abkommen ist jeder Außenstaat verpflichtet, die Grenze für den Rest Europas zuzumachen. Also, die Mauer wird jetzt woanders hingestellt. Die tatsächliche Berliner Mauer war für Westeuropa ganz angenehm. Das war natürlich ein enormer Schutz, der auf einmal weggefallen ist. Es gab in den Verhältnissen beider deutscher Staaten mehrere kritische Punkte – ein kritischer Punkt war auch, dass aus dem Iran sehr viele Leute über Schönefeld einflogen und nach Westberlin gingen. Da konnte sich Westberlin nicht wehren, weil die Mauer eine Ostsache war und Westberlin keinen eigenen Grenzschutz hatte, nicht in dem Maße. Ost-Berlin ließ sie alle rüber. Damals hat die Bundesrepublik sehr heftig protestiert und verlangt, dass die Mauer dichtgemacht wird. Das klingt komisch, weil es ihnen sonst immer darum ging, dass die Mauer weg soll. Aber zu bestimmten Zeiten braucht man eine Mauer. Gegenwärtig brauchen wir nach dem Schengener Abkommen eine. Das ist die hohe Kunst: Wie baue ich eine Mauer, ohne dass es wie eine Mauer aussieht.

BN: Wie sehen Sie die Entwicklung in der ehemaligen DDR? Man liest immer wieder, dass der ganze Prozess vom Westen gesteuert wird, der mehr an der Durchsetzung des Antikommunismus als an der Vergangenheitsbewältigung interessiert ist.

CH: Aufgearbeitet wird die Vergangenheit ganz sicher nicht, das haben wir nie geschafft. Nicht einmal die Vergangenheit von 1870/1871 wurde aufgearbeitet, geschweige denn die der Kaiserzeit, der Weimarer Republik, der Nazizeit. Warum sollen wir jetzt auf einmal speziell bei der DDR etwas klüger verfahren können?

BN: Den Versuch gibt es. Die Bonner Politiker behaupten immer, wir machen es diesmal besser als nach 1945, gründlicher.

CH: Das ist Tradition, das wird jedesmal behauptet. Das wird auch so bleiben. Nur mit dem Antikommunismus, das sehe ich nicht ganz so. Für den Antikommunismus damals, zur Zeit der McCarthy-Ära, gab es ganz handfeste ökonomische Gründe, eine Bedrohung aus dem Osten. Das ist heute nicht mehr da. Folglich, wenn es da noch Antikommunismus gibt, und antikommunistische Ideologie, ist sie gleichzeitig etwas lächerlich. Es gibt keine echte Bedrohung für den Kapitalismus, warum soll es da noch Antikommunismus geben? Dass es eiserne Antikommunisten gibt, antikommunistische Tendenzen, das ist gar keine Frage, aber das sind letzte Gefechte.

Man versucht ein bisschen diese Geschichte der DDR aufzuarbeiten, natürlich mit Interesse, mit Interessen, die sich dann durchschlagen. Es geht durchaus auch um eine nachträgliche Delegitimierung der DDR. Ohne diese etwas albernen Versuche der Delegitimierung würde es diese Ostalgie oder Nostalgie nicht so stark geben, und je stärker die eine wird, desto stärker wird die andere sein. Selbstverständlich ist in Ostdeutschland der Westen präsent, alle wichtigen Stellen sind im Grunde in westdeutscher

Hand. Professor Jens Reich sagte mir, in seinem Institut im Osten Deutschlands seien bis auf ihn alle (zehn) Professoren aus dem Westen, während die Reinemachefrauen alle aus dem Osten stammen. Auch in dem ideologischen Bereich der Aufarbeitung dominiert der Westen. Es hat einen Sieg gegeben: der eine Staat ist verschwunden, der andere ist als Sieger übrig geblieben, oder ist übrig geblieben und dadurch Sieger geworden, und der arbeitet die Geschichte auf. Ich hatte auch, ehrlich gesagt, nicht die Illusion, dass es anders wird, ich hatte nur überlegt, ob es Möglichkeiten gäbe, es anders zu machen.

Aber auch für die »Sieger« ist das nicht immer so einfach. In einer berühmten Kleinstadt Ostdeutschlands gibt es sieben wichtige Funktionen, im politischen und kulturell-politischen Bereich, und die sieben treffen sich gelegentlich. Sie sind alle aus dem Westen und haben alle Probleme in dieser Stadt. Sie sind etwas verloren, sie merken, sie kennen sich da nicht gut aus, und es ist ganz wichtig für sie, sich auszutauschen, und daher treffen sie sich als die »glorreichen Sieben«. Das gefällt mir, da ist Ironie drin. Sie sind die Sieger, kämpfen aber allein auf verlorenem Posten. Daran erkennt man das Verzwickte der Situation. Es geht nicht anders, ich bin davon überzeugt; und wenn, würde es anders keinesfalls besser gehen.

DC: Eine Frage zum *Tangospieler*: Was mich an diesem Buch interessiert, ist, dass es das erste längere Stück Prosa ist, in dem nicht in der Ich-Form erzählt wird. Was waren die Gründe?

CH: Es gab immer Texte, wo ich in der dritten Person gearbeitet habe. Vielleicht hat es damit zu tun, dass ich von der Dramatik komme. Vielleicht gibt die erste Person für mich beim Schreiben eine zusätzliche Möglichkeit. Es gibt neben dem Erzähler, dem tatsächlichen Erzähler, was ich bin, und manchmal dem vorgegebenen Erzähler, der das scheinbar erzählt, noch eine dritte Möglichkeit, die einer Maske oder einer Unbestimmtheit. In dem *Fremden Freund* sagt die Person unentwegt etwas, und gleichzeitig wird etwas anderes mitgeteilt, was der Erzähler gar nicht sagt, was er nicht sagen kann, weil er nicht aus der Rolle herausgehen darf.

Für mich war das ganz spannend bei *Von allem Anfang an*. Ich wusste überhaupt nicht, wie ich das erzählen kann, oder mit wem, und war sehr glücklich, als ich das Kind hatte. Da wusste ich, ich war an die Temperatur gekommen. Ich war unsicher, ob ich alles, was ich erzählen will, über die kindliche Sicht ins Buch bekomme. Ich merkte aber bald, dass ich insofern einen ganz glücklichen Griff getan hatte, dass ein Zwölf-, Dreizehnjähriger sehr genau sieht. In diesem Alter gucken sie sehr genau hin, was da passiert. Sie verstehen nicht alles, sie können es manchmal nicht einordnen, oder sie werten es falsch, aber das kann der Leser in seinem Kopf wieder zurechtsetzen. Der Leser hat mehr Lebenserfahrung als das Kind, aber das Kind sieht viel genauer. Wenn wir einem Ehestreit zuhören müssen, ist das unangenehm, und wir würden lieber rausgehen. Aber ein Kind hat so etwas noch nicht erlebt und ist viel interessierter an dem Ehestreit. Für das Kind gibt es dieses Unangenehme an der Sache nicht. Es ist direkter, neugieriger. Bei *Vor allem Anfang an* war der Glückspunkt, dass ich mit jenem Zwölf-, Dreizehnjährigen alles beschreiben konnte, was ich gesehen habe.

Aber ich hatte, wie beim *Fremden Freund*, die Schwierigkeit, dass dieses Kind natürlich bestimmte Dinge nicht wahrnehmen bzw. sagen kann, die nicht zu seinem Erfahrungsbereich dazugehören, aber die ich eventuell dem Leser auch mitteilen muss. Ich glaube, das ist etwas, was ein Buch für den Leser spannend macht. Dass man nicht mehr nur diesen allwissenden Erzähler hat, der im zwanzigsten Jahrhundert ohnehin ein bisschen langweilig ist. Ich habe versucht, die Erzählerrolle anders aufzubauen. Da ist die so genannte Rollenprosa, diese erste Person, für mich ganz hilfreich. Wie weit ich das weitertreiben will, weiß ich nicht, es reizt mich schon, mit dieser dritten Person zu arbeiten. Aber keine Frage, der Erzähler in dem *Tangospieler*, der in der dritten Person berichtet, ist gottähnlicher für den Leser. Das, was dieser Erzähler sagt, stimmt.

BN: Hat sich etwas verändert in Ihrem Selbstverständnis als Schriftsteller, durch die »Wende« und durch die Wiedervereinigung? Sehen Sie Ihre Rolle anders?

CH: Meine Rolle sehe ich eigentlich nicht anders. Ich habe mich immer »Chronist« genannt, und das hat sich für mich nicht geändert. Es gibt eine Sache, die ich als nicht unangenehm, sogar als angenehm empfinde: in den sozialistischen Ländern, in der DDR, gab es einen enormen Druck auf den Autor, auf den bekannteren Schriftsteller, einzustehen für andere Sachen. Das ist weitgehend weg. Konkreter gesehen, diese öffentliche Rolle ist geringer geworden. Ich weiß, dass es Kollegen gibt, die da Schwierigkeiten haben, weil sie sich an diese öffentliche Rolle ein wenig gewöhnt haben. Ich hatte in meiner Zensur-Rede von 1987 über die falschen Gewichte gesprochen, die unsere Literatur scheinbar gewichtig machen. Das waren damals politische Gewichte. Weil es keine Presse gab, waren die Bücher dieser DDR-Autoren und aus den sozialistischen Ländern besonders wichtig. In den Büchern stand immer mehr als in der Zeitung. Und das, habe ich 1987 gesagt, würde sich sofort ändern, würden wir eine Presse haben. Das hat sich auch geändert, mit Ausnahmen. In der Presse wird über den Skandal berichtet, das muss nicht mehr der Autor machen. Dieser Druck auf den Autor ist weg, und das ist für mich eine Erleichterung.

BN: Entsteht vielleicht ein anderer Druck durch Kritiker wie Reich-Ranicki, die z. B. verlangen, dass die Literatur sich auf bestimmte Probleme einstellen sollte, ganz besonders die Aufarbeitung der DDR-Vergangenheit? Gibt es eine Art Zensur im Westen?

CH: Ja, es gibt einen Druck, keine Frage. Das merkte ich auch ganz stark bei mir. Von mir hatte der Wenderoman zu kommen. Ich glaube, dass das *Napoleon-Spiel* besonders eine Enttäuschung war. Man hatte von mir gehofft, ich würde einen Roman schreiben, der die endgültige Verurteilung der DDR wäre. Es interessierte mich gar nicht. Wenn der Staat noch lebendig wäre, und virulent und spannend, wäre es auch spannend gewesen, so etwas zu schreiben, aber über einen Leichnam ... Nach der Jagd wird der Bär immer größer. Also es gibt einen Druck, aber er ist natürlich nicht vergleichbar mit der Zensur. Gewisse Zwänge wird es immer geben, durch den Markt, das Feuilleton. Aber das ist ein Druck, dem man ausweichen kann und muss, wenn man weiterschreiben will.

BN/DC: Herr Hein, wir danken Ihnen für dieses Gespräch.

4

Unvollständige Rekonstruktion: Über das Lektorat des Buches *Von allem Anfang an* von Christoph Hein[1]

ANGELA DRESCHER

Für einen Lektor stellt es eine Art unsittlichen Antrag dar, über das Lektorat an einem Manuskript berichten zu sollen. Der Herausgeber der Werkausgabe Hans Falladas und langjährige Lektoratsleiter im Aufbau-Verlag, Günter Caspar, schrieb in einem Essay über diesen Berufsstand:

> Der Lektor kann ein Vertrauter des Autors werden, wenn er in der Lage ist, guten Rat zu geben. Nimmt der Autor ihn an, so wechselt der Ratschlag den Urheber. Ein kluger Lektor wird nirgendwann ausposaunen, wie und womit er dem Autor geholfen hat. [...] Der Lektor sollte immer hinter dem Werk stehen und das in der doppelten Bedeutung des Wortes.[2]

Dass ich mich dennoch dabei ertappte, nach Rechtfertigungen zu suchen, um diesen Grundsatz des Lektoren-Ethos umgehen zu können, hat drei gute Gründe, einen egoistischen und zwei altruistische:

1. die Gelegenheit, auf einen unverzichtbaren, aber vom Aussterben bedrohten Beruf aufmerksam machen zu können;
2. die Chance, junge Menschen von einem Irrweg abzubringen, und
3. die Möglichkeit, Christoph Hein Rückendeckung zu geben.

Der erste Grund ist dem Selbsterhaltungstrieb geschuldet. Der Beruf des Lektors ist jung, gerade einmal hundert Jahre alt. Die Entwicklung der Verlage erforderte um die Jahrhundertwende eine Arbeitsteilung zwischen Verleger und Lektor. In Deutschland holte sich 1896 als erster Samuel Fischer einen Lektor in seinen Verlag, den Essayisten und Prosaisten Moritz Heimann. Meist kennt man Lektoren nur, wenn sie selbst Schriftsteller waren –

Oskar Loerke, Franz Hessel, Hermann Kesten zum Beispiel –, denn der Lektor verstand sich lange Zeit als diskreter, sensibler Berater des Autors, der im Hintergrund zu bleiben hat. Noch einmal Günter Caspar:

> Der Lektor ist ein erster Leser, ein Gesprächspartner des Autors, oft ein Berater, manchmal ein Anreger, seltener ein Vertrauter und Freund, und für jüngere, neue, beginnende Autoren sicher auch ein Nothelfer. Er muß sein Handwerk beherrschen, Literatur kennen, Maßstäbe besitzen und Sachverstand [...]. Vor allem aber braucht er ein paar Eigenschaften: Er muß wissen, wie man mit sensiblen Leuten *um*geht, und er muß wissen, was man bei ihnen manchmal um*geht* und um was man gegebenenfalls auch *herum*geht. Er muß den Umgang pflegen, und er muß über den Umgang schweigen. Er darf mit seinem Autor nicht umspringen, und er muß sich, notfalls, seiner Haut wehren. Ein guter Lektor wird zu seinem Autor in einer freundlichen, achtungsvollen Beziehung stehen, dessen Bücher aber wird er schätzen und mögen und ins Herz schließen. Kann er das nicht, dann wird die *Arbeitsehe* schnell geschieden.[3]

Das ist vor fünfzehn Jahren geschrieben, in einem Land, das es nicht mehr gibt. Mittlerweile hat sich auch das Berufsbild des Lektors gewandelt, die rasant gestiegene Zahl der jährlich erscheinenden Bücher, der Konkurrenz- und Effizienzdruck der Verlage bringen es mit sich, dass immer mehr Titel von immer weniger Lektoren verantwortet werden. Noch versucht man, den Spagat zwischen diesem geschilderten Lektor alter Schule und einem modernen Manager und Promoter hinzubekommen; es ist aber abzusehen – und in vielen Verlagen ist es bereits so –, dass der Literaturmanager überwiegt, dass Lektorate immer mehr an Außenmitarbeiter vergeben werden. Wer zwanzig und mehr Titel pro Jahr bearbeiten muss, dabei für mehrere Sprachen zuständig ist, oft gleichermaßen für Belletristik und Sachbücher, sich außerdem als Talent- und Projekt-Scout betätigt, für Verträge, Kalkulation, Präsentation mitzuständig ist, der kann sich um die traditionelle Arbeit mit dem Autor am Manuskript kaum noch kümmern.

Der Aufbau-Verlag ist ein Verlag mittlerer Größe, in dem man Wert legt auf gute Autorenbeziehungen und gut redigierte Manuskripte. Nicht zuletzt fordern die meisten Autoren diese Sorgfalt energisch ein, denn wenn sie erst einmal an ein gründliches Lektorat gewöhnt sind, geben sie sich nicht mehr mit oberflächlicher Arbeit zufrieden. Das geschieht übrigens aus Eigennutz und um sich so gut wie möglich vor den Angriffen von Rezensenten und Literaturwissenschaftlern zu schützen. Davon später.

Eines hat sich für den Lektor in den vergangenen Jahren nicht geändert, und das sind die verschiedenen Autorentypen, mit denen er zu tun hat:

> Kein Autor ähnelt dem anderen, und keiner bleibt lange Zeit derselbe. [...] Debüts können etwas Besonderes sein: Vielleicht hat man tatsächlich ein Talent entdeckt [...] Ärgerlich ist es, wenn man mit einem eingebildeten Autor zu tun hat: Meist sind es die geringeren Talente, die sich groß dünken. Ärgerlich ist es, wenn der Autor sein Produkt nicht sorgsam herstellt: Meist sind es die genialisch Faulen, die ohne den gründlich redigierenden Lektor nicht auskommen. [...] Am besten kommt man mit den wirklichen Talenten aus, mögen sie noch so komplizierte und schwierige Leute sein.[4]

Die Beschreibung meiner Arbeit an Christoph Heins Manuskript *Von allem Anfang an* könnte vielleicht davon überzeugen, welchen Nutzen ein Lektor für den Autor, für die Literatur und damit auch für die Germanistik stiften kann.

An diesem Punkt meiner Überlegungen rief ich Christoph Hein an – ein paar Skrupel waren geblieben –, um ihn nach seiner Meinung zu diesem Vortrag zu fragen. Nun ist er ein ausnehmend diskreter Mensch, vor allem was seine Person und sein Schreiben anbelangt. Gerade darum jedoch stimmte er sofort zu, denn man kann sich hinter nichts so entspannt verbergen wie hinter vielen möglichst widersprüchlichen Meinungen zu sich selbst, eine Taktik, die er äußerst erfolgreich seit langem betreibt.

Der Vortrag selbst schien mir nicht allzu schwierig, hatte ich doch meine Arbeit an Christoph Heins Manuskript redlich und wahrscheinlich nicht ungeschickt geleistet – schließlich schmeichelt der Erfolg eines Autors auch ein wenig dem Lektor, und *Von allem Anfang an* ist ein erfolgreiches, sehr gelobtes Buch.

Als ich in meinem mit unzähligen Manuskripten zugepflasterten Büro nach der ersten Fassung von Christoph Heins Manuskript zu suchen begann, um an Beispielen die von uns vorgenommenen Veränderungen schildern zu können, fand ich die überarbeitete Version von *Von allem Anfang an*, fand die vorletzte Fassung, das Satzmanuskript, den Umbruch – was ich nicht fand, war die ursprüngliche Version, weder als Manuskript noch als Diskette.

Mittlerweile war mir eingefallen, dass ich das Manuskript redigiert hatte, und dass ich Christoph Hein die Redaktion gebracht und mit ihm durchgesprochen hatte. Er hatte dann den Text überarbeitet und mir eine neue Diskette geschickt. Christoph Hein war so ratlos wie ich: die ursprüngliche Version hatte er gelöscht, meine Redaktion zum Altpapier geworfen. Kurz, es gibt kaum mehr Spuren meiner Arbeit. Alles, was ich im folgenden darzustellen versuche, ist eine Rekonstruktion.

Christoph Hein wurde immer heiterer, als ich ihm klarmachte, dass sich die verschiedenen Manuskriptfassungen nur ungenau beschreiben ließen: er mag es, wie gesagt, Spuren zu verwischen. Mit einer gewissen Genugtuung meinte er, es würde gar nichts schaden, wenn ich nicht allzu genau von meiner Arbeit berichten könnte, die ja doch eine gewisse Unvollkommenheit seiner eigenen *sichtbar* machen würde, denn etwas sichtbar zu machen und den Autor zu *verhaften*, wäre es, was die Germanisten wollten.

Damit bin ich bei meinem zweiten Grund angelangt. Jemand muss es einmal sagen: Die Germanistik ist ein interessantes, unterhaltsames, aber unnützes Wissenschaftsfach. Unnütz zum einen, weil sich kein Autor, den ich kenne, wirklich für die Ergebnisse dieser Wissenschaft interessiert, und zum andern, weil die Möglichkeiten, sich selbst mit den Kenntnissen zu erhalten, die man in diesem Fach erworben hat, minimal sind, vgl. Punkt 1 meiner Ausführungen. Das Beispiel zeigt obendrein, dass die moderne Technik in Zukunft ein wesentliches Betätigungsfeld der Literaturwissenschaft verhindern wird: die Untersuchung der Entstehungsgeschichte eines Werkes und seiner verschiedenen Fassungen. Wer dennoch mit dem Virus Literatur infiziert ist und sich nicht von diesem Studium und dieser Wissenschaft abbringen lässt, dem kann ich nur raten, Computerspezialist zu werden, um in der Lage zu sein, sozusagen Computerarchäologie zu betreiben und in den geheimnisvollen Urgründen von Festplatten nach gelöschten Versionen, verworfenen Texten, missglückten Versuchen fahnden und diese wiederherstellen zu können.

Nach dieser langen Vorrede kann ich endlich von der Genese des fraglichen Manuskriptes – soweit ich sie kenne und mich erinnern kann – berichten. Zugleich werde ich damit meinem dritten Grund nachkommen. Ich will versuchen, eine Vorstellung vom Schaffensprozess eines Autors zu vermitteln. So paradox es klingen mag: indem ich über ein unvollkommenes Stadium berichte, also Entstehungsschichten und Verworfenes aufdecke, möchte ich erreichen, dass der der Öffentlichkeit zugänglich gemachten Version mehr Wertschätzung entgegengebracht wird.

Hinter der scheinbaren Leichtigkeit des Erzählens sollte die Schwierigkeit des Schreibens aufscheinen. Denn nicht nur ein guter Lektor muss sich trotz aller Vertrautheit und der Bekanntschaft mit Krisen und Unvollkommenem eine Ehrfurcht vor Autor und Werk bewahren, auch die Literaturwissenschaft kommt ohne diese Ehrfurcht nicht aus. Für beide gilt, was Kurt Tucholsky sich selbst als Grundsatz für seine Kritiken auferlegte:

> Jeder, der kritisch tätig ist, sollte täglich dreimal dieses Gebet beten: Damit, daß du kritisierst, bist du dem Werk nicht überlegen; dadurch bist du ihm nicht überlegen, dadurch bist du ihm nicht überlegen.[5]

Christoph Heins Buch *Von allem Anfang an* wäre an sich ein sehr dankbares Beispiel, um Lektoratsarbeit zu demonstrieren. Zum einen gehört Hein zu den Autoren, die von sich heraus einen Lektor fordern, die dankbar über kritische Hinweise sind und mit diesen Hinweisen produktiv umgehen (was nicht bedeuten muss, dass sie auf jeden Vorschlag, jeden Einwand eingehen). Zum anderen ist die besondere, offene Struktur gerade dieses Buches eine wirkliche Herausforderung für den Lektor gewesen.

1. Entstehungsgeschichte

Christoph Hein gehört zu den Autoren, die nicht über Pläne sprechen, Konzepte erörtern, von entstehenden Manuskripten erzählen. Ganz im Gegenteil. »Bücher, über die man redet, schreibt man nicht«, heißt es in einem Brief vom 10. April 1996, in dem er zum erstenmal von einem neuen Text berichtet:

> Es soll ein Roman sein, allerdings formal etwas eigenartig. Es gibt eine Mittelpunktsperson, um die sich alles und dann doch nicht alles dreht. Vielleicht Kindheitserinnerungen, aber einiges spricht dagegen. Etwas Erzählendes. Und ich hoffe, Sie werden es mit Vergnügen lesen. Mehr als diesen letzten Satz sollte ich eigentlich nicht sagen. Vor dem Oktober werde ich nichts weiter erzählen oder abgeben. (Und wenn die Götter ungnädig sind, dann schweige ich über den Oktober hinaus.)

Ich weiß nicht, ob Sie sich vorstellen können, was eine solche Mitteilung für den Lektor bedeutet. Natürlich war ich geschmeichelt, dass ich überhaupt so frühzeitig von einem Manuskript erfuhr, denn im Falle Christoph Heins stellt das einen ungeheuren

Gunstbeweis dar. Andererseits könnte ein Manuskript, wenn es im Oktober an den Verlag gegeben wird, gut im Frühjahr erscheinen – gesetzt den Fall, es wäre alles vorbereitet. Dazu müssen Ausstattungsvorschläge erarbeitet werden, Werbetexte geschrieben, die Vertreter müssen Textproben kennen usw. Ein wenig vom Inhalt muss man da schon wissen und vor allem einen Titel haben. Als ich also drei Monate später deswegen vorsichtig nachfragte, erhielt ich einen sehr kühlen Brief:

> Ich sagte doch nur sehr vorsichtig [...], daß ich hoffe, Ende Oktober das Manuskript abgeben zu können. Ich bin vorher nicht fertig. Und das Gesamtmanuskript entsteht – wie immer – im letzten Moment. Und dann würde ich gern erst mit Ihnen daran arbeiten, bevor ich den Text auf die Reise gebe. [...] Ich bitte daher, daß der Verlag den Titel um ein halbes Jahr verschiebt. Dann ist für Vertreterkonferenz und Werbung alles rechtzeitig vorhanden – und wir zwei können seriös arbeiten. (24. Juli 1996)

Das ist, nebenbei gesagt, eine sehr untypische Vernunft-Haltung für einen Autor. Erfahrungsgemäß ist ein Autor, wenn er einen Text abgeschlossen hat, so euphorisch, dass er die Tage zählt, bis er als Buch erscheint. Nur erfahrene, sehr selbstkritische Schriftsteller wissen, dass sie dem eigenen Empfinden, etwas Außerordentliches geleistet zu haben, gerade in diesem Stadium nicht trauen können, weil sie zu wenig Abstand zu ihrem Text haben – dass sie also unbedingt den unvoreingenommenen Blick eines Fremden, des Lektors eben, brauchen.

Was nun dieses angekündigte Manuskript anbelangt, war Christoph Heins Zurückhaltung berechtigt. Der Arbeitsplan konnte nicht ganz eingehalten werden, und in jenem Jahr, 1996, erfuhr ich nicht mehr als seinen Titel: 'A. M. B. – Kleines Buch'.

Niemand konnte sich etwas unter diesem Titel vorstellen, doch am 30. Januar 1997 hatte er sich bereits verändert und erklärte sich von selbst: 'Anna Magdalena Birke und ich. Kleines Buch'. 'A. M. B.' war also die Abkürzung eines Namens gewesen, welche Geschichte sich dahinter verbergen sollte, wusste ich dennoch nicht. Mittlerweile wurde aber das Manuskript für Ende Februar avisiert, und es gab sogar eine Angabe für den Umfang, etwa 200 Seiten.

Offensichtlich waren die Götter diesmal gnädig, es muss die verschollene erste Fassung im Februar eingetroffen sein, denn am 10. März bedankte sich Hein für meine Kürzungs- und anderen

Lektoratsvorschläge, schickt eine Überarbeitung, nennen wir sie Variante 2, und vermerkte, dass er noch Änderungen im Kopf habe. Es gab einen zweiten Lektoratsgang, und am 25. März lag dann Manuskript und Diskette mit Variante 3 vor. Hein erwartete ein drittes Lektorat. Danach entstand Variante 4, das Satzmanuskript, die Fassung, die Sie alle kennen.

Ich habe das hier so umständlich referiert, um einen Eindruck vom Arbeitsaufwand zu vermitteln. Übrigens ist ein untrüglicher Gradmesser für die Qualität eines Textes, ob man ihn auch beim vierten Lesen interessant und lesenswert findet, ob man immer noch Neues in ihm entdeckt. Es gibt wenige Texte, die man schließlich im Umbruch – in diesem Fall beim fünften Mal – ohne Überdruss liest. Dieser hier gehörte zu meinem Glück dazu – ich langweile mich nicht gern.

2. Buchtitel

Es war bereits erwähnt worden: der zweite Titelvorschlag lautete: 'Anna Magdalena Birke und ich. Kleines Buch'. Im Verlag war man nicht besonders glücklich damit, und zwar weder mit dem Haupt- noch mit dem Untertitel. Beide hielt man für wenig werbewirksam und nicht gerade aussagekräftig. Den meisten Autoren fällt es schwer, einen neuen Titel zu finden, haben sie doch das Manuskript über einen langen Zeitraum mit dem ersten Titel assoziiert. Hein machte relativ schnell einen neuen Vorschlag, denn bereits am 18. Februar nannte ich das Manuskript in einer verlagsinternen Mitteilung *Von allem Anfang an*.

Der Titel ist einem Dialog im Kapitel 'Ende der Großen Ferien' entnommen, in dem Tante Magdalena sagt:»Dem Leben muss man von allem Anfang an ins Gesicht sehen« (VA, 140), um die Kinder über einen Streit ihrer Eltern zu beruhigen. Noch in der 3. Variante griff der halbwüchsige Daniel kurz darauf diese Formulierung auf und beschrieb damit, wie er in einen Schlamassel geraten war. Ich glaube mich an eine weitere Stelle zu erinnern, die den Umarbeitungen ebenfalls zum Opfer gefallen ist. Wahrscheinlich wollte der Autor, nachdem er sich für diesen Titel entschieden hatte, das Stichwort bewusst nur einmal auftauchen lassen.

Von allem Anfang an ist ein glücklich gewählter Titel, weil er Inhalt und Stimmung des Buches auf das Schönste trifft, weil er etwas andeutet, ohne etwas zu verraten, weil er klingt, weil er haften bleibt – ein Titel, wie er nicht alle Tage gefunden wird.

Kontrovers wurde hingegen der Genretitel diskutiert: 'Kleines Buch'. Würde man mit diesem hübschen understatement nicht auch das Buch als Nebenwerk abwerten? Am Ende zäher Diskussionen erschien es ohne Genrebezeichnung. Manche Rezensenten haben es als Erzählungssammlung bezeichnet, Christoph Hein selbst nennt es Roman, und irgendwann wird der Verlag das sicher auch auf das Titelblatt setzen, und das nicht nur, weil man heutzutage ungeniert alle Texte über 100 Seiten um der Verkäuflichkeit willen so bezeichnet. Ich jedenfalls hatte noch in meiner Vertretermitteilung geschrieben:

> 'Kleines Buch' ist der treffende Ausdruck für diese Szenen einer Kindheit und Jugend, in den fünfziger Jahren, die da mit leichter Hand erzählt werden und einen engeren Zusammenhang haben als bloße Erzählungen und ein kleineres Konfliktpotential, als für einen Roman nötig wäre.

Aber über die Genrebezeichnung können sich nun die Germanisten den Kopf zerbrechen.

3. Vom Anfang

Der Anfang schlägt den Ton an, verleiht dem Buch die Richtung und ist darum besonders heikel. *Von allem Anfang an* hatte anfangs einen eher unbefriedigenden Anfang, eine Art Vorkapitel von vielleicht acht bis zehn Seiten. Rudimente davon finden sich in der Buchfassung von S. 6 bis 17, wobei diese Fassung sich aus Stücken zusammensetzt, die zum Teil in anderen Kapiteln standen.

Ursprünglich begann der Roman mit einer etwas umständlichen Beschreibung der Wohnung und des Gartens von Tante Magdalena, die an einen klassischen, weit ausgreifenden Familienroman erinnerte und gegenüber dem später episodisch Erzählten zu voluminös wirkte; der Beginn war langatmig und wenig geeignet, den Leser in den Text zu ziehen. Christoph Hein hat einmal erwähnt, dass er dieses Manuskript ursprünglich als zusammenhängende chronologische Geschichte geschrieben, dann diese Form jedoch aufgebrochen hatte, da sie ihm zu sperrig war für das leichte Erzählen, das ihm vorschwebte. Möglicherweise war der Anfang ein unbearbeiteteres Rudiment des Ursprungstextes als die anderen Kapitel.

Nachdem wir lange über diese Problematik gesprochen hatten, überraschte mich Christoph Hein dadurch, dass er eine Episode schrieb und voranstellte, die im Grunde den Schluss der

Geschichte vorwegnimmt, die sie einbettet und dann schließlich den Blick des Erzählers zurückzoomen lässt. Durch diesen kleinen Trick bekam die Geschichte sofort Tiefe, und der Roman erreichte auch Geschlossenheit (ein weiteres Problem in der ersten Version war der offene Schluss), ohne seine Offenheit aufgeben zu müssen.

Welch heikle Balance so ein Text halten muss, zeigt eine andere Überlegung des Autors. Nachdem er das Auftaktkapitel 'Krieg zur See' umgeändert hatte, sollte der erste Satz beginnen: »An dem Tag, an dem ich die Republik verraten hatte ...« Dieser Anfang hätte aber sofort dem gesamten Roman einen vordergründig politischen Stempel aufgedrückt, und da das Gegenteil Christoph Heins Intention war – nämlich zu zeigen, wie indirekt, hintergründig und unspektakulär Politik auch bei spektakulären Entwicklungen in die Biographie der einzelnen eingreift –, wurde ein unspektakulärer Anfangssatz gewählt und die politische Interpretation von Daniels Schulwechsel an späterer, dennoch versteckt prominenter Stelle eingebaut (VA, 16).

In diesem Auftaktkapitelchen befand sich übrigens schon in der ersten Version eine Passage, die gern zitiert wird, weil sich der Erzähler zum einzigen Mal an den Leser wendet – ein Erzähler, den man gern mit dem Autor identisch setzt – und scheinbar eine Absichtserklärung zum Text abgibt (VA, 10f.). Diese Stelle ist zwar gekürzt worden, blieb aber im Text, obwohl sie offensichtlich einen Bruch in der Erzählhaltung darstellt. Sie gehört zum Spiel des Autors mit Fiktion und Realität, oder der Fiktion von Realität und Autobiographischem, worauf noch zurückzukommen sein wird.

4. Anordnung der Kapitel

Es folgt eine ziemlich verwirrende Darstellung über die Varianten bei der Kapitelreihung, der selbst ich nicht einfach folgen kann, weil nicht nur die Kapitel mehrfach verschoben wurden, sondern sich obendrein ihre Titel änderten.

Variante 1: ist aus den genannten Gründen nicht zu rekonstruieren; Christoph Hein hat Notizen über:
> Vorkapitel
> Krieg zur See
> Das Ende der großen Ferien
> Leuchtschrift
> Am Russensee
> Der Evangelist Lukas

	Flüssige Luft
	Schöne Bescherung
	Die schlummernde Venus und die Hausordnung
Variante 2:	Vorkapitel
	Krieg zur See
	Schöne Bescherung
	Das Ende der großen Ferien I
	Am Russensee
	Das Ende der großen Ferien II
	Flüssige Luft
	Der Evangelist Lukas und die Artisten
	Die schlummernde Venus und die Hausordnung
	Glace surprise
Variante 3:	Krieg zur See
	Schöne Bescherung
	Flüssige Luft
	Ende der großen Ferien I
	Am Russensee
	Ende der großen Ferien II
	Der Evangelist Lukas und die Artisten
	Die schlummernde Venus und die Hausordnung
	Glace surprise
Variante 4:	Krieg zur See
	Schöne Bescherung
	Flüssige Luft
	Großvater und die Bestimmer
	Am Russensee
	Der Evangelist Lukas und die Artisten
	Ende der großen Ferien
	Die schlummernde Venus und die Hausordnung
	Glace surprise

Nur der Übersichtlichkeit halber will ich festhalten, dass aus 'Das Ende der Großen Ferien I' in der 4. Fassung 'Großvater und die Bestimmer' wurde, aus 'Der Evangelist Lukas und die Artisten' nur 'Der Evangelist Lukas', 'Glace surprise' hieß früher 'Leuchtschrift'.

Das Lektorat des Buches Von allem Anfang an

Es fällt auf, dass das einzige Kapitel, das trotz der Tauschaktionen seinen Platz behalten hat, das erste ist, 'Krieg zur See'. Alle anderen wurden mehrfach neu sortiert. Der Hauptunterschied zwischen den Varianten 1 und 2 besteht darin, dass die einzelnen Kapitel zunächst eine weitaus willkürlichere Anordnung hatten, die zwar Momentaufnahmen aus der Kindheit und Jugend eines Jungen Mitte der fünfziger Jahre zeigte, eine Entwicklung dieses Jungen und der Familie aber eher verdeckte als verdeutlichte. Das Problem war, dass damit für den Leser ein recht mühsames, in sich widersprüchliches Puzzle entstand, durch das der Zugang zur Geschichte verdeckt und verkompliziert wurde, ohne damit etwas an erzählerischem Raffinesse zu gewinnen. Der Vorschlag, die Kapitel umzusortieren, wie dann in Variante 2 geschehen, lief auf eine größere Stringenz der Handlungsführung durch die chronologische Anordnung der Einzelgeschichten hinaus. Das war weniger einfach, als es der heutige Text ahnen lässt, denn auch die Geschichten selbst mussten der Gesamtgeschichte angepasst werden. Am ursprünglichen Text könnte man beweisen, wie verwirrend es ist, wenn man die einzelnen Sachverhalte und Bezüge wie Altersangaben, Jahreszeiten, historische Ereignisse oder Geschehnisse innerhalb der Familie miteinander koordinieren muss, wenn man immer beachten muss, wer was in welchem Alter zu welchem Zeitpunkt gekonnt, gekannt und gewusst hat. Bestimmte Sachverhalte müssen u. U. früher erzählt werden – ich erinnere mich vor allem an Informationskollisionen zwischen 'Der Evangelist Lukas' und 'Ende der großen Ferien' und 'Am Russensee' –, wenn man die Reihenfolge wechselt. Besonders knifflig war es, die verschiedenen Altersangaben aufeinander zu beziehen, ohne dass Widersprüche und Ungereimtheiten blieben.

Schwieriger noch, als Sachverhalte logisch zu ordnen, ist es, auch die charaktermäßigen, die psychischen Entwicklungen nachvollziehbar bleiben zu lassen. Manche Kapitel hätten an verschiedenen Stellen stehen können. Ausschlaggebend für die Anordnung war in diesen Fällen eine gewisse innere Dramaturgie. 'Flüssige Luft' zeigte einen naiveren Jungen als er z. B. in 'Ende der großen Ferien' gezeichnet wurde, deshalb wurde dieses Kapitel nach vorn verschoben. Gerade in Davids Alter verändert man sich innerhalb weniger Monate.

Genauso wichtig wie die Klärung der Handlungsabläufe ist es, Motive, Beobachtungen und Eigenheiten nicht aus den Augen zu verlieren, um einem Text größere Geschlossenheit und

Verzahnung zu verleihen. Wenn die Kinder anfangs so fasziniert sind von Tante Magdalenas Spieluhr und den geheimnisvollen Kartons in ihrer Kammer, fragt sich natürlich auch der Leser, was es damit auf sich hat. Ursprünglich wurde beides nicht mehr erwähnt; schließlich hatte Christoph Hein, auf diese Szene hingewiesen, den schönen erzählerischen Einfall, am Ende noch einmal darauf zurückzukommen, ohne das Geheimnis jedoch zu lüften. All diese in sich verschränkten Änderungen kann man insgesamt kaum nachvollziehen. In jedem Fall wurde mehr als eine Reihenfolge geändert, zumal nicht nur die Kapitel in sich bearbeitet, sondern auch Szenen und Absätze in andere Kapitel eingebaut wurden – ein diffiziler Balanceakt, bei dem der Lektor zwar mehr oder minder Hilfestellung oder Anregung geben kann, der Autor aber darüber entscheidet, wann sein Text im intendierten Gleichgewicht ist.

Letztendlich dienten diese Puzzlereien nur dazu, ein möglichst genaues Bild dieser neuen, ausgedachten Realität zu schaffen. Das trifft übrigens für jede Prosaform zu. Selbst ein noch so phantastischer Roman muss in sich, innerhalb der dort aufgestellten Gesetze, funktionieren.

5. Stilistisches

War es schon schwer zu beschreiben, wie und warum manche Kapitel umgestellt wurden, so könnte man sich vollends in Einzelheiten verlieren, wenn man auf die redaktionelle Feinarbeit eingehen wollte.

Ein Lektor hat, wenn er redigiert, etwas von einem Chamäleon. Wie jeder Autor stilistische Eigenheiten hat, macht auch jeder spezielle Fehler, und oft ist es schwierig, zwischen Eigenheit, Marotte und Fehler zu unterscheiden. Und manchmal – um alles noch komplizierter zu machen – ist eine Unrichtigkeit, ein schräger Ausdruck treffender als ein »richtiger«, der vielleicht glatt und nichtssagend ist. Besonders schwierig werden solche Entscheidungen, wenn umgangssprachliche Elemente verwendet werden oder aus der Sicht eines Kindes bzw. Jugendlichen erzählt wird. Außerdem wandelt sich auch die Hochsprache: was vor einigen Jahren noch als falsch galt, wird mittlerweile oft akzeptiert.

Das Chamäleon Lektor muss sich nun in den Stil des jeweiligen Autors einfühlen, damit er ihm Vorschläge innerhalb seines Stils machen kann. Zugleich muss er Abstand bewahren, um Stilblüten, schiefe Vergleiche, grammatikalische Unkorrektheiten usw., vor denen kein Autor gefeit ist, zu erkennen. Eine ständige Gratwanderung, die dadurch nicht leichter wird, dass in der Regel Manuskripte verschiedener Autoren parallel redigiert werden müssen. Übrigens habe ich bei diesem Punkt beträchtliche Skrupel, Beispiele zu nennen. Stilistische Ausrutscher korrigiert man, ohne viel Aufhebens davon zu machen. Es sollen daher nur kurz einige Problemfelder angedeutet werden. Besonders tückisch ist im Deutschen der Konjunktiv, dessen Regeln weitaus verschwommener und aufgeweichter sind als im Englischen. Eine weitere Falle stellen Fragen der Kongruenz von Satzgliedern dar. Z. B. hieß es:»[...] mit einer raschen Bewegung stellte sie *den* Topf *oder die* Schüssel, *die* sie in die Hand hatte [...] ab.« Das wurde korrigiert in:»[...] stellte sie *die* Pfanne oder *die* Schüssel, *die* sie in der Hand hatte, [...] ab« (*VA*, 21).

Natürlich gibt es grammatikalische Ungenauigkeiten (»Der Sonntagmorgen war für mich verloren, er war so unerfreulich und bedrückend wie die Vormittage der Woche. *Sie waren* für mich sogar ärgerlicher [...]« – geändert in:»*Er war* für mich sogar ärgerlicher« (*VA*, 169)), unkorrekte Satzkonstruktionen (»Ich sagte ihr, dass es noch viel zu früh sei, dass sie erst nach dem Mittagessen erwartet würden, aber sie bettelte weiter, und schließlich versprach ich *es* ihr, sobald ich aus dem Wasser zurück sei« – geändert in:»versprach ich ihr *loszufahren*, sobald ich aus dem Wasser zurück sei« (*VA*, 102)), monotone, unbeabsichtigte Wortwiederholungen (»[...] auf dem Schulhof *fasste* er stets nach dem den Hof *umfassenden* Zaun [...]« – geändert in:»*umgrenzenden* Zaun« (*VA*, 22)), Doppelungen, erzählerische Nachlässigkeiten (»*Während der Schulzeit* war ich mit Dorle oft allein bei Tante Magdalena« – gemeint ist *nach dem Unterricht* oder *der Schule*, wie man umgangssprachlich sagt, nicht jedoch in den Ferien (*VA*, 12)). Solche Unkorrektheiten unterlaufen jedem Autor, oft entstehen sie, weil ein Text mehrfach umgeschrieben wurde oder gekürzt, so dass sich die Bezüge ändern.

Interessanter und aufschlussreicher aber sind Wiederholungen gewisser Informationen (so traf Daniel im Anfangskapitel beim letzten Besuch Tante Magdalena mit offenem Haar an, dadurch war dann die Schlusspassage dieses Kapitels abgeschwächt), falsche Sachverhalte (im Kapitel 'Glace surprise' saß die Familie ursprünglich im November in einem normalen Straßencafé (vgl. *VA*, 183)), oder Begriffsungenauigkeiten (»[...] selbst der *Putz zwischen* den Feldsteinen war fest [...]«: *Putz* nennt man die Schutzschicht *auf* Mauern, *zwischen* Steinen ist der *Mörtel*).

Beispiele aus diesem tückischen Problemfeld können deutlich machen, dass der Lektor eine umfassende Allgemeinbildung braucht und auch Entlegenes registrieren sollte – irgendwann wird er selbst sehr ausgefallene Kenntnisse benötigen. Jeder Information muss er mit wachsamem Misstrauen begegnen. Alles muss hinterfragt werden, man braucht praktischen Alltagsverstand (im Kapitel 'Schöne Bescherung' hieß es, dass die Kinder Teig in der Schüssel mit Holzlöffeln rühren mussten, den die Mutter dann ausrollte, damit sie Plätzchen ausstechen konnten; Teig, der ausgerollt wird, ist viel zu fest, um gerührt zu werden, man muss ihn kneten, vgl. (*VA*, 32)) und Sinn für Logik. Und auch in dieser Hinsicht muss man ständig zwischen Genauigkeit und Großzügigkeit entscheiden und schließlich dem Autor überlassen können, welche »Fehler« er machen möchte. Nicht alles, was richtig ist, ist in der Kunst wahr.

Dennoch lautet die Lektorenregel Nr. 1 beim Redigieren: traue keiner Sachaussage eines Autors. Das ist geradezu Pflicht des Lektors, denn wenn er eine falsche Aussage nicht erkennt, tun es die Literaturwissenschaftler oder die Kritiker ganz gewiss. Der Lektor ist u. a. zum Schutz des Autors angestellt.

6. Orthographisches

Es versteht sich von selbst, dass der Lektor für eine korrekte Orthographie und Zeichensetzung zu sorgen hat. Nur wenige Autoren haben dafür einen Sinn, und meist wird ihre Aufmerksamkeit naturgemäß mehr von Aufbau, Handlungsführung und Stilistik als von Kommas u. ä. in Anspruch genommen.

Bei *Von allem Anfang an* liegen die Dinge aber komplizierter. Vor einigen Jahren wurde in Deutschland eine Rechtschreibreform beschlossen, die auf weitgehende Kritik gestoßen ist, besonders bei Autoren, weil sie durch die veränderte Schreibweise von Worten einen Verlust an Eindeutigkeit fürchten, aber auch die Verwischung von Wortstämmen, -herkunft usw. Während sich die meisten Schriftsteller vehement gegen diese Reform sträuben, hat Christoph Hein von diesem Manuskript ab die neuen Regeln benutzt, allerdings in manchen Fällen in abgewandelter Form. Wenn sowieso alles verändert wird, kann jeder nach Belieben seine Regeln bestimmen, meint er, und so hat er denn auch oft rein gefühlsmäßig entschieden, was ihm von den neuen Regeln zusagt: die veränderte Schreibung des ß, die Getrennt- und Zusammen-,

Groß- und Kleinschreibung, die Zeichensetzung, die Schreibung von Fremdworten und die Trennungsregeln, nicht aber Dreifach-Konsonanten bei Wortzusammensetzungen wie z. B. »Spinnetze« oder Vokalveränderungen wie bei Stengel/Stängel. Diese kleine Provokation hat manche Leser so erbost, dass sie Leserbriefe geschrieben haben, einer hat sogar sein Buch zurückgeschickt.

Lektoratsarbeit – das sollte deutlich werden – besteht aus unzähligen Einzelproblemen und -problemchen. Es wäre langweilig und beckmesserisch, weitere Beispiele aufzuzählen und Ihnen damit auszuliefern. Der einzige Erkenntnisgewinn wäre möglicherweise der, dass auch bedeutende Autoren Fehler machen, bzw. dass ihre Manuskripte nicht von Anfang an fehlerfrei und makellos sind. Kluge Autoren wissen, dass ihr ärgster Feind die Selbstzufriedenheit ist, und suchen sich Verbündete zu ihrer Bekämpfung wie zum Beispiel einen Lektor.

Die Frage, was denn bei einem Kunstwerk Begriffe wie *fehlerfrei* oder *makellos* bedeuten, sei einmal dahingestellt. Der Lektor hat jedenfalls die Chance, ihm zu ein bisschen mehr Vollkommenheit zu verhelfen, bevor dann der Kritiker oder Literaturwissenschaftler darüber Gericht hält.

Kunst ist, wie Uwe Johnson sagt, eine Version der Wirklichkeit, nicht deren Spiegel. In diesem Sinne gilt es, den inhärenten Maßstab für diese Wirklichkeit zu finden, die der Autor entworfen hat. Zu diesem Entwurf gehört übrigens die Fiktion, die Wirklichkeit zu sein. Je versierter ein Autor ist, desto perfekter gelingt ihm diese Simulation. Glauben Sie also einem Autor nicht alles, was er – oder besser sein Erzähler – im Text behauptet: die Behauptung gehört zum Kunstwerk, zur Erzählerfigur in ihrer Fiktion und im Spiel des Autors, das auf mehreren Ebenen gleichzeitig stattfindet.

Eine dieser Spielformen ist es, Autobiographie vorzutäuschen. *Von allem Anfang an* arbeitet mit Mitteln des Biographischen, ist aber keinesfalls eine Autobiographie. Selbst wenn Elemente aus Christoph Heins Biographie zu erkennen sind (er erklärt, 10 Prozent des Erzählten seien Rudimente eigenen Erlebens, 90 Prozent erfunden – aber wer sollte wiederum diese Aussage nachprüfen können?), sind sie untrennbar in Erfundenes verwoben: eine erfolgreiche Strategie, um – wie er sagt – Lügen glaubhaft machen zu können. Eines seiner Lieblingszitate lautet denn auch sehr frei nach Platon: »Alle Schriftsteller sind Lügner«.

So gesehen, ist ein Lektor ein Komplize, der hilft, die Lügen zu perfektionieren und als Wahrheit erscheinen zu lassen. Und darum ist es letztlich in beider Interesse und dem Zufall zu danken, wenn nur eine unvollkommene Rekonstruktion ihrer gemeinsamen Bemühungen veröffentlicht werden kann.

Anmerkungen

[1] Anm. d. Hrsg.: Dieser Beitrag wurde ursprünglich am 15. Oktober 1998 als Vortrag im Germanistischen Seminar der Universität Wales Swansea gehalten.
[2] Günter Caspar, 'Im Umgang. Eine Paraphrase', in *Im Umgang. Zwölf Autoren-Konterfeis und eine Paraphrase* (Berlin und Weimar, Aufbau, 1984), S. 202.
[3] Ebd., S. 197.
[4] Ebd., S. 202.
[5] Kurt Tucholsky, 'Die Aussortierten', in *Mit 5 PS durch die Literatur. Essays und Rezensionen* (Berlin und Weimar, Aufbau, 1973), S. 476.

5

Die versteinerten Verhältnisse zum Tanzen bringen?
Der Autor Christoph Hein auf der Bühne

KLAUS HAMMER

In seinem erst 1981 veröffentlichten Essay 'Waldbruder Lenz' erzählt Christoph Hein gleich anfangs eine Geschichte, die er in einem Comic-Heft fand:

Ein Landstreicher erklärt einem ältlichen Priester des Vatikans die biblische Schöpfungsgeschichte, wonach die Erdkugel ein Wollknäuel ist, welches Gott aus dem Schoß gefallen sei und nun langsam von ihm wieder aufgerollt werde. Unser Leben sei insofern rückläufig, die Vergangenheit, unsere Zukunft und das Finale der Welt absehbar, es hänge am Fadenende. Auf die Frage des entsetzten Priesters, wo denn, bei Gott und allen Teufeln, dies in der Bibel stünde, entgegnet der Landstreicher: So direkt steht es natürlich nicht drin. Aber du bekommst es sehr schnell mit, wenn du verstehst, zwischen den Zeilen zu lesen. (Öa, 70)

Die künstlerischen Strategien »beim Schreiben der Wahrheit« (Brecht) waren in der Literatur der DDR vielfältig. Die Kunst, sowohl mit verstellter Stimme zu sprechen als auch »um die Ecke« zu lesen, wurde mit der moralischen Verpflichtung verbunden, den geknebelten Journalismus und den unterbundenen öffentlichen Diskurs in und mit der Kunst zu ersetzen. Viele Autoren setzten ihren Ehrgeiz darin, die Sprache der Herrschaft nur in ihrer Oberflächenstruktur benutzt, so die Organe des Machtapparates genarrt und »Kassiber« unter das Volk gebracht zu haben. Der Autor dissimulierte und verrätselte, konstruierte nach dem Modell von Anagramm oder Palimpsest, Labyrinth oder Rebus, und der eingeweihte Leser tüftelte und entschlüsselte.

Christoph Hein allerdings wies den Versuch einer Funktionalisierung von Literatur zum Zweck einer verschwörerischen Verständigung mittels der »Sklavensprache« strikt von sich. Er bestand darauf, Literatur schreiben zu wollen, und forderte diese

Freiheit – uneingeschränkte Öffentlichkeit – für alle. Er hat die
»versteinerten Verhältnisse« beschreiben wollen, und diese sollten
anfangen zu tanzen. Nicht der Vorgang sei das eigentlich Fürchterliche, sondern sein Benennen. In den letzten 800 Jahren sei es
immer ein Verbrechen gewesen, wenn bestehende Verhältnisse
genau benannt wurden (*TuK*, 89).

Die Ideale sind desavouiert, die Botschaften verschlissen, das
Leben scheint ein falsches, leeres, sinnloses und auswegloses –
Hein unternimmt die Bestandsaufnahme eines Zustandes, nicht die
Schilderung eines Entwicklungsprozesses. Während in seiner
Prosa gesellschaftliche Realität und Psychologie der Figuren
gleichermaßen minutiös aufgezeichnet und vernetzt erscheinen
(und die Notation geringfügiger Verhaltensänderungen hier das
Aufregende und »Unerhörte« der Begebenheit ausmacht), bleibt
der Autor in seinen konventionell gebauten Stücken vornehmlich
registrierender Chronist, der allerdings mehr an den Folgen als den
Fakten interessiert ist. Auch hier durchdringen sich Persönliches
und Gesellschaftliches, in scheinbar belangloser Konversation wird
gesellschaftliche (Nicht-)Entwicklung deutlich, banale zwischenmenschliche Vorgänge offenbaren Bestürzendes. Alle seine Dramen sind »historische Gegenwartsstücke«, weil Heins Blick in die
Vergangenheit auch immer einer in die Zukunft ist. »Gegenwart
wird ohnehin verhandelt. Für das Nichtstattfinden von Zeitung/Berichterstattung ist Theater kein Ersatz«, erklärte er schon
1978 (*Öa*, 100). Es sind Komödien, denn sie handeln von lächerlichen Kalamitäten mit tiefen, ernsten Bedeutungen. Es sind Spiele
um Kunstfiguren, Schau- und Denk-Spiele, in denen sich überall
komisch abgründige Fallen auftun. Sie heben sich in ihrer Abfolge
direkt und indirekt auf, führen weiter oder setzen dagegen – die
»gewöhnliche Haltung von Produktivität«, die das Theater (wieder) als Anstalt des öffentlichen Nachdenkens über große gesellschaftliche Gegenstände begreift, als »Schaubühne und Instrumentarium menschlicher Fantasie« (*Öa*, 119).

1
Hein hat nie in Abrede gestellt, dass die ihn umgebenden Verhältnisse auch sein Schreiben beeinflusst haben. In seiner Rede im
September 1989 über die in der DDR verdrängte Hinterlassenschaft des Stalinismus bekannte er, dass es ihn psychisch und physisch krank mache, in einem Land zu leben, dessen Bürger es
verlassen wollen: »es macht mich krank, weil die Gesellschaft

irgendwo krank ist« (*AK*, 155). Die Diagnose der Gesellschaft in seinen Texten ist auch die der Krankheit der Gesellschaft. In der Geschichte der Ärztin Claudia (in der Novelle *Der fremde Freund* von 1982), die da scheinbar fühllos über sich selbst berichtet, die alles unter Kontrolle, »alles im Griff« hat, versuchte der Autor (so in einem Gespräch 1991)

etwas von dem zu benennen, was ich gesehen habe, was vorhanden, fast unübersehbar war. Es war für mich eine DDR-Geschichte. Aber sie wurde in vierzig Ländern übersetzt, und auch an den Briefen aus sehr unterschiedlichen Ländern merkte ich, daß da offenbar noch etwas war, was auch in anderen Ländern vorhanden ist. In der *New York Times* hieß es dann auch: Die Frau lebe in Ostberlin, aber das Barometer stehe auf der gleichen Stelle wie in New York. Also ist da irgend etwas Übergreifendes, und ich vermute nachträglich, daß es eben etwas mit dem Stand der Zivilisation zu tun hat, die ja doch in den sonst politisch so unterschiedlichen Ländern vergleichbar ist. (*CB*, 29)

Indem Claudia sich weigert, sich selbst zu überprüfen, und alles verdrängt – das Wiederfinden der begrabenen Vergangenheit, die heilende Macht der Erinnerung –, nimmt die Oberfläche von vorbeiziehenden »alltäglichen Abziehbildern« (*fF*, 7) den Platz des abwesenden Ich ein. Das Ich Claudia wird durch den Beobachter Claudia abgelöst, an die Stelle von Selbsterleben, Selbsterfahren tritt kühle, distanzierte Registration. Und gerade weil so die Verbindungen zwischen Vergangenheit und Gegenwart total unterbrochen sind, kann es auch keine Zukunft geben. 1986 plädierte Hein für die ihm gemäße Haltung der Aufklärung, »die das Bestehende eindeutig und genau analysiert. [...] Wenn ich meine gegenwärtige Situation mitleidlos und distanziert genug, ohne Haß und Eifer betrachten kann, auch gnadenlos genug, dann, denke ich, ist dies eine Chance, einen künftigen Weg zu finden«.[1] Die Aufklärung der Gegenwart hängt also ab vom Verstehen der Vergangenheit, dem Wissen meiner eigenen Geschichte und der Geschichte der Gesellschaft. Der Kontrast zwischen (abwesendem) Ich und (anwesendem) Beobachter in Claudias Text dürfte also auf mehr hinweisen als auf den Bericht einer blockierten Identität. Ihre soziale Emanzipation ist praktisch mit einem völligen emotionalen Defizit erkauft. Heins Aufklärung der äußeren Erscheinungen sind Oberflächenprotokolle der Überlebensstrategien eines perfekt funktionierenden Ich. Die emanzipierte und funktionelle Beziehung zwischen Claudia und Henry, diesen beiden Fremden, wird aufrechterhalten durch das Nichtvorhandensein von Kommunikation, durch Kälte, Langeweile und Entfremdung. Beide versuchen zu leben, zu überleben, indem sie sich von ihrer Vergangenheit wie Zukunft lösen. Ihre Gegenwart aber ist erfüllt von der Leere des Wartens darauf, dass etwas geschieht. Das »Mir geht es gut« (*fF*, 212) von Claudia ist die schlimmste Bankrotterklärung des Ich und damit einer Gesellschaft, die dem einzelnen Identität, das Leben in sich selbst, verweigert. Es ist aber darüber hinaus die Frage nach dem Preis der Zivilisation in der modernen Gesellschaft, sowohl im Osten als auch im Westen. Von Bitterkeit und Komik zugleich ist die Geschichte des 36jährigen Hans-Peter Dallow in der Erzählung *Der Tangospieler* (1989) geprägt, der, nachdem ihn ein »Unfall« (*Ts*, 110) für 21 Monate ins Gefängnis gebracht hatte, nun wieder in Freiheit mit zweifelhaftem Erfolg nach einer freien Entscheidung sucht. Ebenso aber die Geschichte seines Konkurrenten Roessler, der, wiederum eines »Unfalls« wegen, auf der Karriereleiter des Wissenschaftsbetriebes ausrutscht, dem abgestürzten Dallow die »glückliche« Gelegenheit bietend, dieselbe hinaufzufallen.

Gerade diese »Unfälle« werfen ein ironisch-satirisches Schlaglicht auf Paradoxes in der Stellung beider Historiker im und zum zeitgenössischen historischen Geschehen. Dallow war damals nur eingesprungen als Klavierspieler, ohne Kenntnis des umgeschriebenen Tangotextes, der eine so drakonische Strafe nach sich zog. Doch kehrt er am Ende, nunmehr wiederum Nutzen ziehend aus dem grotesken Missgeschick des anderen, Roesslers, ins Historische Institut zurück und kann sich den Gag leisten: »eine Bedingung [. . .] keine Vorlesungen früh um sieben« (*Ts*, 204). Erst will er die Nachrichten gehört haben.

Hier, an diesen Wendepunkten der Erzählung, setzt Hein die Realität als Groteske ein. Normalität und Banalität haben Dallow eingeholt, sie sind stärker als die unerhörte Begebenheit seiner Haft. Dallow erscheint als die männliche und politisierte Ausführung der Kälte, die im *Fremden Freund* so erschreckte. Mit seiner Entlassung aus dem Gefängnis hatte die Erzählung eingesetzt. Wie verhält sich der zufällig und versehentlich Verurteilte in der wiedererlangten Freiheit? Am liebsten würde er wieder in den alten Gleisen unter den vertrauten Bedingungen weiterlaufen. Er ist unfähig zur Freiheit, und es fehlen auch die Räume dafür. Er kann noch weniger als vorher Entscheidungen treffen, er sehnt sich nach einer Situation, in der wieder für ihn Vorsorge getroffen wird.

Im westberliner Rechtsanwalt Dr. Wörle des Romanes *Das Napoleon-Spiel* führt uns Hein dann einen Mann vor, dessen Lebensphilosophie das Spiel ist. Es reicht von den kindlich-erotischen Spielen über das Billardspiel mit sich allein bis zur Tötung eines Menschen. Napoleon sieht er als den größten Hasardeur der Weltgeschichte an; dessen Russlandfeldzug sei allein Sucht am Spiel gewesen. »Auch ihm ging es nicht darum zu gewinnen [. . .]. Er mußte spielen, um weiter leben zu können. Darum der Spielzug Moskau. Auch er nahm dafür Tote in Kauf« (*NS*, 130), so argumentiert Wörle. Er sucht innere Leere, Bindungsarmut und Werteverluste mit den Aktivitäten seines wechselnden Spiels zu kompensieren. Dabei verliert er immer mehr als Mensch, geht seiner menschlichen Substanz verlustig. Während die Ärztin Claudia und der Tangospieler Dallow in Gleichgültigkeit verfallen sind, mit Überdruck und Gefühlskälte auf den Verlust von Werten und Beziehungen reagieren, sucht Wörle sich mit seinem Spielaktionismus zu betäuben. Er ist noch unverletzlicher als die beiden Figurenvarianten aus dem Osten. Wörle ist das glücklichere Pendant zu Claudia, die dem Selbstmord nahe schien. Wörle kann zwar der Überdruss umbringen, aber für Selbstmord ist er nicht der Mann. Er hat noch genügend Spiele auf Lager. Seine Sorge ist, als banaler Mörder verurteilt zu werden. Es ist sehr hilfreich, wenn ihm so ein Wort wie »Solidarität« fehlt. Der Gebrauch von Freiheit schließt immer auch den Missbrauch mit ein. Wörle handelt aus Langeweile, zu erklären aus dem deformierten Zustand der Zivilisation. Die schrecklichsten Wahrheiten, auch über sich selbst, lassen sich besser mit einer Maske sagen. Schreiben hat sehr viel mit Spielen zu tun. Erinnerungen und Ausblicke reduzieren sich auf den Überdruss am Bekannten und die Angst vor der Wiederholung. Hoffnung oder gar Utopie kommen gar nicht mehr vor, die Dimension der Geschichte ist wie weggebrochen. In dem Roman *Horns Ende* hatte Kruschkatz über Horn geäußert, dass der für diesen Tod bestimmt war »wie ein Ochse für den Schlachthof«. Für ihn war Horn nicht »lebenstüchtig«, denn er war »für ein Leben unter Menschen nicht geeignet« (*HE*, 86). Für Wörle ist es gerade Kennzeichen »des Menschen«, nicht allzu selbstlos zu sein. Darum ist nicht der Selbstsüchtige das Monstrum, sondern eher der mildtätige Urwalddoktor. Denn er bleibt die Ausnahme. »Die kleine Schäbigkeit, die uns einen Vorteil bringt, kennzeichnet sie nicht genauer das Menschliche?« (*NS*, 134), fragt Wörle. Nach Kruschkatz gibt es mehrere, einander widersprechende Wahrheiten.

Spodeck vergleicht das Bewusstsein mit tausend Spiegeln, von denen jeder tausendfach gebrochen ist. Der Heinsche Roman hat die Struktur eines Puzzle. Das »Napoleonspiel« endet damit, dass wieder ein neues Spiel ansetzt. Wörle verlangt das Manuskript zurück und will es einem vermeintlichen Schriftsteller geben, der es dann unter seinem Namen veröffentlicht. Kunst ist in diesem Sinne vollendetes Spiel: Sie verarbeitet Wirklichkeit mit Verkehrungen, Spiegelungen, Frakturen und nicht in purer Form.

2

In der Prosa konnte Hein seine Texte bis zu Ende selbst inszenieren. Die Notation minimaler Verhaltensänderungen, die hier so aufregend wirkt, verliert aber auf der Bühne in ihrer szenischen Unmenschlichkeit an Spannung. Was in der Prosa als subtile Zustandsbeschreibung des Denkens und (Nicht-)Fühlens einer Figur in sinnlicher sprachlicher Präsenz aufscheint, mag in der Dramatik deklamatorisch wirken. Aber dazu bedient sich Hein bestimmter literarischer Mittel, theatralischer Instrumentarien und Strategien wie einer szenischen Phantasie, die er in jedem Stück anders einsetzt. »Warum [...] kommt eine neue Zeit immer mit einem Sortiment ausgesuchter Plattköpfe daher, die sich auf ihre schlichte Einfalt überdies noch etwas einbilden« (Cr, 9), so orakelt General Manchester, Cromwells Mitfeldherr, ein Graf und kein landadliger Ackerbauer wie Cromwell. »Nein, dem Karl Stuart mußte man auf die Finger klopfen. [...] Seine Hände steckten beständig in unseren Taschen« (Cr, 9). Die revolutionären Puritaner können sich aber selbst nicht die Taschen füllen, wenn sie sie nicht vorher anderen zu leeren verstehen. Graf Manchester wird noch manches dazulernen müssen. Im Cromwell-Stück entleert sich Geschichte durch »laufende Ereignisse«, verkümmert Geschichte zum Anekdotischen. Nicht aus vorbedachtem Verständnis wird der Grundbesitzer Cromwell mehr und mehr zum Einsatz revolutionärer Mittel getrieben, nachdem er doch angetreten war, um für ausschließlich eigene Interessen zu kämpfen. »Macht korrumpiert und Fanatismus ist kontraproduktiv«.[2] Bald verliert er sich darin, die Macht bloß zu behaupten, sie in kleinlichen pragmatischen Kompromissen zwischen alten und neuen Kräften zu ruinieren. Ein Lehrstück über den tödlichen Mechanismus der Revolution, gebrochen durch spielerisch groteske Elemente. Denn die Quintessenz besteht ja gerade in der ironischen Pointe, dass der Bauer Cromwell besiegt wird durch den Hunger. Die »City«, d. h. die

Kaufleute aus der Ostindischen Kompagnie und ihre Freunde haben ihn künstlich herbeigeführt, sie haben die vollen Lager geschlossen: »Die Armee kann einen König besiegen, aber sie kann nicht Krieg führen gegen Kartoffeln und Rüben« (*Cr*, 51). Das exponierte Individuum, der revolutionäre Führer, wird an einem bestimmten Punkt der revolutionären Entwicklung von dieser selbst überrollt. Angesichts dieser subjektiv unverschuldeten Ohnmacht steht Cromwell vor dem Dilemma, sich als Tyrann der Geschichte zu behaupten oder als Don Quichote abzutreten. »Seine Tugenden und Prinzipien werden korrumpiert, die Freiheit schlägt um in Terror, die Republik verkommt zur Militärdiktatur, die Revolution frißt ihre Ideale«.[3] Hein hat die damals ablaufende Revolution in Portugal »kräftig benutzt«, um die Brechungen zu bekommen, die das Historienstück verhindern sollten (*CB*, 18). Er hat auch Bruchstücke aus Gerichtsreden von Stalins Starankläger Wyschinski montiert. An einer Modellsituation sollte etwas durchgespielt werden, die Bedingungen für Gelingen oder Nicht-Gelingen einer Revolution. Das hatte natürlich zu tun mit den stehengebliebenen, abgebogenen, rückläufigen Prozessen im eigenen Lande, bis hin zu dem vollständigen Ende des Aufbruchs im Stück. Der alte, neue König kehrt zurück. Der Leichnam Cromwells wird aus dem Grab geholt und öffentlich aufgehängt.

In einem Gespräch 1992 meinte Hein sogar, im *Cromwell* bereits das Ende Honeckers vorweggenommen zu haben, wie er ebenso für sich in Anspruch nimmt, elfmal – vom *Cromwell* 1974 bis zu den *Rittern der Tafelrunde* 1989 – das Ende der DDR beschrieben zu haben.[4] Geschichte also als eine »Form von Wiederholung in geradezu kurioser Art und Weise«, die ins Groteske und Absurde umkippt. So wenn Cromwell die eigenen Fehler auf das Volk projiziert (»Eine Kanaille, die nur gelauert hat auf das Mißglücken meiner Arbeit. [...] Sie waren nicht reif genug [...]. Sie sind undankbar und rachsüchtig« (*Cr*, 84–5)) – Projektionen, die in der Geschichte der sozialistischen Revolutionen und ihres Scheiterns angesiedelt sein können. Diese Anachronismen hat Hein als »grobe Mittel« (*CB*, 20) bezeichnet, sie sollen die Geschichte in die Gegenwart verlängern, ihre Unabgeschlossenheit bewusst machen, ohne aber die Vermischung verschiedener historischer Ebenen zu bewirken.

Das war dann aber genau der Punkt, der die Inszenierungen in der DDR (Cottbus 1980; Gera, Eisenach 1984) und in der Bundesrepublik (Essen 1986) voneinander unterschied: Während die

DDR-Aufführungen vom historischen Stoff ausgingen, die Tragödie der »bürgerlichen« Revolution nachzeichneten und die »provokanten Brechungen von Zeit- und Raumebenen«[5] von einem allerdings sensibel reagierenden Publikum selbst entschlüsseln ließen, wurde in Essen ein Gegenwartsstück aus der DDR inszeniert, mit dem willkürlichen Einsatz heutigen Vokabulars, in Form eines Kabaretts, das den Zuschauer zwar zu amüsieren vermochte, aber ihm doch vorkam wie eine ferne, ihn nicht berührende Welt. Die Camouflage, die bei Texten in der DDR solange notwendig und mutig schien, konnte in der Bundesrepublik nur mit einem »DDR-Bonus« aufgenommen werden.

Im Gegensatz zu Cromwell lebt Lassalle in einer Epoche der Restauration: Jener kann mit der Zeit nicht Schritt halten, dieser sich mit ihren (nun kleinen) Schritten nicht abfinden. Die Situation der beiden Titelfiguren scheint komplementär und berührt sich doch in einem entscheidenden Punkt: Das Scheitern kommt für beide zwangsläufig, ist unvermeidliches Moment ihres Aufbegehrens. Im Lassalle-Stück demoliert Hein die Form des großen historischen Schauspiels aus dem 19. Jahrhundert bis zur Unkenntlichkeit. »Er mißachtet auch alle Bauprinzipien eines Dramas. Seine Geschichte läuft bald auf Grund, und dann werden nur noch Trümmer aufgeräumt«.[6]

Der Autor zitiert stattdessen das Salon-Stück, das Konversationsstück mit seiner »kunstlosen« Sprache des Banalen und Trivialen, mit seiner aus kleinen (and kleinlichen) Querelen bestehenden Handlung. Der Figurenaufschluss erfolgt auch hier von der privaten Existenz her, ja eine der banalsten und »privatesten« Episoden aus dem Leben des deutschen Sozialisten-Vorläufers wird zu einer »Pseudospannung« erhoben: Die lächerliche Liebesgeschichte mit einem adligen Gänschen, die mit dem ebenso lächerlichen Tod Lassalles – durch ein Duell, durch einen Schuss in den Genitalbereich – endet. Er ist ja nichts anderes als ein verschleierter Selbstmord. Denn Lassalles Versuch der erwünschten Annäherung an die Klasse der Arbeiter ist gescheitert. Seine persönliche Verkommenheit – seinen Opportunismus – nimmt er ja sehr genau selbst wahr, und andere Alternativen als den Tod sind ihm nicht mehr möglich. Dieser Lassalle ist ein Parvenü, ein Hochstapler, Schürzenjäger, Demagoge und Spieler der Revolution, der sich in eitler Selbstgefälligkeit in ihr sonnt. Er spielt ständig Theater vor sich selbst und vor den anderen. Der Kampf der Arbeiter schien ihm wunderbare Auftritte, Applaus and

Tränen zu versprechen, and danach schminkte er sich wieder ab, und tauschte die Barrikade gegen den Salon ein. Der Leser soll erkennen, dass dieser Mann da immer unterhalb seiner eigenen Geschichte geblieben ist und bleiben muss, der Philosoph, dessen Phiosophie mit dem eigenen Leben ebenso wenig wie mit den Problemen der Arbeiter zu tun hat. Die Verwicklungen, Zwänge und Bedrängnisse Lassalles werden in den Beziehungen zu den ihn umgebenden Typen des bürgerlichen Lachtheaters, den Schwänken eines Labiche oder Feydeau entsprungen, abgebildet. Da gibt es

die den Sohn kompromittierende Alte, der der Gettogeruch noch anhaftet, den erzproletarischen Nichtversteher mit seiner Aufrichtigkeit, den auf die erste Gelegenheit zur Usurpation wartenden Domestiken, das sich zur Tragödin hochspielende, abservierte Ladenmädchen, den päderastischen Feingeist und Proletkult-Snob, die klimakterische Gräfin, die ihren sublimierten Geschlechtstrieb sogar auf die Finanzhilfe für die Arbeiterklasse wendet.[7]

Alle Denunziationsmechanismen laufen in ihnen zusammen. Jeder Streit wird hemmungslos durchgespielt. Jede Peinlichkeit übertrifft die vorangegangene. Kaum hat die eine Geliebte den Herrn zurückgewiesen, duelliert er sich für eine andere. Und diesmal ist es das Ende. Sogleich machen sich die Leichenfledderer ans Werk. Im Schwank lassen sich die Personen ebenso leicht austauschen wie die Örtlichkeiten, in denen sie sich tummeln. Doch bei Hein spiegelt sich die anekdotische Geschichte Lassalles wie in einer »Nußschale« (CB, 22) wieder. Ein abgebrochenes Leben wird beschworen zur Aufhellung zeitgenössischen Dahinlebens. »Das Stück ist vor allem ein Stück Autobiographie«, lässt uns Hein wissen, »eine Möglichkeit, von eigenen Zwängen, Verstrickungen und Befindlichkeiten spielerisch zu erzählen.« Und an anderer Stelle: »Ich habe auch mit dieser Figur zu tun, mit diesem Kleinbürger«, »mit diesen Unerträglichkeiten« (Öa, 29–33).

Was bedeutete Lassalle einem Publikum, das die Geschichte Lassalles nur aus der Perspektive Bismarcks kennt, und was einem Publikum, das sie nut aus der Sicht von Marx kennt? Die historische Begegnung zwischen Bismarck und Lassalle, die beide in ihrem Antiliberalismus übereinstimmten, findet auf Heins Bühne seine private, personalisierte Entsprechung in Lassalles Diener Herbert, der zuvor bei Bismarck in Diensten stand.

Die Anbiederung Lassalles ans Establishment seiner Zeit erfolgt auf der Kammerdienerebene und kündet von einer Funktionärsmentalität, die das Stück als keineswegs historisch abgetan, sondern als fortwirkend aktuell erkennen läßt.[8]

Vermochte sich das deutsche Publikum in Ost und West mit dem Diener Herbert zu identifizieren, dessen Maxime lautet: »Die Gedanken [...] sind in Deutschland immer noch frei. Folglich darf ich mir welche machen, muß sie aber nicht äußern« (Cr, 94)?

Als eine Tragödie über den Rückzug aus der Politik in der DDR und zugleich eine Komödie über opportunistische Anpasser erlebte das Stück auch 1980 in Düsseldorf seine Uraufführung. Sie handelt von einer Revolution, die nie auf die Beine kam, von einer Gesellschaft, die nie durch Umsturz verändert wurde, und schließlich von einem Geschichtsbewusstsein, dem sich Geschichte nicht mehr als fortschreitender, verändernder Prozess darstellt, sondern als Anekdote.

Die DDR-Erstaufführung mit sieben Jahren Verspätung in Erfurt stellt den Salon als Refugium von Veränderern, die gescheitert sind und hier eine bestimmte Art von Wirklichkeitsbewältigung leisten, auf die Bühne. »Im banalen Salonrevoluzzertum eine Art Wetterleuchten verlorener Utopie, zerrieben zwischen den Mahlsteinen gesellschaftlicher Existenzformen«.[9] Zwei schräg gestellte Glaswände lassen stets in die Szene einsehen, machen Verborgenes sichtbar und verfremden zugleich. Transparenz erweist sich als Lebensform: Lassalle macht sich zum selbstgefälligen Clown und die Szene zu seinem Spiegel. Wenn Hein heute eines seiner Stücke zur Aufführung empfehlen sollte, dann wäre es dieses. »Zur Zeit läuft das Stück überall, nicht gerade auf der Bühne, aber sonst überall im Land« (CB, 17). Denn der Geschichtspessimismus gerinnt zum wohlfeilen Klischee; die Erfahrung des Scheiterns wird missbraucht als Konzession dafür, sich wehleidig dem »Fatalismus der Geschichte« zu überlassen.

3
Bei der Wahren Geschichte des Ah Q ist nicht mehr die Brechung und Aufsplitterung der Strukturen durch Anachronismen, durch Sich-Reiben und Sich-Berühren der Zeiten, durch Assoziationsreihen so wichtig, sondern der Spielraum fungiert wieder als Bühnenraum: Zwei Schauspieler sprechen einen einstudierten Text auf der Bühne. Wenn eine Figur aus dem Spiel heraustritt, und sich als

Schauspieler demaskiert, wird dem Leser die Möglichkeit gegeben, ein fremderes, befremdeteres Verhältnis zu den Vorgängen einzunehmen. Tschechow, Lenz, Commedia dell'arte, absurdes Theater mischen sich hier zu einem Spiel um eine Wartesituation, um die Unfähigkeit, utopisch, solidarisch, politisch zu denken und zu handeln, um eine Revolution, die nicht stattfindet, weil die, deren Interesse sie wäre, nicht imstande sind, sie herbeizuführen. Sie warten und ihre Hoffnung hat nicht die Kraft eines Entwurfs oder auch nur eines Traums von besserem Leben. Anarchie geistert als Zauberwort auf der Bühne. Es beschreibt einen Zweifel an allem, eine Haltung, die am Beginn jeder Philosophie gestanden hat. Das Zerstören, um zu einem neuen Anfang zu kommen, zu einer neuen Hoffnung zu finden, um Illusion als Illusion entlarven zu können – um diesen Punkt kreisen die Gedanken der beiden Figuren Ah Q und Wang. Wo der Wunsch nach Genuss reglementiert wird, entwickeln sich egoistische, parasitäre und kriminelle Energien. Gegenüber dem Anspruch der Ideologie, die Utopie habe ausschließlich objektive und nicht auch subjektive Bedeutung, riskiert der Autor den Absturz ins »Triviale« – aber das Triviale erscheint hier als das Wahre. Ein Stück, das über die Verzweiflung einen Funken Hoffnung vermitteln will. Denn Anarchie ist Vergewaltigung auf der einen und etwas Zärtliches, Hoffnungsvolles auf der anderen Seite. Der ihr zugrundeliegende Gedanke ist ein antizipatorischer: Wir haben es hier mit gesellschaftlichen Träumern und Anregern zu tun, nicht aber mit Politikern. Alle Figuren sind irgendwie vergewaltigt. Der Gegenspieler ist eine für sie nicht mehr erfassbare Zeit.

Sie haben [...], [so Hein 1983 vor der Berliner Uraufführung, K.H.] weil sie mit einer für sie unfaßbar ablaufenden Wirklichkeit nicht mehr hinkommen, einfach die ganz normale Erwartung auf eine andere Wirklichkeit. Auf die himmlische bei der Nonne, auf eine revolutionäre bei Ah Q und Wang oder eben Maske, der ja fast alles hinter sich hat, der von sich nur noch erwartet, gut zu funktionieren. Vielleicht, weil er am schlimmsten vergewaltigt wurde.[10]

Aus verweigerter Lust entsteht Aggression: Ah Q hat sich in Gefahr begeben und ist darin umgekommen. Doch ihm war auch kein »Blick ins Getriebe der Welt« (RT, 51) gestattet, wie ihn sein anarchielehrender Kompagnon Wang für sich reklamiert, der vor den damit verbundenen Konsequenzen aber kneift. Das auslösende Moment – Revolution, eine degenerierte Revolution hat es auch hier nicht gegeben und man hat nachträglich versucht, das dafür fehlende Bewusstsein zu schaffen, durch ein Nivellieren der Prozesse, durch Verfälschungen und gewaltsame Überzeugungsarbeit.

Ah Q ist für Hein die Dramatisierung des *Fremden Freundes*: Zwischen den Interessen dahinschwimmend, sich mal den einen, mal den anderen ein wenig anschließend, ohne irgendwo zu Hause zu sein. Er hat selbst Ah Q und Wang in die Nachbarschaft der Sinnsucher und -leugner des absurden Dramas konzipiert, da er ihnen keine Geschichte gibt und jeden Rest von Auflehnung in ihnen in Inkonsequenz münden lässt. Dennoch – und das unterscheidet sie wiederum von den Figuren Becketts – ist in ihnen die humane Alternative stets mitgedacht, auch wenn ihr Hein keine Chance gibt. Aussage steht gegen Handlung; »dem Schicksal eins in die Fresse« (*RT*, 8), sagt Ah Q und lässt das Schicksal walten. Wang: »Die Geschichte liebt Sprünge. Dialektik. Vom Niederen aufsteigend zum Höheren und abfallend ins Triviale« (*RT*, 50). Wie die Geschichte sich auch dreht und wendet, sie ist nichts anderes als eine Kette von absurden Zufällen, die jeder geschichtsphilosophischen Logik entbehrt. Die Intelligenz muss ihren Platz noch finden, um nicht die Kreisbewegungen ihrer Geschichte endlos fortzusetzen.

Heins *Ah Q* wurde offenbar in Frankreich und in der Schweiz besser begriffen als in den beiden Teilen Deutschlands – in der Möglichkeit, sich spielerisch über die eigene Realität zu verständigen. Die clowneske Provokation von Alexander Langs Inszenierung am Deutschen Theater 1983 bestand in dem geheimen Einverständnis mit dem Publikum, das da herauskam. Jekers Kasseler Inszenierung wiederum ließ die Figuren »in eine bedeutungsschwangere Auseinandersetzung eintreten, als müßten sie sich mit neugewonnenen Einsichten« – und nicht mit empirisch und intellektuell gewonnenem Spielmaterial – »erst gegenseitig überzeugen«.[11] In Strasbourg dagegen wurde das Stück 1984 unter dem Titel *Zwischen Hund und Wolf* als tragikomisches Märchen inszeniert, das in eine böse Parabel umschlägt, mit »Figuren im Wechselbad ihrer eigenen und der politischen Geschichte: Distanz und Nähe, voreilige Zweck-Versöhnung und Unvereinbarkeit, wenns um die eigene Haut geht«.[12] Während in Zürich Peter Schweiger – ähnlich wie Alexander Lang in Berlin – 1985 eine komödiantische Auseinandersetzung über »Intellektuellen-Phraseologie, über den Abstand von Ideologie und Realität, über den Elfenbeinturm der geistigen Hochstapler« herausbrachte, ging gleichzeitig in Bern »ein Stück über Diktatur und Folter, über den Zynismus der Mächtigen«,[13] mit eingeschobenen V-Effekten, wenn die Protagonisten das Publikum direkt ansprachen, über die Bühne. Die Analogien und Assoziationen, die der Text zulässt, machen ihn auch heute für die Bühne interessant, weil er sich »sehr raffiniert vernetzt«,[14] dieses Spielerische, Offene, Bewegliche in Zusammenhang mit der sich verändernden wie veränderten Realität bringt.

Die beiden »Intellektuellen im Wartestand«,[15] Ah Q und Wang, haben sich auf den Dachboden – in ihr anarchistisches Wolkenkuckucksheim – zurückgezogen, aber am Ende den defekten Überbau namens Dach nicht repariert. »Die Szene ein Hinterzimmer«[16] könnte dagegen unter *Passage* stehen, das Hein hintersinnig »ein Kammerspiel« nennt. Wieder die »geschlossene Gesellschaft«, wieder die Geschichte, die draußen passiert, während drinnen nur geredet, nur reagiert wird. Ein Typen-Personal, jeder ist in seine eigene Welt verstrickt, und so geht die gemeinsame Welt unter. Nur am Bildrand ziehen, unberührt, die 15 Juden ihres Wegs über die Pyrenäen – keine Fiktion, sondern eine wahre Begebenheit, die die Ausweglosigkeit der historischen Konstellation nur um so bewusster macht. Die betont konventionelle Form des Kammerspiels, die die Handlung ganz linear erzählt, erscheint hier gänzlich unangebracht und entfaltet gerade dadurch seine produktive Wirkung. Die ästhetischen Instrumentarien werden gleichsam in den Gegenstand – die ohnmächtige Wartesituation – hineingenommen. Während draußen die Geschichte eskaliert, sind die Flüchtlinge zum Warten verdammt und damit auf triviale Konversation verwiesen.[17] Selbst der Schluss (Lisa: »Einen Moment wollen wir noch warten« (*RT*, 130)) lässt in diesem Sinne die Frage nach dem Aufbruch, dem Ziel offen. Das Ende des Stückes ist nicht das Ende der Geschichte.

4
Leerstellen, Brüche, Abstände zwischen den Teilen drängen sich in den spannend erzählten Ablauf der Geschichte des *Passage*-Stückes. Als Kurt, ein junger Antifaschist, die Schachpartie vorschnell verloren gibt, hält ihm der Sinologe Dr. Frankfurther, der Züge des im gleichen Jahr aus dem Leben geschiedenen Walter Benjamin trägt, entgegen: »Dummheiten. Denken Sie nach. Zwei, drei Züge voraussehen, alle möglichen Reaktionen des Gegners einplanen, das ist alles. In unserer Situation ist es lebensnotwendig,

das zu lernen« (*RT*, 63). Was der Intellektuelle Frankfurther beim Schach geübt hat – das Brettspiel als »Überlebenstraining in finsteren Zeiten«[18] – kann er für die Praxis nicht nutzen. Er ist dem täglichen Druck von Warten, Hoffen und befürchteter Festnahme nicht länger gewachsen. Sein Selbstmord ist ein letzter, verzweifelter Akt des Widerstandes und tragischerweise doch eine Fehleinschätzung. Dagegen beginnt der jüdische Ex-Hauptmann Hirschburg, der sein plötzliches Unerwünschtsein für ein Missverständnis gehalten hat, angesichts des Verzweiflungsmarsches der Juden die Endlösung als Völkermord zu durchschauen, er bekennt sich zum alten Glauben und erwägt die Überquerung des Gebirges.»Kann uns Vernünftiges helfen? Sagen Sie. Dann muß uns etwas Dummes helfen« (*RT*, 126). Der Hoffnungsträger der ersten beiden Akte, der Intellektuelle, der sein Buchmanuskript zur Rettung übergibt, nicht sein Leben, sondern sein Werk als erhaltenswert befindet, kapituliert. Der Pragmatiker, der mit seinem Schatz an alten Generalstabskarten und seinem verbohrten Glauben an das Missverständnis seiner Verfolgung misstrauisch betrachteter, unerbetener Fremdkörper war, versucht das Unmögliche. In seiner letzten Arbeit *Über den Begriff der Geschichte* (1940) hatte sich Benjamin mit dem Fortschrittsglauben der deutschen Sozialdemokratie und dem linearen Kausalitätsdenken der (literarischen) Universalhistorie auseinandergesetzt. Der Text wird in der ersten der Kunstwerkthesen mit einer Schachpartie verglichen; er soll als ein »Streit um den wahren Begriff der Geschichte [...] in Gestalt einer Partie zwischen 2 Partnern« angelegt sein, wie die zur These gehörige Aufzeichnung erklärt. Das Gleichnis hebt anekdotisch an und wird dann mit Begriffen verfremdet, die das Gleichnis »ins Freie« führen sollen. Selbst in der Situation verzweifelter Ausweglosigkeit wird Hoffnung geboren. Benjamin in einer Aufzeichnung: »Beispiel echter historischer Vorstellung: ›An die Nachgeborenen‹. Wir beanspruchen von den Nachgeborenen nicht Dank für unsere Siege, sondern das Eingedenken unserer Niederlagen.« Das zielt auf den Zeitenumbruch, den nur das Erinnern »rückwärts« überspringen kann. Benjamin richtet sich an die Nachwelt, wenn er den Historiker ermutigen will, »seine Zeit im Medium von verflossenen Verhängnissen« zu betrachten.[19]

Die Schweizerische Erstaufführung 1987 stellte *Passage* in den Zusammenhang von »Fluchtpunkt Zürich«, mit dem daran erinnert wurde, dass das Schauspielhaus Zürich während des Nationalsozialismus für viele deutsche Theaterleute eine Zufluchts- und

Wirkungsstätte war. Auf eine »theaterhafte Überhöhung der Wirklichkeit«[20] zielte die Essener Uraufführung. Den utopischen Aufbruch der 15 Juden, die Grenzüberschreitung im Geiste des »Prinzips Hoffnung« brachte Hansgünther Heyme am Schluss als Allegorie szenisch sichtbar auf die Bühne. Das Ausbleiben der so planvoll angelegten Katastrophe wirkte wie ein »Beruhigungsstoff« für Fernsehzuschauer:[21] »Ein kleines, trauriges Spiel von deutscher Seele, deutscher Seelenlosigkeit«.[22] »Wir erleben Geschichtsunterricht in melodramatischem Gewand«.[23] Der Dresdner Regisseur Klaus Dieter Kirst dagegen schrieb den Text szenisch weiter, häufte Assoziationsmaterial an. Ohne Verleugnung des historischen Kontextes entfaltete sich ein Gegenwartstück: »Stagnation, heillose Bewegung im Stillstand, Frustrationen und Enttäuschungen angesichts ausbleibender Passagen, die Aura undurchlässiger Grenzen – alles das trifft offenbar [...] auf ein Lebensgefühl, das ein Westpublikum nachzuempfinden kaum in der Lage war«.[24] Fragt Hein in *Passage* nach der ständig neuen Prüfung des Möglichen, zwingt er seine *Ritter der Tafelrunde* in einen vergleichbaren Prozess des Umdenkens. Er wird zur aktuellen Entscheidung – für das Überleben auf unserem Planeten, für die Preisgabe eines Ideals, das längst total verschlissen ist, für eine menschliche Form des Zusammenlebens. Heins Stück ist der Legende, dem Mythos näher als der realen Historie, und er erzählt eine Geschichte, die aus jenen fernen Zeiten auch morgen noch und erneut Gültigkeit haben kann: eine End- und Umbruchssituation.

Die Komödie *Die Ritter der Tafelrunde* entstand schon 1985. Vier Jahre später in Dresden uraufgeführt, wurde es zu einem Teil jenes politischen Theaters in der DDR, das dem Umbruch als Forum diente. In dieser Situation musste das Stück rundum als Chiffre einer allen spürbaren Bankrotterklärung des Systems erscheinen. Die Komödie galt als ein prophetisches Schlüsselstück über die letzten Tage des Honeckerschen Politbüros. Hein im Gespräch 1991: »der Zuschauer [war] gar nicht fähig, das zu abstrahieren, und nahm das pur, möglicherweise sogar 1:1, was gar nicht aufgeht bei dem Stück« (CB, 38). Zwischen ihrer ruhmreichen Vergangenheit und der glanzvollen Zukunft, in die der Gral sie führen soll, sind die Ritter der Tafelrunde in einem unbeweglich-tristen Heute steckengeblieben. Auch hier wieder das Boulevardstück in der eigentümlichen Abgeschiedenheit von den Geschehnissen draußen (»Palaverdramatik« nennt es Hartmut Krug).[25] Die Suche nach dem Gral sollte ein Glück verheißen, das das Artus-Reich selbst überflüssig werden ließ. Der Gral verspricht das Paradies auf Erden, ein irdisches Glück ohne Grenzen. Aber niemand kennt es aus eigener Anschauung und keiner kann es genau definieren. Die vielseitige Brauchbarkeit schließt den Missbrauch ein. Die transzendentale Sinnstiftung einer Idee, einer Utopie, entbehrt jenes komplexen Syndroms der »Ichsucht«. Artus: »Die unsterblichen Toten machten uns unverletzlich« (RT, 190). Ein Kampf, der solche Opfer gefordert hat, kann nicht sinnlos sein, weil er es nicht darf. Das ist der Don-Quichotte-Punkt des Stückes, der die Figuren zu Rittern der traurigen Gestalt macht, die durch den (Nicht-) Zusammenstoß mit der veränderten Welt zu anachronistischen Figuren wurden. »Jedes reflektierende Bewusstsein birgt unausgesprochen die Alternative in sich. Der Mythos ist, wiewohl in der Vergangenheit wurzelnd, immer der Zukunft verwandt und damit ein höhnendes oder schmerzliches Bild gegenwärtiger Bemühungen«, sagt Hein.[26]

Der Kurzschluss, das Artusreich in der Krise eindeutig erkennbar hinzustellen, wäre in der Tat verhängnisvoll gewesen.[27] Die Dresdner haben ihn vermieden, die Distanz blieb gewahrt. Obwohl in Dresden peinlich jede Aktualisierung vermieden und das Stück auf einer allgemeinen ideengeschichtlichen Ebene als psychologisches Kammerspiel inszeniert wurde, leistete Heins Text dennoch den Schauspielern wie Zuschauern keinen Widerstand. Er wurde von seiner vordergründigen politischen Bedeutung fast aufgesogen. Auch die bundesdeutsche Erstaufführung im März 1990 in Kassel machte vom ersten Bild an recht vordergründig klar, wer diese Gesellschaft repräsentiert. Hatte die Realität die Voraussetzungen für eine Legende eingeholt und zerstört? Die Camouflage, als »das Widerlöcken gegen das System«[28] jahrzehntelang in der Bundesrepublik verstanden, hatte nach der Öffnung der Mauer ihre Wirkung verloren. Der Regisseur Peter Siefert betonte, er habe sich während der Probenarbeit drei bis viermal einer veränderten Lesart des Stückes gegenübergesehen, bestimmt von der politischen Realität.

> Der Fall ist erledigt, das Geschäft kann beginnen. Längst stehen die Herren mit den Aktenköfferchen, die Konjunkturritter, vor den zerfallenen Mauern. Und der Junior im Herrscherhaus, der gerade seinen alten Herrn in den längst verdienten Ruhestand geleitet hat, wird nur noch mit ihnen verhandeln. Ob er allerdings dabei noch irgendeinen Rest des alten Reiches retten kann,[29]

das blieb offen beim Kasseler Finale. Damit machte Siefert spätestens in den letzten Bildern den Ansatz zunichte, den eigentlich jede Bühne außerhalb der DDR zu prüfen hätte – nämlich auszuloten, ob es, wie Hein meint, tatsächlich um Schwierigkeiten gehe, die nicht nur sein Land beträfen.

Der Verlust aller Mythen, der Niedergang der Normen, die eine Gesellschaft notdürftig zusammenhalten, der Abschied von liebgewordenen, aber ausgehöhlten Werten, die Vernichtung der eigenen Geschichte, die keinen mehr interessiert und die die eigenen Zöglinge schon gar nicht mehr als leuchtende Zukunft übernehmen möchten – dies alles mischt sich an Heins Tafelrunde zur Grundmetapher einer Gesellschaft ohne Zukunft.[30]

»Künftige Literatur«, so Hein in seinem Essay 'Öffentlich arbeiten',»wird Autobiographie sein, keine private, aber doch persönliche, keine repräsentative, aber doch gesellschaftliche Autobiographie« (Öa, 42–4). Ob Heins *Ritter der Tafelrunde* ein solches Stück neuer gesellschaftlicher Autobiographie sein kann, – der Beweis ist auf der Bühne noch nicht erbracht worden. Denn seine Version der Legende von den Artusrittern steht für politische Machtkonstellationen überall in der Welt. Jede gesellschaftliche Idee kann gemeint sein. *Die Ritter der Tafelrunde* können überall tagen – und wurzeln zugleich auf vertrackte Weise in der DDR.[31]

Hein belässt es nicht bei der Bestandsaufnahme von Verdrängungsmechanismen und Gefährdungen, sondern zwingt seine Figuren zur Positionsbestimmung, zur Annahme von Realität. Eine Geschichte, die subjektive Tragik in sich birgt, aber nichts anderes ist als realer Gang der Geschichte, Menschheitsgeschichte. Alle bisherige Entwicklung sucht ihren Gral, das schließt Näherungen, auch Leerlaufen und Scheitern ein. Und das Ende eines Weges ist nichts anderes als der Beginn eines neuen Versuches der Näherung an den Gral, wenn er nicht als etwas verstanden wird, was man morgen schon in der Hand halten kann, sondern als Prozess zu einem Ideal.

Artus vollbringt vielleicht die größte Leistung im Stück, indem er dieser Erkenntnis Raum gibt: Einsicht in die Chancen einer neuen Welt. Er erscheint als Erkennender, der im Untergang des Alten zugleich eine Chance für den Neubeginn sieht.»Aber wenn wir den Gral aufgeben, geben wir uns selbst auf. Und was uns dann quält und verstört, ist ein Hunger auf Hoffnung« (RT, 188). Hoffnung als Droge oder – wie es Hein sieht – Hoffnung darauf,

»daß eine wirklich menschenwürdige Gesellschaft entsteht« (*AK*, 250).

Das seine Ungebundenheit und seinen Spielcharakter betonende literarische Produzieren – trägt es den von Hein ironisch ausgestellten Widerspruch in sich, dass keine Botschaft zu haben seine Botschaft ist? Der Sinn solcher Produkte erschlösse sich dann nicht aus einem »Inhalt«, sondern aus ihrem bloßen Sein in einer bestimmten gesellschaftlich-kulturellen Sphäre, also durch den Verweis auf das, was sie verschweigen und was nötig wäre. Das ist immer noch die vertraute Strategie des Reagierens auf eine »offizielle« Öffentlichkeit, von der man ausgegrenzt wurde oder sich ausgrenzen wollte. Kann sie unter den neuen Bedingungen noch wirksam sein oder muss sie mit zwingender Notwendigkeit umgeschrieben werden? Der rapide Rückgang der Aufführungen seit 1990 könnte es vermuten lassen.

5
In der Komödie *Randow*, 1994 im Kleinen Haus des Staatsschauspiels in Dresden uraufgeführt, erzählt Hein dann schon von kleinen und großen Tragödien aus dem wiedervereinigten Deutschland, von Verlierern und Aufsteigern, von Alteigentümern und Asylsuchenden. Eine bürgerbewegte Malerin hat sich in einem aufgelassenen militärischen Übungsplatz irgendwo an der deutschen Ostgrenze ein Haus gekauft, sie will nur noch der Kunst leben, erprobt die Idylle. Aber sie wird eingeholt von den Problemen mit ihrem Mann und der emanzipierten Tochter. Ihr Haus wird zum Objekt der Begierde von kleinen und großen Haien, Wendehälsen und Wendegewinnlern. Jede der Figuren hat ihre eigene Wahrheit, aber sie passt nicht mehr mit der der Geschichte zusammen.

Hein deckt diese Geschichte mit deutscher Geschichte richtiggehend zu. Es muß alles vorkommen, was deutsche Gemüter bewegt, von der unbewältigten Nazivergangenheit bis zur Überwältigung durch den »real existierenden Kapitalismus«. Von der Invasion durch Asylanten bis zur Emanzipation der Frau. Von ewigen Mitläufern und Stasi-Überläufern bis zu den Vorläufern eines neuen »National-Sozialismus«.[32]

Es ist ein sarkastisches Stück – »aber erst muß alles an Utopien und Visionen abgearbeitet sein, und was dann bleibt, ist etwas wirklich sehr Entscheidendes. Das wäre das, worauf ich gespannt bin«, sagt Hein.[33] Scheint der heute erreichte Zustand zu bestätigen, dass die Geschichte deutscher Revolutionen ein Lehrbeispiel für die Unmöglichkeit wirkungsvollen, beständigen Eingreifens der Unteren in den Geschichtsverlauf ist, ein fortwährendes Scheitern des Versuchs, Geschichte nach eigenem Bild zu gestalten? Gleichen die »entlassenen Kinder der Revolution« wirklich dem Benjaminschen Engel der Geschichte, der vom Sturm der Ereignisse vorwärts getrieben wird, unfähig, das Zerschlagene zusammenzufügen? Subjekt-Werdung wird nur gegen Anpassung und Absage an Heilserwartung möglich. Aber auch nur durch Korrektur einer Geschichtsauffassung, die im europäischen Raum eine lange Denktradition hat, und zwar im religiösen, im aufklärerischen wie im marxistischen Denken. Geschichte nämlich als Entwicklung auf einen erlösten Endzustand hin zu begreifen. Die lähmende Konsequenz dieses Denkens, als Sieger der Geschichte bereits im Paradies angekommen zu sein, sollte uns aufgeschreckt und skeptisch gemacht haben gegen neue Heilsversprechungen. Wir sollten uns stattdessen auf die Kritiker dieser Entwicklungsgläubigkeit besinnen, die vor dem mörderischen Verlauf der Geschichte, der kleinen wie der großen, vor der Permanenz der Katastrophe, der privaten wie der öffentlichen, nicht die Augen verschließen, aber zugleich sich dessen bewusst sind, dass dieser Geschichtsverlauf durch die subjektive Tat unterbrechbar wird – was nicht heißt, aufhebbar. Denn überall dort, wo im Bruch mit der Kontinuität der Leidens-Geschichte die Stillegung oder Umkehrung des katastrophalen Fortgangs gelingt, vermag sich ein Korrektur-Schritt zu vollziehen, vermag Hoffnung zu wachsen. Und die Kunst als Tochter der Erinnerung – so Peter Weiss – hat diesen Augenblick als geschichtliche Erfahrung für kommende Unterbrechungen und Niederlagen weiterzugeben. Hein appelliert deshalb an die menschliche Gelassenheit, es muss ausgehalten werden, mit der Vergangenheit zu leben: »Und das ist ja auch das Menschliche, das ist nun mal so, dass völlig rein eine Sache nicht zu haben ist, weder der Opportunismus noch der Widerstand, sondern dass sich das menschliche Leben in Zwischenbereichen bewegt« (*CB*, 49).

Anmerkungen

[1] Krzysztof Jachimczak, 'Gespräch mit Christoph Hein', *Sinn und Form*, 40 (1988) 2, 343–59 (hier 347).

[2] Michael Skasa, 'Rundköpfe an der Macht', *Süddeutsche Zeitung*, 27. Oktober 1986.

[3] Andreas Roßmann, 'Ein Dramatiker ohne Theater. Über den DDR-Schriftsteller Christoph Hein', *Frankfurter Rundschau*, 23. Oktober 1982.

[4] Peter von Beck and Michael Merschmeier, '"Warum ich in der DDR geblieben bin . . ."', *Theater heute*, 4 (1992), 31–6 (hier 32–3).

[5] Erika Stephan, 'Cromwell von Christoph Hein. Uraufführung: Theater Cottbus', *Sonntag*, 27. Juni 1980.r

[6] Jochen Schmidt, 'Das Bühnenportal als Schlüsselloch', *Frankfurter Allgemeine Zeitung*, 13. November 1980.

[7] Ulrich Schreiber, 'Ein Produkt unserer beschränkten Einbildung', *Frankfurter Rundschau*, 14. November 1980.

[8] Jochen Schmidt, 'Das Bühnenportal als Schlüsselloch'.

[9] Georg Menschén, 'Verlorene Geschichtlichkeit', *Theater der Zeit*, 42 (1987) 5, 52–3.

[10] Georg Edelmann, '"ansonsten würde ich ja aufhören zu schreiben"', *Theater der Zeit*, 38 (1983), 10, 54–6.

[11] Heinz Klunker, 'Christoph Heins *Ah Q* in Kassel', *Theater heute* (1985), 3, 37.

[12] Peter Burri, '*Ah Q*', *Frankfurter Allgemeine Zeitung*, 27. November 1984.

[13] Dominik Hunger, 'Witzig und bluttriefend: *Ah Q* kann alles', *Baseler Zeitung*, 7. Juni 1985.

[14] Andreas Roßmann, 'Zwischen Hund und Wolf', *Frankfurter Rundschau*, 12. Dezember 1984.

[15] Manfred Behn, 'Christoph Hein', in Heinz Ludwig Arnold (Hg.), *Kritisches Lexikon zur deutschsprachigen Gegenwartsliteratur*, 34. Nlg. (München, edition text + kritik, 1990).

[16] Vgl. Michael Skasa, 'Die Szene ein Hinterzimmer', *Die Zeit*, 30 Oktober 1987.

[17] Andreas Roßmann, 'Flüchtlingsgespräche', *Deutschland Archiv* (1988), 7, 703–6 (hier 704).

[18] Ebd., 703.

[19] Walter Benjamin, *Das Kunstwerk im Zeitalter seiner technischen Reproduzierbarkeit*, (Frankfurt am Main, Suhrkamp, 1963), Anmerkungsteil.

[20] Andreas Roßmann, 'Flüchtlingsgespräche', a.a.O., 706.

[21] Ulrich Schreiber, 'Begegnungen der dritten Art', *Frankfurter Rundschau*, 5. November 1987.

[22] Michael Skasa, a.a.O.

[23] Wolfgang Höbel, 'Am Fuß der blauen Berge', *Süddeutsche Zeitung*, 30 Oktober 1987.

[24] Heinz Klunker, 'Nun auch in der DDR angekommen', *Frankfurter Rundschau*, 8. Dezember 1987.
[25] Hartmut Krug, 'Ritter von der Traurigen Gestalt', *Theater heute* (1989), 7, 26.
[26] Ebd., 26.
[27] Vgl. Sibylle Wirsing, 'Der heiße Schauplatz Dresden', *Frankfurter Allgemeine Zeitung*, 25. Oktober 1989.
[28] Ludwig Zerull, 'Heins Tafelrunde – schnell gealtert', *Theater heute*, (1990), 4, 45–6 (hier 46).
[29] Michael Laages, 'Der Verlust der Mythen', *Die Welt*, 5. März 1990.
[30] Ebd.
[31] Hartmut Krug, a.a.O.
[32] Ernst Schumacher, 'Ostdeutscher Zerrspiegel', *Berliner Zeitung*, 23. Dezember 1994.
[33] Christoph Hein, *Sächsische Zeitung*, 17./18. Dezember 1994.

6

'Die Vergewaltigung [. . .] ist nicht das Thema meiner Erzählung': Rape and Female Identity in the Work of Christoph Hein

BETH LINKLATER

Christoph Hein's short story 'Die Vergewaltigung' was first published in *Neues Deutschland* in the weekend edition of 2/3 December 1989. Any aesthetic visualization of rape is highly controversial, raising accusations not only of trivialization, silencing, pornography and voyeurism, but also of possible identification with either the victim or the attacker. Yet in an interview Hein asserted: 'die Vergewaltigung der Großmutter ist nicht das Thema meiner Erzählung' (*AK*, 202). The theme is, he emphasizes, 'Verdrängung'. Rape in this instance is, according to the author, used merely as an example of the GDR's repression of an undesirable past. However, it is my contention that this theme cannot be understood simply in terms of historical fact. Moreover, in the light of Hein's earlier adoption of the same motif in plays, novels and short prose pieces, it is possible to read his use of rape not only in terms of historical silencing, but also of sexual identity, specifically of female identity.

In this article I examine rape in Hein's work and analyze the meanings that this theme acquires. In the context of GDR literature, Hein stands out as a writer who adopts a variety of sexual themes – including rape – thereby challenging the taboos surrounding this subject. He makes it a part of GDR reality, both past and present. Hein does not dwell upon the rapist, nor does he explore what makes men rape. Rather he attempts to consider the meaning of the act from the female character's point of view. He concentrates on the crucial issues of subjectivity, power, silencing and nature. This article is set in a tradition of feminist critiques of literary rape, which aim, in the words of Lynn Higgins and Brenda Silver, to 'help identify and demystify the multiple manifestations, displacements and transformations of what amounts to an insidious cultural myth'.[1] Sexual violence is read back into textual silences, highlighted, taken literally rather than as a symbol. The female body is made real, marked both physically and psychologically by the violence done to it. I begin, therefore, with an introduction to some of the complexities inherent in the aestheticization of a motif so fraught with ambiguity.

The meaning of rape is highly contested, particularly since the 1970s feminist movement successfully brought the topic into the public domain. In a culture where sexuality determines personal identity, its intrusive and depersonalizing nature is especially offensive. Emotionally loaded, it escapes denotation, crossing boundaries of the socio-historical, legal, military, aesthetic and moral. As Higgins and Silver assert, rape is about 'who gets to tell the story'; a story – written literally onto the body – that focuses attention on the mind. In terms of gender relations and sexual politics, the act has come to signify the most visible aspect of a social ideology of male dominance; whereby the suggestion that male sexuality is always violent is reductive and essentialist, and does not allow for a proper analysis of the conditions that encourage sex crimes.[2] In court women have traditionally had to prove that they resisted rather than encouraged sexual advances. Legal constructions of rape have focused upon the issue of consent, thereby attempting to differentiate between rape and seduction. Yet if the act is looked at from the perspective of the victim, rather than the intention of the aggressor, there is often no substantial difference, for both involve physical force. Frequently there can be no single 'truth' about what happened, raising the danger that the event itself disappears.

The meanings of fictional rapes are even more highly contested, each reader bringing her own experiences to bear on an author's personal portrayal. As Deborah Cheney argues, 'the viewers cannot merely "look at" rape, they are forced to engage with it as a concept and come to terms with it as an act/state of being/reality in which they are implicated'.[3] Norman Bryson goes further, outlining the 'impossibility of portraying rape, of rape existing for us as an image'.[4] Thus the most famous portrayals of rape, such as in Kleist's story *Die Marquise von O...* and Thomas Hardy's novel *Tess of the D'Urbervilles*, are often the most ambiguous. When the author is a man, the contest of signification is further complicated, engendering questions of how both rapist and raped are seen, by whom and in what context. Historical, mythologized or religious versions of rape may comment upon and even influence present reality. But ultimately they remain outside it, simply one more element in accounts of the rise and fall of cities or nations. With its shocking and very real results rape can never be simply aesthetic, it cannot function purely as a metaphor. The meaning of the act cannot be separated from the form of the depiction, whereby the artistic language of violation can often descend into cliché. Neither can it remain unrelated to what has gone before, to its various refracted forms in multiple media.

In terms of GDR literature rape was either taboo (as the furious debate surrounding Annett Gröschner's 'Maria im Schnee' as late as 1988 shows),[5] or historicized in terms of more general violence – particularly war-time violence. In these representations it is only the war that renders men brutalized enough to behave brutally. The creation of distance rather than empathy, is, for example, typical of Christa Wolf's novel *Kindheitsmuster*, where 'vergewaltigen' is a 'düster-geheimnisvolle[s] Wort' and the rape of Rosemarie Steguweit is a 'große tränenreiche' film scene.[6] Nevertheless, in the context of GDR historiography, literary recognition of the violence perpetrated by the Red Army in 1945 was of crucial importance.[7] Where the Russian soldier had to be regarded solely as German saviour, such portrayal crossed boundaries of socialist realism, socialist politics and socialist/bourgeois ethics. Fictional rapes gained, therefore, symbolic value in terms not just of violence, but also of 'Verdrängung' (Dahlke, 5). Hein's statements in interview both acknowledge and develop this aspect of the East German literary system.

Within the contexts of rape in literature, and more specifically in GDR literature, Hein's writing is of notable importance. As a broad concept sexuality is used in a wide variety of forms. In *Von allem Anfang an*, for example, Daniel's sexual awakening dominates his childhood memories – which in this respect recall those of Thomas in *Horns Ende*. The numerous superficial sexual encounters of both Dallow and Wörle reflect an inability to come to terms with their society. Sex is a sadomasochistic 'Spiel', a game in which women, the playing pieces, are described solely in terms of their physical attributes. Particularly telling is, for example, the scene in which Dallow forces sex upon a young student desperate to listen to the news of the entry of Soviet troops into Prague. Her tears and desperation arouse only lust. Sexual relations in *Horns Ende* are also defined in terms of failure and humiliation. All of the numerous relationships portrayed in *Der fremde Freund* are characterized by a similar lack of understanding and commitment, on a physical as well as a mental level. For Claudia, this inability to communicate is partly the result of gendered relationships towards the sexual, of the 'Ausüben von Herrschaft' (fF, 105). Other sexual topics Hein tackles include abortion, pornography, prostitution and sexual violence. The sexual motif most carefully developed in his work is, however, rape.

The most famous rape in German literature is that of Kleist's Marquise von O. A mark of punctuation – the notorious dash – expresses without words the complex ambiguity surrounding the rape/seduction of the Marquise. Ironically, the elision serves to emphasize the violence, raising the possibility of making it visible – a process represented in the Marquise's pregnancy. Hein's story 'Die Vergewaltigung' deals with the violence of the Russian 'Befreier' in similarly concise fashion. The sexual assault is mentioned twice, not as a defining event in Ilona's grandmother's life, but rather as an afterthought. The opening sentence of the narrative simply states the facts. It could almost be a police report:

> Zwei Tage nach dem siebzehnten Geburtstag von Ilona R., Tochter eines Landarbeiters in einem Dorf östlich von Prenzlau, wurde ihre vierundsechzigjährige Großmutter im August 1945 von zwei marodierenden Soldaten der sowjetischen Streitkräfte vergewaltigt. (EK, 131)

The second description of the rape – 'Die angetrunkenen Soldaten vergewaltigten darauf die Bäuerin und verließen danach das Gehöft, wobei sie zwei Kisten mit Apfelwein, die sie im Keller gefunden hatten, mitnahmen' (EK, 131–2) – is just as brief. Other stories in the collection display the same distanced terseness and it is this that reviewers praised, using terms such as 'prägnant', 'knapp', 'kühl', 'spröd', 'beherrscht', 'staubtrocken', 'karg' and 'fest gebaut'.[8] This art was compared with that of Hebel and, notably, Kleist – whom Hein himself claims as one of his 'Vorbilder in der deutschen Literatur' (AK, 203).

It would seem, then, that the claim 'die Vergewaltigung der Großmutter ist nicht das Thema meiner Erzählung' is justified. Indeed the following seven pages of the text deal with Ilona's exemplary career, as is suggested by the opening words of the story. Ilona's grandmother herself plays down the rape and refuses to identify her attackers. 'Was heult ihr dummen Küken?', she asks; 'Hab ich mir ein Bein gebrochen?' (EK, 132). In terms of the wider pattern suggested above, the rape is simply symbolic of war atrocities, of the power of silencing within history, of 'Verdrängung' – all themes reinforced by the constant renaming of the Frankfurter Allee. However, the selection of such an explosive term as the title of the piece (for the rape is certainly the 'unerhörte Begebenheit' at the centre of this anecdotal narrative), the evocation of Kleist and, moreover, the links between this violation and those portrayed in Hein's other texts, allow a reading of the rape that does make it the main theme of the story.

The succinct descriptive style in which Hein portrays the attack by Russian soldiers recalls firstly that in which he informs the reader of the rape of a Dutch farmer by French officers in the title story of his earlier prose collection *Einladung zum Lever Bourgeois*: 'Eine holländische Bauerin war vergewaltigt worden, man fand sie dann zusammen mit ihrem Kind in der Stallung tot auf' (*NfM*, 10). In both cases the act appears as an element of war, 'Alltag der Armee' (*NfM*, 10). In the play *Die wahre Geschichte des Ah Q*, the stage direction according to which Ah Q rapes and murders the nun is similarly brusque: 'Ah Q vergewaltigt die Nonne' (*RT*, 56). As Phillip McKnight states:

> Wang sleeps through it, though he is in the same room – a withdrawal which is a commentary itself. The scene is enacted in the back of the set, with no overt violence, to ensure that the dramatic focus is not on the act itself.[9]

Indeed, in a 1983 interview Hein also qualifies this rape, claiming that it is 'eine Vergewaltigung aus einer anderen Vergewaltigung heraus. Hier wird etwas relativiert, ohne daß die Sache damit aufgegeben wird'.[10] All five characters, he argues, 'sind irgendwie vergewaltigt', casualties of a 'nicht mehr erfaßbare Zeit', the worst rape being that of Wang rather than of the nun. Hein's concept of rape here again goes beyond the single act of violence, referring more widely to socio-political contexts. Yet his work does not deal simply with general acts of oppression, but with female victims who are concretely abused. The nun is the only female character in the play, one whose identity as 'eine heilige Frau' (*RT*, 23) depends upon her renunciation of sexual intercourse and her devotion to helping others. It is thus especially ironic that she should be attacked (*RT*, 21), repeatedly mocked and then violently abused. Ironic also is the description of her death as a musical number, 'die Nonne in Bedrängnis' – 'eine Nummer zum Totlachen' (*RT*, 30).

Like Ilona's grandmother, the nun is raped after revolution, an act of 'Befreiung' which brings suffering rather than release. *Die wahre Geschichte des Ah Q* is, as the author claims elsewhere, 'ein Machostück', and in this instance too rape cannot function merely as literary symbol (*TDB*, 99).

'Befreiung' is, of course, a term loaded with crucial historical significance. In 'Die Vergewaltigung', it is used twice by Ilona during her 'Jugendweihe' speech, where she speaks of the 'Tag der *Befreiung*' (*EK*, 135; my italics), and refers to the Russians as those, 'die Deutschland vom Faschismus *befreit* hatten' (*EK*, 136; my italics). In a further intertwining of the personal and the historical, however, Hein also uses the phrase in connection with the rape. Ilona's grandmother is described as the 'Befreier' of her daughter-in-law and granddaughter: 'Die alte Frau verriegelte notdürftig die zerstörte Tür und *befreite* dann ihre Schwiegertochter und ihre Enkelin aus der Räucherkammer' (*EK*, 132; my italics). Her actions evoke those of Gudrun Gohl in *Horns Ende*, who goes to her death rather than betray her daughter. It is to her mother that Marlene Gohl's dream conversations are addressed. In the third of these conversations Marlene describes her rape:

> Mein Mann hat mich nicht geküßt und mich nicht gestreichelt. Er hat mich gepackt und auf die Erde geworfen, daß ich glaubte, ich werde ohnmächtig. Er hat meine Kleider zerrissen, weil er rasch zu meiner Muschi wollte. Zuerst habe ich gelacht, weil er so furchtbar ulkig war, aber dann heulte ich, denn es tat weh, Mama, es tat weh. [. . .] Er hat mich mit der Faust geschlagen, so daß mein Mund voll Blut war. (*HE*, 284–5)

Throughout *Horns Ende* Marlene, who refers to herself as 'eine Prinzessin', creates a fairytale dream of her wedding to her gypsy prince Carlos. It is thus particularly harsh that her sexual violation is also repeatedly outlined in terms of marriage. The fact that this victim is mentally disturbed, combined with her references to her dead mother, further compound the horror of the scene, as does Hein's choice of childish sexual terminology. Marlene's reaction is deeply sincere, which again makes this event one of the most memorable in the novel: 'Es war nicht schön, Mama. Ich habe geglaubt, ich sterbe. Ich habe die ganze Nacht geweint' (*HE*, 283). She describes her utter loneliness, the pain and the blood, the absence of any tenderness. The fact of Marlene's rape is, moreover, reasserted through the links with Gertrude Fischlinger's sexual suffering at the hands of her husband. Marlene's frequent allusions to her wedding veil (*HE*, 142) echo Gertrude's wedding night, when her torn, bloodied veil becomes the symbol of her humiliation (*HE*, 65–6).

Marlene's narratives are, as Heinz-Peter Preußer argues, 'zutiefst problematisch', but they are not 'in sich nicht haltbar'.[11] Rather, it is their very problematic nature that makes them so interesting. Paradoxically, her unstable and irrational visions offer both 'blindness and insight' (Preußer, 138), a powerful alternative 'truth' to that of the other accounts in the novel. And, as Bärbel Lücke contends, 'das gilt ganz besonders für die Schilderung ihrer Vergewaltigung, die sie zwar nicht als solche erfaßt, die aber gerade dadurch den Mißbrauch der Wehrlosen, die Gewalt und Brutalität des Vorgangs schonungslos offenlegt'.[12] In the light of what many critics describe as Marlene's 'humanity', the rape, in the words of Heinz Bulmahn, emphasizes how 'even the most innocent and sensitive are tyrannized, underscoring the suffocating effects of the isolation and provincialism of Guldenberg'.[13] McKnight further links the rape to events during the War, asserting that 'once again, an anonymous individual from the town has violated the Gohls in the most despicable manner' (McKnight, 67). *Horns Ende*, like 'Die Vergewaltigung', thematizes the repression of the past in the GDR, the rewriting of history to suit the victor. Yet Marlene is not raped by Russian soldiers in wartime, but by a drunken man in a park. This image, so powerfully presented, thus acquires much broader meanings, beyond the constraints of history.

Marlene's anguished calling for her mother draws attention to the fact that it is women who are usually the victims of sexual assault. It also recalls the rape of Hein's most famous protagonist, Claudia. Chapter Five of *Der fremde Freund*, considered by many critics to be the turning point of the novella,[14] closes with Claudia's imagined conversation with her mother, one of the significant moments in the work, where she lets down her defences and reveals her inner struggle with herself: 'Ich will nicht, Mama, ich will nicht' (*fF*, 71). This rape is the most interesting of Hein's portrayals of the subject. A highly complex depiction, it draws attention to Claudia's mental state whilst ostensibly focusing upon her body. Situated at the centre of many other strands of the novella – including the vital issue of Claudia's identity – it hovers on the borders between rape and seduction, asking the crucial question as to *whose* meaning is attached to the act of sexual violence.

Caught up in this questioning, critics have tended to ignore the rape altogether, or simply to circumvent it in phrases such as that used by Graham Jackman: 'the virtual rape of Claudia'.[15] A similar process of semantic circumvention can be observed with regard to Marlene's rape. Most often the act is never mentioned and critics concentrate on the male narrators and their views of history. In reference to the rape, Bernd Fischer writes of Marlene's 'ungeheueres Leid',[16] Klaus Hammer of 'fremde Gewalt, die ihr angetan wird'.[17] Where the emphasis is placed on the manner of the act rather than simply the act itself ('die brutale Vergewaltigung durch einen Betrunkenen'), it is noticeable that this is by a female critic (Lücke, 83). Preußer likens the 'Liebesakt in der Natur' between Claudia and Henry to that between Dr Spodeck and Christine in *Horns Ende*. In both cases, he claims, 'handelt es sich um Übertretungen einer Tabuisierung, um verbotene und gerade dadurch befreiend lustvolle Liebe'. The protagonists lose themselves 'an die Natur und an die begehrende andere Person' and 'der Körper [diffundiert] in seine Umgebung' (Preußer, 143). But he neglects to add that the latter scene is non-violent and consenting, indeed it is these factors that produce its clichés of 'aufblähenden Blutes', 'der tausend sich öffnenden Augen meiner Haut' and 'der schwarzroten Blume ihres Fleisches' (*HE*, 211–12). It is also told from Spodeck's perspective; Christine does not have a voice. In similar vein, David Roberts and Graham Jackman 'naturalize' or mystify the rape through Freudian terminology of 'primeval, natural forces' (Jackman, 176) and 'die irrationale Gewalt der Wiederkehr des Verdrängten'.[18] This critical erasure, most notably of the element of fear, reproduces the more general social silencing of rape. Where critics such as Phillip McKnight and Julia Hell do analyse the event in more detail, they do not fully explore the multifarious meanings of the rape scene.[19]

Forebodingly, the chapter begins with sexual intercourse, after Henry's sudden appearance at Claudia's flat following an unexplained absence. Despite sex the relationship between the two remains conspicuously distanced. Henry and Claudia then set off into the countryside to photograph a ruined mill, the description of which strongly echoes the dream sequence with which the novella opens – itself described as 'fast wie eine Kamerafahrt' (*fF*, 5). It is similarly tense, Claudia sweating nervously as she climbs, whilst

Henry remains below – bored and alone. It is into this tension that the announcement that he is married bursts, shattering Claudia's carefully constructed equilibrium. Her reaction to the news is expressed in terms that suggest mental, if not yet physical rape: 'Ich war unfähig, einen Gedanken zu fassen. [...] Ich fühlte mich gedemütigt, hintergangen. [...] Ich fühlte mich maßlos gekränkt' (fF, 67). She must, then, reaffirm her 'Distanz zu Menschen', and it is at this point that she makes the famous statement 'Ich war gegen mich gewappnet' (fF, 68). At the same time, though, she admits the desire for security expressed in the imagined dialogue with her mother.

Having described this context of betrayal, Brigitte Böttcher argues: 'Henrys Versuch, [...] Nähe herzustellen durch körperliche Nähe, kann jetzt nur Vergewaltigung sein. Jeder für sich, heißt die Devise' (Böttcher, 148). The narrative accordingly builds up to the rape in a dramatic and detailed scene in which Henry chases Claudia through the forest. The tersely constructed sentences and the repeated use of the verb 'keuchen' (which occurs twice in the opening dream sequence in connection with the five runners) heighten the impression of fear created. The structure of the narrative itself suggests 'etwas Nötigendes, Zwingendes' (Öa, 160). At first Henry seizes Claudia's arm and hits out at her face. He shakes her whole body, ripping her clothes. The blows he aims recall those he himself suffered earlier at the hands of the tractor driver, and point forward to the second car accident of the novella in which he again hits Claudia (fF, 158). In both instances, Claudia justifies his actions. In the first instance Henry *needs* to hit her, in the second (which Claudia analyzes at length and in significant detail, giving the lie to her assertion that nothing has happened (fF, 162)) he *must*, a victim of his 'männliches Selbstwertgefühl, ein Mischmasch aus Verklemmungen und Hochmut' (fF, 161). The eventual description of the rape is characteristically brief and clear:

> Er packte meine Schulter, warf sich auf mich, wir fielen auf feuchten Erdboden. [...] Er riß an meinen Sachen, und ich klammerte mich an ihn. [...] Er streifte mein Kleid hoch, zerrte an der Hose. (fF, 69–70)

In this instance, however, an element of confusion is introduced by Claudia's ambivalent reactions to the attack, symbolized firstly in the contrasting descriptions of nature which immediately follow the rape passage:

Ich grub die Finger in seinen Nacken. Vor meinen Augen tanzte ein Zweig mit stumpfen, glanzlosen Blättern. Ich spürte, wie Tränen mir ins Ohr liefen. Und immerzu dieser Zweig, ein fahles Blattgrün, durchsetzt von Lichtern und den bräunlichen Schatten des Waldes. Schatten und Licht, Hell Dunkel, Vordergrund Hintergrund, die Kühle der Erde, die Baumwurzel, die meinen Rücken wund rieb. Nein, dachte ich, nein. (fF, 70)

McKnight has recognized the associations within this description to the vulnerable spots left by the linden leaf on Siegfried's back. Gertrud Bauer Pickar concentrates upon the twig on which Claudia focuses, which, she argues, 'corresponds to her own state', pale, sickly and disappointed.[20] Jackman twice notes the presence of the biblical 'serpent' ('eine Natter' (fF, 69)) in the 'Adam and Eve scene' which represents 'Hein's version of the Fall' (Jackman, 189, 175).

More important, perhaps, are the references to the opening dream sequence and to Claudia's account of her abortions, which serve to heighten the confusion – all three passages leaving the impression of 'Ein Nebel oder Grau oder Nichts'; 'unerreichbar' and 'letztlich unverständlich' (fF, 7). The manner in which Claudia digs her fingers into Henry's neck suggests the actions of her dream 'Begleiter', who bores his nails into her arm. The representation of the leaves as 'stumpf' recalls the bridge railings ('stumpf in die Luft ragend'), the 'Blattgrün' evokes the 'Zypressengrün' background of the dream landscape, the cool earth the fact that the dream narrator 'fröstelt' (fF, 5). The abortions offer a particularly clear example of both Claudia's alienation from her own body and, as Jackman writes, of the 'sexual violence which recurs in the text' (Jackman, 174). They represent an 'Eingriff' of which Claudia is 'das Objekt' (fF, 105), and are described in terms which directly evoke both the rape and the dream:

Dann sind da Wälder, ein kühler, verhangener Himmel, der Weg, der zu einer Brücke führt, brüchigen Resten. Ich verkrieche mich im Gras, unter den Bäumen. Ich spüre kratzende Zweige, die Kälte des Erdbodens, feuchte Blätter. (fF, 107)

Her legs are 'gewaltsam gespreizt' and Claudia is 'festgehalten', unable to speak. Her desperate plea 'ich will nicht, ich will nicht mehr' echoes that made to her mother at the end of Chapter Five.

Yet this is an experience she herself has chosen, the first child was 'zu früh', the second unwanted. 'Mit den Kindern', Claudia claims, 'hatte ich nichts zu tun' (fF, 104). Similarly confusing is the fact that Claudia's tears turn to laughter, a defence she persuades herself is the correct one: 'Ich schüttelte mich vor Lachen. Nur nicht aufhören, dachte ich und lachte weiter, immer weiter' (fF, 69). Likewise, her anger and despair develop into an even stranger mixture of 'jäh aufbrechende Lust' and 'endgültige Einsamkeit' (fF, 70). It is this famous description of sexual desire that has led critics such as Jens-F. Dwars to describe the rape as 'lustvoll genossen', thereby denying Hein's careful juxtaposition of conflicting emotions.[21] The description of the light Claudia feels on her closed eyes as a 'heller Schleier' sets up one further linguistic connection between herself and Marlene and adds to the ambiguity, as does her inability to express the meaning of what has happened: 'Was sollte ich sagen. Ich verstand mich ja selbst nicht' (fF, 70). This again evokes the dream passage, at the end of which Claudia is left with a feeling of shock, of 'ausgestandene Hilflosigkeit' which is 'unfaßbar' and 'unauslöschlich' (fF, 7). After the attack, in a structural echoing of the concrete violence perpetrated, the text, as Hell puts it, 'breaks off, brutally' (Hell, 316). Language, as Dwars has observed, similarly collapses into 'lose Bilder und vereinzelte Wortreihen', signifying the 'Verschwinden sinnstiftender Einheit' (Dwars, 10).

During the dream the face of Claudia's 'Begleiter' is unclear, 'traumverschwommen' (fF, 5). During the rape Henry's face is described as a 'groteske Maske' – similarly hiding the man that Claudia recognizes. Claudia is thus violated by a man she knows, but also by a stranger, a 'fremder Freund'. Her rape is both violent and sexual, acknowledging not only the wider framework of violence residual within western sexuality, but also the possible eroticism of dominance and submission.[22] It embodies elements of different types of sexual violence, which cannot be easily categorized for legal purposes, and cannot easily be understood. In some senses, as Niven argues, the oppression 'supports [Claudia's] own efforts' (Niven, 133). The same ambiguity is present in Dallow's vividly described sexual encounter with Elke, which is both violent and erotic (Ts, 102–4). The attempt to portray, rather than to explain these multiple dilemmas is a central concern of Hein's work. In *Der fremde Freund* this is emphasized not only through the references to the dream and abortion sequences, but also through the context in which the rape is set. Both in the very first chapter and again in Chapter Twelve, the reader is introduced to Anne, who has 'vier Kinder und einen Mann, der sie alle zwei Wochen einmal vergewaltigt [...] Er brauche das, sagt sie' (fF, 14). Claudia, who is to suffer the same fate, does not sympathize with Anne. In a dramatically ironic statement she keeps her distance: 'was habe ich mit ihren Vergewaltigungen zu schaffen. Sie hats weiß Gott verdient, daß sies allein trägt' (fF, 15).

Following the rape, Claudia stays with Henry and appears unchanged. McKnight maintains that this 'functions as a symbol of political or psychological unchangeability' (McKnight, 30). Yet this particular crime does not merely represent the stagnation of socialist politics, any more than it is solely symbolic of a society where 'social interaction is devoid of human intimacy' (Bauer Pickar, 267). Similarly, Marlene's rape does more than 'establish symbolically the continuity between fascism and Stalinism' (McKnight, 31). Unlike the other five characters in *Horns Ende*, she is not only a victim of generalized 'social Vergewaltigung', as is implied by Gisela Shaw.[23] Dallow's sex with the young student does not just 'create an association between the girl and Czechoslovakia as victims of statutory rape' (McKnight, 109). And in *Exekution eines Kalbes* rape is not exclusively illustrative of 'a pervasiveness of human failure and societal ills' (Zehl Romero, 74). In all of these instances, Hein is concerned at a more immediate level with female identity – whether this be erased by patriarchal egotism (as in the case of the student) or expressed in all its intricacy (as in Claudia's case). As Julia Hell comments, therefore, 'close attention to categories of gender' is necessary in order to gain full 'access to the tensions and conflicts' of these texts (Hell, 309).

The 'complex intersections of rape and representation' (Higgins and Silver, 1) characteristic of Hein's writing arise from the intrinsic links with the equally complex issues of subjectivity, power and voice. The victim of rape has her subjecthood wrenched from her in a particularly clear and vicious manner. Henry's attack on Claudia dramatically emphasizes her feelings of alienation and confusion. As in the dream she becomes 'namenlos' and 'unerklärlich' (fF, 7). Marlene's violation is also described in terms of immense loneliness. In a process similarly symbolized in loss of name, her identity is completely eradicated. 'Marriage' to a stranger has left her unable to speak of her self: 'Nur seinen

Namen soll er mir sagen, damit ich weiß, wie ich heiße' (*HE*, 285). Her subjectivity is determined by that of her rapist. The conventional response to this loss of self, and thereby of voice, is silence. The victim is forced – or chooses – to repress the event, rather than to relive her humiliation. Embedded within the silence are guilt, anguish and fear. It becomes both reflection and expression of common threats by rapists that if the victim 'tells' she will suffer further. In Maya Angelou's *I Know Why The Caged Bird Sings*, for example, Marguerite, raped by her mother's lover, retreats into silence which lasts a year. Mr Freeman had threatened her brother's safety if she told anyone what he had done. This highly influential novel has, in this respect, a long tradition. Philomela's story is one of the most familiar in mythology. After having raped her, Tereus proceeded to cut out her tongue, so that she could not express what had happened. In later versions of the myth, Philomela, tongueless, was changed into a nightingale. For Hein, silence is both a structuring principle and a major motif. As Klemens Renoldner argues, 'er operiert an und mit dem Verborgenen, mit Andeutung und Aussparung. Er kalkuliert mit dem Schweigen'.[24] Critical documentation of this theme has, though, occurred primarily with reference to history rather than to rape. Yet the two are clearly connected. In all of Hein's work *public* histories are inseparable from *personal* narratives. Both political and sexual oppression are repeatedly expressed in terms of silence.

In *Von allem Anfang an* for example, Daniel's mother responds to her repeated pregnancies with reticence. Racine's answer to rape and murder is also silence, accompanied by various intellectual attempts to justify this quiescence:

> Hier eloquent zu detaillieren wäre unangebracht. [. . .] Und schließlich, was hätte er ausrichten können. Er, ein kleiner Geschichtsschreiber, gegen die allmächtige, allgegenwärtige Armee. Nein, da sind keine Schuldgefühle, weder damals noch heute. (*NfM*, 11)

It is in this connection that Racine asks himself, in a question which recurs numerous times in Hein's later writing, whether the ability to repress a crime represents 'die Bedingung der menschlichen Rasse, in Gesellschaft zu leben' (*NfM*, 12). After her rape Marlene asks her mother: 'warum darf man es nicht erzählen, warum darf man nicht die Wahrheit sagen, sondern soll lügen und behaupten, daß es schön sei?' (*HE*, 283). Her physical humiliation is, as

Preußer states, 'nicht zu vergessen und nicht zu beschönigen, auch: nicht zu verschweigen' (Preußer, 139). Yet it is Marlene's fate that she should never be listened to. Like Cassandra, her visions are not believed. Words are 'verrückt' (*HE*, 283), and in effect silence – as she has learned from her father – is the only option. The attempt to express her pain to her living aunt, rather than her dead mother, thus results only in her being punished further. The story she is telling is that of the inability to tell the story.

'Sprachlosigkeit', as Brigitte Böttcher argues, 'bestimmt alle Beziehungen Claudias' (Böttcher, 86). Claudia's text too speaks of, and with, silence. After the rape, as they return to Berlin, Henry switches on the car radio to disrupt Claudia's muteness.[25] Her subsequent regression into childhood is a return to learned voicelessness, as is made clear in Chapter Nine, where the formative experiences of youth are portrayed in terms of silence, sexuality and sexual taboos. Claudia's gymnastics instructor teaches her to view her body solely as 'an instrument for domination and exploitation' (Jackman, 184). Her history teacher, Herr Gerschke, is forced to leave the school because of an affair with a pupil,[26] whereupon Claudia's mother 'enlightens' her daughter, generating a dark nightmare of sex as ugly, dirty and sinful:

> Schreckliche Krankheiten, sieche Gestalten voller Auswüchse und Eiter, ein Leben, das nur noch den Tod erhofft, waren mahnende, eindringliche Gespenster, die mich für Jahre verfolgten. [. . .] Jahrelang war mein Kopf mit verquasten Bildern von Sexualität verklebt. (*fF*, 141–2)

Claudia's appeal to her mother following the rape thus ironically refers back to these lectures upon the dangers of sex. It also, as Hannes Krauss has identified, refers to *Kindheitsmuster*, in which 'Geschlechtskranke' is one of the taboo 'Glitzerworte' that Nelly learns, connoting 'Schuld und Verschweigen'.[27] The arrival of Soviet tanks on 17 June 1953 again occasions dreams of 'sieche, widerliche, geschlechtskranke Leute' (*fF*, 146), and persuades Claudia of the necessity of silence. In a careful interweaving of public and private repression, the taboos surrounding sex and sexual violence are thus simultaneously portrayed and challenged.

Silence is not, however, always negative. Speechlessness can also suggest resistance, restoring the active power of decision-making to the passive victim. In Hein's work the psychological and silent repression caused by bodily force is often challenged, or at least expressed, through physical articulation. The effects of Ilona's concealment of the rape of her grandmother, for example, are mainly bodily: 'Sie lag auf dem Bett, von einem heftigen Weinkrampf geschüttelt' (*EK*, 138). The last line of the story emphasizes this physical impression: 'Und nur gelegentlich noch wurde ihr Körper von einer nervösen Zuckung geschüttelt, so als würde sie noch im Schlaf schluchzen' (*EK*, 138). Ilona's crying fit recalls the responses of Marlene, the nun in *Ah Q* and Dallow's nameless young student to their attacks, all of whom sob at length. The latter weeps both for herself and for Czechoslovakia. Crying cannot change what has happened, but it can at least offer an alternative to silence.

In *Der fremde Freund* the body, routinely degraded, is the site upon which Claudia's emotional alienation is made transparent. Her obsession with skin and sweat reveals her fear of what she cannot control. Her intensely physical laughter during the rape is dwelt upon at length, the verb 'lachen' is repeated seven times in one paragraph. It is 'laut und hysterisch', a combination of fear, anger and amusement. A 'Verlachen des sich souverän gebenden Mannes' (Dwars, 9), it reasserts her subjecthood in the face of patriarchal power which threatens to destroy her. It is also a reaction which Claudia used when she was beaten by Hinner (*fF*, 160). In the story 'Ein sächsischer Tartüff' (*EK*, 73–9), female laughter again functions as subversive of male sexuality. Lina Pappke's response to attempted seduction is to laugh 'angesichts der ergrauten Männlichkeit' (*EK*, 79) of her would-be Don Juan. In respect of *Der fremde Freund* Julia Hell has asked 'whether the text ever goes beyond the mobilization of traditional gender codes, whether it ever challenges their "naturalness"' (Hell, 316). She contends, for example, that we are invited to read motifs such as Claudia's repressed longing for motherhood as a sign of her 'true' femininity. Hein's 'counter discourse', she states, only functions 'within a dominant discourse – namely that of gender' (Hell, 321). Claudia's laughter challenges the very codes of gender Hein elsewhere mobilizes and reinforces. With this one gesture at least, women rebel against their status as victim. Ironically it is this very rebellion which reinforces Henry's need to rape.

Less challenging is Hein's association of rape and nature. The link between female subjectivity and romantic nature is at the heart of Western Enlightenment thinking. Natural woman represents refuge, escape, the biological, the passive, the nurturing mother and a chaos that must be controlled. Rape that takes place within nature enacts this control, it is 'a punishment for rebellion'.[28] In the Callisto myth by Ovid, Callisto is raped and impregnated by Zeus in a forest and is turned into the Great Bear star constellation. She is thus tamed and made natural. Other mythical rapes that occur in the natural world include those of the bringer of fertility Persephone – whilst gathering flowers – and Daphne, who is changed into a laurel tree. Hardy's Tess is also raped in the woods, and is similarly exiled. The rapes of both Marlene and Claudia take place outside city boundaries. Marlene is linked to nature through her dreams, which come 'aus dem Wald' (*HE*, 53). Passages such as 'Was könnte ich denn sagen, wenn die Sonne auf die Erde niederschwebt und der Wald zu leuchten beginnt? Wenn meine Blumen sich öffnen, um mich zu begrüßen?' (*HE*, 54–5) strengthen the Romantic impression of her narratives. Yet, as Lücke maintains, 'dagegen stehen auch düstere Bilder der Natur', and 'diese "Nachtseite" ihrer Ahnungen scheint auch die Vergewaltigung vorauszunehmen' (Lücke, 90). Nature is given heightened importance for Claudia's sense of self through her passion for landscape photography. Peter Pfeiffer claims, for example, that 'die Fotos karger Landschaften' are 'die *authentischen* Dokumente von Claudias unauthentischem Leben'.[29] Claudia herself connects her photography with her two abortions (*fF*, 103) – expressing a direct link with her sense of self. The dream sequence, which begins 'Ich oder die Person, die vielleicht ich selbst bin' (*fF*, 5), also signals the importance of both nature and identity for the narrative that follows. In other ways too the female Claudia is identified with the natural environment, in which the male Henry, like Dallow, clearly does not belong:

> Es bedeutete ihm offensichtlich nichts, zwischen Bäumen hindurchzulaufen, auf federnden Moosboden zu treten, die Stimmen und Geräusche eines Waldes zu hören. Die Landschaft gehörte nicht zu ihm, er konnte sich nicht in ihr bewegen. [...] Er war ein Stadtmensch. (*fF*, 66–7)

It is in this landscape that Henry reasserts his dominance over Claudia.

In terms of nature Hein thus relies heavily upon conventional stereotypes of femininity. It is these stereotypes which produce similarly clichéd interpretations of the rape scene – emphasizing the setting rather than the act: 'beide sind in einem Taumel der Affektion, zurückgefallen in einen vorzivilisierten Naturzusammenhang'.[30] Yet the clichés do serve a purpose. Hell argues very convincingly that Claudia's assumed links to the natural/female make the theme of alienation so powerful in *Der fremde Freund*. The damaging effects of modern civilization can be considered much more damaging (and in literary terms more powerful) when embodied in a female character. This, she continues, is why Claudia is a more persuasive character than her male counterparts Dallow and Wörle. Claudia's rape thus represents destruction of the feminine (and with it the Utopian) as well as of one female. It is noticeable, then, that where Hein links masculine sexuality with nature it is in a more positive sense. In *Von allem Anfang an* Daniel's discovery of his sexuality similarly takes place outside the city boundaries in a 'Russenwald' (*VA*, 97). Moreover, he too feels 'eine Baumwurzel und einen Kienapfel, die sich in meinen Rücken bohrten' (*VA*, 93–4). Yet Daniel is not being raped. Dr Spodeck is drawn to 'die arglose, anheimelnde Verlassenheit der Natur' (*HE*, 319), and his account of his passionate forest encounter with Christine also emphasizes natural elements. This scene too, though, has no connotations of violence.

In numerous interviews and essays Hein has asserted that he wants nothing more than to be a chronicler of history.[31] Yet despite these repeated protestations, as Hammer states, 'in seinen einfachen Alltagsgeschichten verstecken sich – im Untertext – ganz andere, viel komplexere Geschichten. Sie stehen dem entgegen, was der Erzähler oder Figurenbericht vorgibt' (*CB*, 7). Furthermore, as Ricarda Schmidt recognizes, 'er lenkt die Sympathien und Erkenntnisse der LeserInnen sehr wohl'.[32] It is disingenuous in the extreme for an author to claim to want to have nothing whatsoever to do with morality and then to tackle with such repeated force a subject such as rape. In these portrayals of sexual violence the female body does not merely signify victimhood, it is a *female* body, a female self. Furthermore, if Hein's victims live they do not simply forget the rape incident and move on, the consequences of the rape are repressed, silenced and physically felt. His fictional rapes problematize female identity, they are not simply vehicles for his stories. They uncover structures that erase female subjectivity and, at a deeper level, recognize male complicity in upholding a system of violence. This theme, therefore, offers one of Hammer's 'komplexere Geschichten', and clearly 'steht dem entgegen, was der Autor vorgibt'.

Ultimately, it is the complexity of this theme which creates its interest. One could equally argue that Hein's more ambiguous texts, produced within a literary system which revised violence out of history, themselves contribute to an erasure of the *Gewalt* from *ver*gewalt*igen*. The attempts of Ilona's grandmother to come to terms with the brutality inflicted upon her, her personal *Vergangenheitsbewältigung*, are founded in *Verdrängung*. By making this the main theme of his story, Hein himself may appear trapped within boundaries both national and gendered. This is perhaps also at the root of his fears that *Der fremde Freund* would provoke strong feminist criticism.[33] Other male authors who represent sexual crimes stand accused of reproducing 'a perspective premised on men's fantasies about female sexuality', and of creating 'codified access to and possession of women's bodies' (Higgins and Silver, 2). Yet despite the problems inherent in its depiction, rape, as Tomaselli writes, must not be conceived of as 'a subject no one dares to name', nor must representations of sexual violence against women come to appear natural or inevitable, 'ingrained and rationalized'.[34] When rape is silenced, neglected or trivialized, as has traditionally been the case, the victim continues to suffer – in the courts, on the streets and in works of literature. In this sense, then, Hein's representations of violation, however violent, must be welcomed.

Notes

[1] Lynn Higgins and Brenda Silver, 'Introduction: rereading rape', in Lynn Higgins and Brenda Silver (eds.), *Rape and Representation* (New York, Columbia University Press, 1991), 1–11, here 2. Subsequent page references in the text.

[2] Particularly important here is the work of Susan Brownmiller, *Against our Will: Men, Women and Rape* (Middlesex, Penguin, 1975/1986). Her dramatic statements on rape were highly influential, especially in America. They include, for example: 'It [rape] is nothing more or less than a conscious process of intimidation by which *all* men keep *all* women in a state of fear', 15.

[3] Deborah Cheney, 'Visual rape', *Women's Studies Occasional Papers, University of Kent at Canterbury*, 20 (1990), 13.

[4] Norman Bryson, 'Two narratives of rape in the visual arts: Lucretia and the Sabine Women', in Sylvana Tomaselli and Roy Porter (eds.), *Rape*

(Oxford, Blackwell, 1986), 152–73, here 153. Subsequent page references in the text.

[5] Annett Gröschner, 'Maria im Schnee', *Sondeur*, 5 (1990), 48–55, and 'Anekdoten', *Sondeur*, 5 (1990), 55–7. The critics' opinions on this text, and the text itself, were not allowed to appear in the journal *Temperamente. Blätter für junge Literatur*, as had been planned, and were published instead, 'unofficially', in *Bizarre Städte* and *Sondeur*. Commenting on her text, Gröschner said: 'Im Nachhinein fürchte ich nämlich, ich habe ein erfolgreich aufrecht gehaltenes Tabu übertreten' (56). The taboos she challenged concerned not just the fact of the rape itself, but also aesthetic and political conventions. The themes, the setting, and the style of Gröschner's narrative offended. Her sketch is detailed, precise and frighteningly naturalistic. For a general introduction to rape in GDR literature, see Beth Linklater, *'Und immer zügelloser wird die Lust'. Constructions of Sexuality in East German Literatures. With Special Reference to Irmtraud Morgner and Gabriele Stötzer-Kachold* (Bern, Lang, 1998).

[6] Christa Wolf, *Kindheitsmuster* (Darmstadt and Neuwied, Luchterhand, 1979), 297 and 330.

[7] This is not to deny the rapes carried out by marauding troops of other nations. However, as Birgit Dahlke points out, those inflicted on the German women by the Russian troops fitted more easily into established nationality paradigms. The English, French and Americans were considered too charming (or too reserved) to rape, and thus 'waren die Übergänge zwischen Gewalt und Freiwilligkeit fließender' (Birgit Dahlke, 'Tagebuch des Überlebens: Vergewaltigungen 1945 in ost- und westdeutschen Autobiographien?', as yet unpublished paper, 2. Subsequent page references in the text).

[8] See, for instance, Beatrice von Matt-Albrecht, 'Spröd und meisterlich. Christoph Hein's Erzählband *Exekution eines Kalbes', Neue Zürcher Zeitung*, 10 February 1994, 25, and Andreas Isenschmid, 'Nachrichten vom beschädigten Leben', *Die Zeit – Literatur*, 18 March 1994, 4. See also Christiane Zehl Romero, 'In the shadow of the rainbow: on Christoph Hein's *Exekution eines Kalbes* and Christa Wolf's *Auf dem Weg nach Tabou*', in Margy Gerber and Roger Woods (eds.), *Changing Identities in East Germany: Selected Papers from the 19th Hampshire Symposium* (Lanham, UP of America, 1996), 63–86. Subsequent page references in the text.

[9] Phillip McKnight, *Understanding Christoph Hein* (Columbia, University of South Carolina Press, 1995), 147. Subsequent page references in the text.

[10] Christoph Hein, 'Ansonsten würde man ja aufhören zu schreiben ...', *Theater der Zeit* (1983) 10, 54–6, here 54.

[11] Heinz-Peter Preußer, 'Hoffnung im Zerfall. Das Negative und das Andere in *Horns Ende*' (*CB*, 134–46, here 138). Subsequent page references in the text. Preußer argues that Marlene's language is too complicated for a mentally disturbed girl, and he thereby denies the insight offered in her narratives: 'Die Sprache der Marlene ist so unstimmig wie keine andere in *Horns Ende*. [...] Das eingeschränkte Bewußtsein wird nicht noch in seiner Sprachlichkeit reflektiert' (*CB*, 138). Marlene obviously has a symbolic function within the narrative (she offers an alternative to the

alienation of modern civilization). Yet it is assuming too much about her disability to argue that she cannot be believed as a character in her own right as well. In the rape scene in particular the reader empathizes with Marlene as a woman, rather than as a cipher.

[12] Bärbel Lücke, *Christoph Hein. Horns Ende* (Munich, Oldenbourg, 1994), 88. Subsequent page references in the text.

[13] Heinz Bulmahn, 'Christoph Hein's *Horns Ende*. Historical revisionism – a process of renewal', *Studies in Twentieth Century Literature*, 15 (1991) 2, 247–62, here 257.

[14] McKnight, for example, calls the rape a 'key event in the novella' (McKnight, 27). Brigitte Böttcher describes it as 'den Höhepunkt, den Umschlagspunkt der Novelle' (Brigitte Böttcher, 'Diagnose eines unheilbaren Zustands. Christoph Hein: *Der fremde Freund*', *neue deutsche literatur* (1983) 6, 145–9, here 147. Subsequent page references in the text). Other critics argue that the turning point is rather the trip to 'G', Henry's murder, Claudia's internal dilemma, her abortions, or even her life itself: thus Niven maintains that 'the whole novella is one long unheard-of event' (William J. Niven, 'The vanquished self: Christoph Hein's *Drachenblut* and *Der Tangospieler*', *Journal of European Studies*, 22 (1992) 2, 127–41, here 128; subsequent page references in the text). For Hein's comments, see *Öa*, 154–64, particularly 161.

[15] Graham Jackman, 'The fear of allegory: Benjaminian elements in Christoph Hein's *The Distant Lover*', *New German Critique*, 66 (1995), 164–92, here 175. Subsequent page references in the text.

[16] Bernd Fischer, *Christoph Hein. Drama und Prosa im letzten Jahrzehnt der DDR* (Heidelberg, Carl Winter Universitätsverlag, 1990), 105.

[17] Klaus Hammer, '*Horns Ende*: Versuch einer Interpretation' (*CB*, 121–33, here 125).

[18] David Roberts, 'Das Auge der Kamera: Christoph Hein's *Drachenblut*', in Paul Lützeler (ed.), *Spätmoderne und Postmoderne: Beiträge zur deutschsprachigen Gegenwartsliteratur* (Frankfurt am Main, Fischer, 1991), 224–43, here 242. Subsequent page references in the text.

[19] Julia Hell, 'Christoph Hein's *Der fremde Freund/Drachenblut* and the antinomies of writing under "real existing socialism"', *Colloquia Germanica*, 25 (1992), 307–35. Subsequent page references in the text.

[20] Gertrud Bauer Pickar, 'Christoph Hein's *Drachenblut*: An internalized novella', in Sabine Cramer (ed.), *Neues zu Altem. Novellen der Vergangenheit und der Gegenwart* (Munich, Wilhelm Fink Verlag, 1996), 251–78, here 257. Subsequent page references in the text.

[21] Jens-F. Dwars, 'Hoffnung auf ein Ende. Allegorien kultureller Erfahrung in Christoph Hein's Novelle *Der fremde Freund*' (*TuK*, 6–15, here 9). Subsequent page references in the text.

[22] Much has been written on the relationship between rape and so-called 'normal' sexual violence. Catherine Mackinnon, for example, argues that heterosexuality 'institutionalizes male sexual dominance and female sexual submission' ('Feminism, marxism, method and the state: an agenda for theory', *Signs*, 7 (1982), 515–44, here 533). Rape, then, is merely the extreme version of an established pattern, 'a sex crime that is not a crime when it looks like sex' (Catherine Mackinnon, 'Feminism, marxism,

method and the state: toward feminist jurisprudence', *Signs*, 8 (1983), 635–58, here 649).

[23] Gisela Shaw, 'Christoph Hein, the novelist as dramatist manqué', in Arthur Williams, Stuart Parkes and Roland Smith (eds.), *Literature on the Threshold: The German Novel in the 1980s* (New York, Berg, 1990), 91–105, here 100. Subsequent page references in the text.

[24] Klemens Renoldner, 'Vom Pathos der Sachlichkeit. Der Erzähler Christoph Hein' (*TDB*, 128–37, here 130).

[25] The second time Henry hits Claudia, following the next car accident, it is he who returns home in silence. One further link between this second incident and the rape is to be found in Claudia's reference to herself as a little girl. This time, however, she denies the need for her mother: 'Ich bin kein kleines Mädchen mehr, damit muß ich mich abgefunden haben' (*fF*, 162).

[26] Jackman writes of the 'imaginary rape by Herr Gerschke' (Jackman, 183), but I would argue that this is overstating the case. The figure of Herr Gerschke also appears in *Von allem Anfang an* as Herr Greschke (*VA*, 37).

[27] Wolf, *Kindheitsmuster*, 58 and 62. Cf. Hannes Krauss, 'Durch die Christa Wolf Referenz wird Claudias politische und sexuelle Abrichtung in einen hier überraschenden Kontext gestellt: die jahrhundertealte [. . .] Tradition der sanften, äußerlich gewaltfreien, Unterdrückung und Konditionierung von Kindern' ('Schreibend das Sprechen üben oder: Worüber man nicht reden kann, davon kann die Kunst ein Lied singen oder Als Kind habe ich Stalin gesehen – Zur Prosa Christoph Heins', in Axel Goodbody and Dennis Tate (eds.), *German Monitor No. 29, Geist und Macht. Writers and the State in the GDR* (Amsterdam, Rodopi, 1992), 204–14, here 208).

[28] Kathleen Wall, *The Callisto Myth from Ovid to Atwood* (Kingston and Montreal, McGill-Queen's University Press, 1988), 5.

[29] Peter Pfeiffer, 'Tote und Geschichte(n): Christoph Hein's *Drachenblut* and *Horns Ende*', *German Studies Review*, 16 (1993) 1, 19–36, here 25. My italics.

[30] Heinz-Peter Preußer, *Zivilisationskritik und literarische Öffentlichkeit. Strukturale und Wertungstheoretische Untersuchung zu erzählenden Texten Christoph Heins* (Bern, Lang, 1991), 99.

[31] Numerous possible examples include 'Denn Schriftsteller sind, denke ich, Chronisten. Schreiben ist nach meinem Verständnis dem Bericht-Erstatten verpflichtet' (*AK*, 99); and 'Der Autor, der ja auch ein Historiker ist, ein Schreiber von Geschichten mit einer vergleichbaren Zielstellung, nämlich Chronist der Zeit zu sein' (*AK*, 116).

[32] Ricarda Schmidt, 'Erlaubte und unerlaubte Schreibweisen in Honeckers DDR. Christoph Hein and Monika Maron', in Robert Atkins and Martin Kane (eds.), *German Monitor No. 40. Retrospect and Review. Aspects of the Literature of the GDR 1976–1990* (Amsterdam, Rodopi, 1997), 176–96, here 180.

[33] 'Ich hatte zwar von Feministinnen eine große Kritik erwartet, aber die ist ausgeblieben' (*TuK*, 81).

[34] Sylvana Tomaselli, 'Introduction', in Tomaselli and Porter, *Rape*, 1–15, here 2.

7

'Spiele aus Notwehr':
Re-reading Christoph Hein's
Critique of the West in *Das Napoleon-Spiel*

DAVID CLARKE

The critical reception of Christoph Hein's 1993 novel *Das Napoleon-Spiel* was generally negative, and sometimes damning. On the whole, reviewers depicted Hein's portrayal of the novel's protagonist and narrator, Wörle, as an attack on egoism, cynicism and opportunism in the West, all of which many assumed to be central to the author's allegedly limited understanding of capitalism. Wörle was, therefore, reduced to a model of the 'Erfolgstyp in der kapitalistischen Gesellschaft' or 'eine Großmetapher auf die Spielwelt des entfesselten Egoismus',[1] and where the reviewer in question regarded Wörle as atypical of the kind of individual produced by Western society, Hein was accused of falling back on 'vulgärmarxistisch[e] Vorurteil[e]'.[2] The GDR exile Chaim Noll claims: 'Aus den Westdeutschen macht der Autor tückische Monster, ganz wie sie früher in den Fibeln seiner Provinz geschildert wurden'.[3] The irony of this approach to Hein's text, as David Robinson also observes, is that it reproduces the orthodox socialist realist demand for typicality in the literary figure which was a feature, for example, of GDR reviews of *Der fremde Freund*.[4] Thus Thomas Rietzschel complained: 'diese Karikatur [Wörle] läßt keinen Typ erkennen',[5] and Günther Grack argued that Wörle remained a 'Kopfgeburt' as far as the realities of the FRG were concerned.[6]

However, such an interpretation of Wörle's game-playing, which is the central (and, indeed, dominant) motif of the text, leaves aside the issue of Wörle's sense of compulsion to continue his games, and especially his need to find new games to which he can progress once he feels he has exhausted the possibilities of the one in hand. Whilst it is true that the manipulation and exploitation of others for one's own profit is a feature of capitalism, to regard Wörle merely as exemplary of such behaviour firstly ignores the fact that Wörle is relatively uninterested in material gain (for example, NS, 48). Secondly, it overlooks another possible explanation for this mania which, if investigated more closely, can indeed be seen as a critique of Western capitalist society,[7] but one which is subtler and more fundamental than the novel's initial reception would suggest. This critique can most easily be comprehended when *Das Napoleon-Spiel* is seen in the context of Hein's pre-*Wende* writing.

To understand Hein's view of the capitalist West, it is also necessary to understand his conception of human nature and of the kind of society which he believes to be best suited to that nature. Throughout Hein's work it is possible to identify the working out of a central paradox, which is perhaps best summed up by Hein himself in a 1986 essay, where he compares what he calls (borrowing a term from Pascal) the comforting 'Vernunft des Herzens' with another kind of reason which attempts to overcome illusions and see the world as it really is:

> Der Widerspruch dieser sich gleichenden und doch verschiedenen Funktionen verschiedener Vernunft verweist uns auf eine Kluft zwischen dem richtig Erkannten und der menschlichen Möglichkeit, damit zu leben. Wir benötigen die Wahrheit über uns und unsere Umwelt, und wir benötigen gleichzeitig einen beruhigenden, beschönenden und verfälschenden Schleier über dem Erkannten, um es aushalten zu können. (*Öa*, 171)

Hein's point, developed in this and other essays of the 1980s, is that, faced with the chaos of the world and of their own psyches, human beings naturally search for some kind of interpretative framework which can provide them with a sense of order. This framework has variously been described by Hein as a 'Weltbild', a set of 'Ewigkeitswerte' (*Öa*, 13), or 'eine nützliche zweite Haut' which protects us from coming to terms with the world as it really is (*Öa*, 50).

The following examples of Hein's use of the symbol of the map may serve as an illustration of this point. In *Passage* (1986), Hein's play about the German emigration in the Second World War, the Jewish *Reichswehr* officer Hirschburg refuses to give up his identity as a German and an officer, despite having been forced, on account of his race, to flee the country he once served. Hirschburg stubbornly holds to the values he associates with Germanness, and particularly with the German army, and refuses to confront the possibility that the community which has rejected him does not share those values. In this way, he is blinded to the true nature of National Socialism. That is, however, until he encounters a group of orthodox Jewish emigrants from a community near Auschwitz, who tell him about the reality of National Socialist atrocities (*RT*, 126). Until this revelation at the end of the play, Hirschburg insists on carrying bulky military maps which are no longer of practical use to him. These function as a symbol for the world-view whose validity he is not yet able to call into question, and which he adopted in order to find his place in the world (just as the military map helps the soldier to orientate himself in a foreign landscape which is full of dangers). Significantly, it is only when forced to accept the reality of Auschwitz (which is incompatible with this world-view) that he leaves these maps behind on his journey. However, this abandonment of one set of values does not imply a nihilistic rejection of all such means of making sense of the world. Instead, this act is accompanied by a return to the religious faith of his ancestors. In this way he retains his ability to see the world as a comprehensible and ordered place, and regains the ability to act decisively, believing that God will provide (*RT*, 127).

In Hein's book for children, *Das Wildpferd unterm Kachelofen* (1984), Jakob Borg and his friends decide to go on a treasure hunt with a map which Jakob has made himself. They run into trouble when they try to utilize this work of the imagination as a valid model of part of the world (that is, their local park), and begin to invent reasons why the map appears to be such a poor representation of the land in which they hope to find buried treasure. They speculate, for instance, that certain features of the map might have disappeared in an earthquake (*WK*, 42–3), and make some changes to it. However, when they finally try to dig for treasure, they find nothing, and Jakob arrives at the conclusion that his map may be problematic: '"Ich fürchte, ich habe einen Fehler gemacht. Ich will mich gleich hinsetzen und eine neue [Karte] malen"' (*WK*, 55). The irony of the above situation is that, although Jakob is finally able to abandon his inappropriate map, he immediately sets about creating another, which (the reader may well surmise) will equally be an artificial construction, and thus just as dubious as the first. However, as in the case of Hirschburg, we see how Hein portrays a human tendency to, as it were, return to the drawing-board when our means of making sense of the world are shown to be inadequate. What is significant here is that the search for the treasure is not abandoned, but the means of that search have been revised;

even if the original map fails, some means of giving order to the world is still required.

Sociologists have described the individual's experience of modernity in terms of a 'metaphysical loss of "home"',[8] that is to say 'the collective and individual loss of integrative meanings' along with the institutions which upheld such meanings. This situation becomes problematic, it is claimed, when the individual's awareness of the absence of a shared and stable means of coming to terms with the world leads to an experience of 'anomie', in other words to a condition in which reality appears uncertain and is threatened with meaninglessness.[9] In the examples cited above, we see individuals being forced to give up their affiliation to a set of shared meanings (symbolized in each case by a map). However, rather than this process resulting in anomie, it leads to the adoption of an alternative set of meanings which can equally fulfil this role, as represented, for instance, by Hirschburg's return to Judaism.

Marxism sees the constant overturning of all values (and thus also anomie) as a direct result of capitalism,[10] and it therefore becomes an integral part of the project of the socialist state to call a halt to this process.[11] As can be seen from the example of the GDR state, the socialist regime attempts to impose a certain interpretation of the workings of society and, in this way, to offer a new 'map' by means of which all of its citizens can experience the world as an ordered and meaningful place. The GDR which Christoph Hein describes, however, is a socialist state whose ideology frequently fails to provide an adequate means of making sense of the world for its citizens, but which is prepared to use violence and coercion in order to maintain the *status quo*. Hein's criticism of the socialist state is to be understood, I would argue, not in terms of a rejection of its project of establishing a shared interpretation of the world, but rather as an attack on the tendency of the SED regime to enforce the outward acceptance of that interpretation even where it stands at odds with the experience of the individual. Thus Hein's figures often find that their desire to share in an interpretation of the world with others, which nevertheless allows them to make sense of their own personal experience, is hemmed in by the regime's need to impose its interpretation, and thus to hold on to power.

The figure of Claudia in *Der fremde Freund* provides a good example of this situation in her childhood relationship with

Katharina. Claudia's discussions with Katharina can be seen in terms of an attempt to find 'sicher[e] Wert[e]' (*Öa*, 22) in a world where such certainty is lacking, for instance by helping her to make sense of the disturbing events of her childhood (particularly those of 17 June 1953) in the face of her parents' silence. However, this friendship is also characterized by the desire of the two girls to adopt a common world-view, choosing between Katharina's Christianity and the ideology of the SED state (*fF*, 147). Although by no means the only reason for the ultimate failure of this project, the interference of the state in this attempt to establish a set of shared beliefs is indicative of its intolerance of ideological competitors and its unwillingness to allow its citizens to formulate and express collective meanings which are not its own. The same is equally true in the case of the eponymous historian in Hein's 1985 novel *Horns Ende*, who is ousted from the party and eventually driven to suicide for his humanistic attempts to integrate the experience of the victims of historical progress into the official account of the past.

In the protagonist of Hein's last major GDR prose text, *Der Tangospieler* (1989), the reader is confronted with a figure who is incapable of living outside the institutions of the state, and who displays the need to become, as it were, a cog in a larger machine. Having been expelled from the party and his job as an academic historian (where he once taught year in, year out the state-approved version of history), Dallow finds in his prison cell a 'vertrautes Umfeld, ein Zuhause, in dem er geborgen war' (*Ts*, 58), but cannot cope with the freedom that, on his release, seems 'unheimlich und fremd' (*Ts*, 58). As elsewhere, Hein makes use of the symbol of the map to depict Dallow's situation. In this case, a railway map represents both Dallow's need to see the course of his own life in the context of a greater whole and his uncomfortable awareness that his own personal 'map' has become separated from that authorized by the state:

> Ihm gefiel die Karte, auf der das Land nur aus den Erfordernissen und Interessen der Bahngesellschaft gesehen war. Verzeichnet waren darauf nur jene Städte und Verkehrsbindungen, die für die Bahn eine Bedeutung hatten. Wo es keine Schiene gab, zeigte die Karte weiße Flecken, Niemandsland, Wüste. Dallow malte sich in Gedanken seine eigene Landkarte. Dieses lächerlich kleine Straßendorf wäre auf seiner Karte der zentrale Punkt, die Hauptstadt. [...] Ein paar Städte und Landschaften würden in den nächsten Jahren hinzukommen, aber

auch dann reichte für seinen persönlichen Weltatlas noch immer eine seiner Handflächen aus. Ich bin halt keine Eisenbahngesellschaft, sagte sich Dallow. (Ts, 77)

Here, the state-run institution of the railway becomes a metonymic representation of the state apparatus as a whole, which claims the exclusive right to map out or order reality, whilst the individual's personal map, born of his own life experience, appears 'lächerlich klein' by comparison, and is threatened with erasure by the 'weiße Flecken' in the official description of the world.

Hein's own statements on the function of literature can be read as a reaction to this situation. In his essays of the 1980s, for instance, he dismisses as 'Makulatur' any literature which panders to 'das Bedürfnis nach sicheren Werten' (Öa, 13), and describes his own work, in contrast, as 'gesellschaftliche Autobiographie' (Öa, 34). His writing is, he claims, 'Mitteilungen von Individuen in der Welt, einer Welt, die ich nach meinen Kenntnissen, Fähigkeiten, Haltungen mir aneignete, die ich bin' (Öa, 34), yet it gains its social significance from the power of the unflinchingly recorded individual perspective to challenge the world-view of the reader. In Hein's opinion, it is not so much 'das berichtete Ereignis, der genannte Zustand' which brings the reader to see the world in a new way, but rather the confrontation with a representation of that 'Ereignis' or 'Zustand' which challenges the 'sichere Werte' reinforced by 'Makulatur':

Die Lage, der Zustand, das Geschehen konnte allgemein bekannt sein und scheinbar hingenommen werden, das Benennen jedoch [...] führte zu einem Aufschrei der Freude oder des Schreckens und zu eingreifenden Maßnahmen. (Öa, 48)[12]

By extension, Hein's definition of literature can be seen as a challenge to a state ideology which tries to uphold a set of ideas about the world by coercion, even when the gap widens between those ideas and the world they claim to make sense of. Thus Hein opposes his own positive conception of literature, defined as a confrontation with lived experience, to the 'Makulatur' of the 'staatserhaltende Phrase' (Öa, 15).

Nevertheless, as I have already suggested, Hein does not see the overcoming of outmoded or inappropriate conventional ideas about the world as the first step towards an abandonment of the notion of shared meanings. His scathing view of Western intellectuals, for example, is founded on the notion that, unlike their Eastern bloc counterparts, they have lost the capacity to experience a sense of 'Solidarität und Engagement' (*Öa*, 146). Thus in his essay on Peter Sloterdijk's *Kritik der zynischen Vernunft* (1983), for example, Hein attacks a Western intelligentsia which, by failing to commit itself to a clear and stable set of values, reduces every issue to a 'cause' interchangeable with any other:

> Da war oder ist man für die Frauen und für die Sintis, für die Homosexuellen und gegen den Numerus clausus, für die französische Küche und die Abtreibung und gegen Gewalt, für den Wald und gegen 'BILD', für den New York-Urlaub und gegen die Hundescheiße. (*Öa*, 146)[13]

The ironic humour of this description should not detract, it must be noted, from the seriousness of Hein's criticism of the attitudes portrayed, which he in fact sees as being typical of the Federal Republic as a whole (*Öa*, 135).

In the wake of the *Wende*, Hein extends this criticism of Western society to point out what he regards as its fundamental flaw. In the face of claims that the end of the Cold War heralds the 'end of history', in which liberal (and, therefore, capitalist) democracy is left as the only 'competitor standing in the ring as an ideology of potentially universal validity',[14] Hein insists 'daß Veränderungen sich auch weiter selber verändern werden, das ist völlig klar, wir sind an gar keinem Schlußpunkt'.[15] For Hein, no society can survive if it fails to meet what he sees in May 1990 as a fundamental human need for a 'common idea':

> Eine menschliche Einrichtung, sei es eine Familie oder sei es ein Staat, die nur noch – und sei es bestens – funktioniert, aber die nichts darüber hinaus verbindet, die von keiner gemeinsamen Idee getragen und verbunden ist, ist tot und wird verfallen. (*MJ*, 61)

Whilst the GDR could not overcome the loss of its common idea through the use of 'Panzer', capitalism will, Hein predicts, equally fail to survive by offering its citizens an 'umfängliches Bankkonto' as a substitute for a shared world-view (*MJ*, 61).

Hein's identification of this deficiency in the capitalist system is also reflected in his changing attitude to the function of writing after 1989. Instead of a literature which forces the reader to face the discrepancy between established ideas and experience, Hein talks in 1994 of the value of literature as a creator of common values: 'Unser Gespür für Recht und Ordnung wurde durch Aschenputtel und Froschkönig geweckt, durch den Kleistschen Kohlhaas geschärft' (*MJ*, 154). This role, he feels, is essential in a capitalist society which demands of the individual that s/he be totally flexible, that is, that s/he be ready to abandon the values which constitute personal identity when the market demands: 'Das Lesen [...] ist ein traditioneller Wert, und es schafft traditionelle Werte. Das Individuum im heutigen Produktionsprozeß darf sich nicht länger auf eine einzige Identität festlegen lassen' (*MJ*, 157).

To turn finally to Hein's first major post-*Wende* work, *Das Napoleon-Spiel*, I will argue in the following that the criticism of Western society which can be read in the figure of Wörle is indicative of the author's concern at what he regards as the lack of a common idea in capitalist society. Whilst his fictional descriptions of the GDR may have taken the SED regime to task for its attempt to impose by force the acceptance of a particular world-view, Hein is equally critical of Western society's abandonment (as he sees it) of what Jürgen Habermas describes as the distinctly modern project of creating a unifying set of values in a post-traditional world.[16]

The text of *Das Napoleon-Spiel* consists of two fictional letters written by the protagonist Wörle to his lawyer, Herr Fiarthes. The first (and by far the longer) letter is written from a prison cell, where Wörle is awaiting trial for the murder of Bernhard Bagnall, whom he has killed by means of a blow from a billiard cue to the temple in a Berlin *U-Bahn* carriage. Wörle explains to Fiarthes that this bizarre murder was not a crime as such, but rather an 'unerläßliche Tötung' (*NS*, 13), which Wörle was forced to carry out in order to save himself from the suicidal state of depression into which he is likely to sink if he is not able to experience the 'Kitzel des Spiels' (*NS*, 37). Wörle identifies himself as one of a race of 'Spieler', whose patron saint is Napoleon (*NS*, 121) and who rise above the 'Masse', distinguished from them by a rejection of the security which, Wörle claims, is necessary to the existence of the latter: 'Die Masse will Sicherheit, nicht Spiel, und das trennt uns' (*NS*, 137). A player such as Wörle must engage in ever more complex and risky games if he is to preserve his sanity: his childhood schemes to outwit his adoptive brother, his success as a lawyer, his accumulation of wealth and his political activities are all part of his game-playing, as is his passion for billiards, which he uses as a medium for planning his various other games. However, when these lose their appeal, he turns to murder as offering new and interesting game-playing possibilities. Wörle carefully selects his victim Bagnall as 'das perfekte Neutrum' (NS, 170) – a man of so little consequence that it seems impossible to imagine anyone having a motive for killing him – and hopes thereby to orchestrate an apparently motiveless crime (NS, 13), which will so confuse the judicial system that he will be set free. After his release, Wörle will be able to move on to his next game.

Twentieth-century literature provides a number of examples of the way in which the theme of game-playing can be used as a means of examining the human need (which Hein himself identifies) to experience the world as an orderly and meaningful place. In some modernist texts, for instance, the frustration of this need by the apparent chaos of the world of experience is expressed in a flight from that world into the game. This is the case, for example, in texts like Hermann Hesse's *Das Glasperlenspiel* (1943), Stefan Zweig's *Schachnovelle* (1943), or Vladimir Nabokov's *The Defence* (1930), where the modernist game allows the player access to an artificial, yet ordered realm. However, such games cannot impose a comparable order on the chaos of the real world, and the relationship of the player to that world is consequently problematic; the attempt to bring together the ordered world of the game and the real world here results in madness and/or death. On the other hand, in the fiction of Friedrich Dürrenmatt, the motif of the game comes to symbolize the disruption of conventional means of making sense of experience. In Dürrenmatt's detective story *Der Richter und sein Henker* (1950),[17] and also particularly in his later novel *Justiz* (1985), which shows many similarities with Hein's *Das Napoleon-Spiel*,[18] the game-player is conceived of as an amoral figure who recognizes the purely formal nature of the conventional ideas which shape the individual's understanding of the world, and who can therefore exploit the tendency of others to cling to those same ideas in order to get away with his crimes.

In *Justiz*, the reader is presented with a figure highly reminiscent of Hein's Wörle: a billiard-playing lawyer called Dr Kohler, who uses his billiard table as the medium for planning a murder for which, although he commits the crime in broad daylight, he goes unpunished.[19] Like Wörle, Kohler employs another lawyer to defend him whilst he waits in jail for his plan to come to fruition. Significantly, Kohler's young lawyer Spät is an orphan who has been brought up in a state orphanage, and who, like Hein's Dallow, is drawn towards the security apparently offered by such state institutions: he describes himself as 'ein Retortenmensch' who can only survive in a 'Waisenhausordnung', in which the official discourses of order and justice are not subverted by the 'Raubtierordnung der Menschen'.[20] It is Spät's need to see society as an ordered place which makes him so susceptible to Kohler's manipulations, but he is by no means alone in this. In fact, it is Kohler's understanding of his fellow citizens' inability to break free of preconceived notions about the world which allows him to get away with his crime. Thus he is correct in believing that the legal system and the society which puts its faith in that system both lack the structures to cope with this apparently motiveless killing, which, for example, the chief of police describes as 'ein Verstoß gegen [. . .] die Logik'.[21]

Wörle's strategy in murdering Bagnall similarly challenges tried and tested means of making sense of the world, as can be seen in his attack on the Enlightenment and its legacy. This, he states, was 'eine Fantasterei von Burschen, die die Welt nicht kennen' (NS, 76). The law which it has produced, he tells Fiarthes, cannot take account of the 'Bündel und Gewirr von Ursachen und Gründen' (NS, 90) which lie at the heart of human actions and which cannot be made transparent and knowable:

> Der Wahnsinn und die Leidenschaft, und wir alle sind nicht frei von ihnen, sind nicht justitiabel. Sie sind mit unseren Gesetzbüchern gottlob nicht erfaßbar, denn wohin gerieten wir, wenn wir dies zu untersuchen hätten, wenn wir über das Nicht-Sagbare befinden und urteilen müßten. Ein Gericht hat im Grunde nicht über einen Fall und die Wahrheit zu urteilen, sondern lediglich über das uns Begreifbare. (NS, 91)

For Wörle, those who (like Dürrenmatt's Spät) hold on to 'das uns Begreifbare' in order not to face the true chaos of the world, are to be dismissed as 'Knechte'; they can be manipulated by players like Wörle, who are capable of living without such illusions.

In Wörle's view, the progressive expansion of personal liberty represents a fate which the 'Knechte' are fundamentally ill-equipped to cope with. Indeed, the drive of the masses in the nineteenth century to secure freedom from their masters is presented as the equivalent of the biblical Fall (NS, 146), where paradise is lost when the servant claims his right to act independently of the master, who provides him with 'Sicherheiten, unerschütterliche Werte, eindeutige Handlungsanweisungen und eine Moral'; 'ein durchaus angenehmes Paradies' (*NS*, 150), as Wörle sees it. However, as the reader of *Das Napoleon-Spiel* becomes increasingly aware, Wörle's sense of superiority towards the 'Knechte' is called into question by his own game-playing obsession. Unlike Dürrenmatt's Kohler, who seems secure in his sense of mastery over those who cling to illusions of order, Wörle is driven ever onwards to find new games which, on closer analysis, fulfil a not dissimilar function to the comforting received ideas of the 'Knechte'. This can perhaps best be understood by examining Wörle's childhood, where the roots of his mania lie. As Hannes Krauss points out in his review of Hein's novel, a considerable amount of information is provided by Wörle on his early years, whereas the games of his adult life are only sketched in with little detail.[22] The question as to whether this should be regarded as a literary deficiency is perhaps less interesting than the fact that Wörle's later games may be seen as a reaction to the fates of those he encounters in his early life, and who provide stark examples of the dangers which present themselves to individuals who believe that their understanding of the world and their place in it are immutable. Wörle's own mother, for instance, the reader is told, dies of sorrow after having been forced to leave behind her home in Stettin when fleeing from the advancing Russian troops at the end of the Second World War. Frau Wörle's whole existence is founded upon her role as the wife of a wealthy factory owner and small-town society lady, yet this position is taken away from her by events beyond her control. A similar fate befalls Frau Rupert, Wörle senior's personal assistant, who dedicates her life to her work in the Wörle family's confectionery factory (*NS*, 19), displaying such loyalty that her identity merges with the firm she serves. As Wörle's father says: 'Schoko-Wör [his factory], das ist eigentlich unsere Frau Rupert' (*NS*, 20). However, when the factory is eventually closed at the end of the War, Frau Rupert commits suicide. The final such figure is Wörle's own adoptive brother, who stays in the GDR after the young Wörle escapes to West Berlin to complete his studies. After having been thrown out of his job as a history lecturer following his protest against the actions of the Warsaw Pact countries in Czechoslovakia in 1968, he is rehabilitated as a *Gymnasium* teacher on the condition that he takes over an unpopular party function in his school. Although this is only an attempt to salvage his career, the brother allows himself to become identified with the GDR state and its ideology to the extent that, when this regime finally falls, he is condemned to fall with it (NS, 200).

There is also evidence to suggest that Wörle himself has undergone a similar experience of disillusionment to that of, for instance, his mother. Wörle describes the years before 1945 as a 'Paradies' (NS, 27), a term which recalls the 'Knechtsdasein' (NS, 147) that he denigrates. In his father's sweet factory, the pre-pubescent Wörle is allowed to sit on the knees of the female employees, a practice from which both parties gain an unacknowledged erotic pleasure. However, both the young boy and the women are preserved from having to face the reality of their actions by the use of the nickname 'Engelshaar', which confers upon the young Wörle the harmless status of the small child he has long since ceased to be. In this way, the perhaps more dangerously adult nature of this eroticism is made harmless by a refusal to see its true nature, imposing upon it a certain charm coupled with a veneer of respectability:

> Wir ließen den bunten Schmetterling weiter fliegen und hüteten uns, ihm die Flügel auszureißen. Wir weigerten uns, die unansehnliche Raupe zu sehen, der er entschlüpfte. Wir wollten etwas genießen und schlossen daher die Augen. (NS, 19)

In retrospect, Wörle portrays his erotic experiences with the women on the production line as a part of the highly predictable life which he would have been able to live in Stettin had history not intervened. He imagines that, had he been allowed to stay longer in the factory, he would one day have been invited by the women to come into their shower-room, in order, it is implied, to complete the sexual initiation which would have marked his passage into adulthood (NS, 25). The adult world of Stettin which Wörle imagines he would become part of with the help of the women, and also by virtue of his privileged position as the son of a wealthy factory owner, is itself described as secure and predictable. He would, he supposes, have spent a few years as his father's junior before marrying the daughter of one of the factory's suppliers and running the firm himself until the end of his days (NS, 15–16).

With the loss of his father's factory, however, comes for Wörle also the loss of this paradise, and it is after his evacuation from

Stettin that Wörle truly becomes a 'Spieler' (NS, 34). Yet, in his game-playing postwar life, his childhood, and particularly the afternoons at the factory with the women, remains an ideal of harmony which is now replaced by the compulsion of the 'Spieler', driving Wörle throughout his adult life. As he says of his early years: 'Mir bereiten nur noch meine Erinnerungen ungeteiltes Vergnügen – denn meine Spiele sind kein Spaß, es sind Spiele aus Notwehr' (NS, 27).

Wörle, then, has also experienced the fragility of the kind of comforting order which the 'Knechte' he despises place over the uglier and more threateningly chaotic realities of the world, the end of the Second World War representing a disillusionment of the same kind as suffered by his mother and Frau Rupert. Wörle is thereby transformed into the ultimate cynic who recognizes the fragility of all attempts to impose an ordering structure on the chaos of existence and who can use this knowledge to exploit the need of others (the 'Knechte') to hang on to such structures. Thus he exploits his defence lawyer's sense of duty to his profession and its ethical code in order to overcome the disgust that Fiarthes feels when he has heard Wörle's tale. Thus, equally, he exploits the court's need to place all crimes into certain preordained categories of 'Wahrscheinlichkeit' (NS, 91) in order to escape punishment for his apparently motiveless murder of Bagnall.

However, as the texts by Hesse, Zweig and Nabokov cited above suggest, the game itself can be seen as an attempt to create a personal order, even if in Das Napoleon-Spiel that order does not exist purely in an abstract realm, but rather serves as a means of gaining a sense of mastery over real situations. Furthermore, Wörle's compulsive game-playing does not differ to any great extent from the way in which, as he claims, the 'Knechte' subordinate themselves to those authorities or institutions which offer them 'unerschütterliche Werte'.[23] Wörle's compulsion to play games becomes the 'Mittelpunkt' (NS, 82) of his life in much the same way as her role in prewar society became both the 'Lebensmitte' and 'Lebenssinn' (NS, 29) for his mother, a parallel reinforced by Wörle's repeated equation of the end of the game with his own death (for example, NS, 35). Also echoing Frau Rupert's demise, he even suggests that, if he exhausted all of his game playing possibilities, he would be forced to commit suicide (NS, 82). Thus, whilst looking down on those who (he believes) abdicate their freedom, he is caught up in games which he himself describes as subordinating everything to the final victory (*NS*, 155), as having 'eiserne Regeln' (*NS*, 175), and which eventually lead him, he claims, into being forced to kill Bagnall (*NS*, 162). In this way, the games certainly give a structure to Wörle's life and, much like the values of the 'Knechte' in their subordination to higher authorities, restrict his freedom.

On the other hand, Wörle's compulsion to move on to ever new and different games provides him with a sense of the unpredictable and potentially chaotic, allowing him to convince himself that he is not a victim of that same need for order which is characteristic of the 'Knechte': 'Es ist ja eigentlich der Kern des Spiels, daß es keinerlei Gewißheiten gibt, die aus der Erfahrung gespeist sind' (*NS*, 115). As long as a particular game continues to present Wörle with unknown situations, he is able to feel that he is acting absolutely spontaneously and freely without reliance on any received order or previous knowledge, whilst at the same time giving himself over to the pursuit of an artificial goal which gives his life a structure and a purpose. In this way, Wörle succeeds in creating for himself a 'Lebensmitte', a project to which he subordinates himself as an individual, yet which appears to him as a constantly self-renewing vehicle for his own freedom, exercised in cynical detachment from the ordering values and projects proposed by society and taken up by the 'Knechte'. When he discovers that a particular game has become too familiar, and thus too close a parallel to the certainties preferred by the 'Knechte', he is obliged to give it up, yet the extent to which the abandoned games gave meaning to his life can clearly be seen in the sense of 'Lebensleere' (*NS*, 154) and 'Sinnlosigkeit' (*NS*, 97) he must suffer until he can find a new one to play.

Wörle's situation is to some extent reminiscent of the 'postmodern condition' described by Jean-François Lyotard. Lyotard claims that 'postmodernity' is characterized by localized 'language games' which form a bond between a particular group of people at a particular point in time, but which make no claim to universality. Throughout their lives, individuals progress through a series of such language games or 'temporary contracts' with other human beings or institutions, these contracts replacing 'permanent institutions in the professional, emotional, sexual, cultural, family and international domains'.[24] Elsewhere, Lyotard sees the ability to move from game to game, perhaps even inventing new ones, as characteristic of a new 'paganism',[25] that is to say a creative, indeed artistic attitude to the various bonds and structures which define the life of the individual, offering the possibility of a greater freedom for self-expression.[26] Whilst the reader may recognize the movement from one 'game' to another in *Das Napoleon-Spiel* as being analogous to that described by Lyotard, Hein's description of Wörle's obsession does not contain this element of liberation, but is rather experienced as oppressive and potentially deadly. In fact, the figure of Wörle appears to echo the more critical perspective of Frederic Jameson (a Marxist commentator on the 'postmodern'), who, like Hein, sees this series of 'temporary contracts' as a 'free play of masks and roles without content or substance' resulting from 'the waning of collective hope in a particularly conservative market climate'.[27] In other words, Wörle exists in a capitalist society which, like that described by Lyotard, offers no overarching or privileged values and meanings which could create the 'Solidarität und Engagement' (*Öa*, 146) Hein sees as essential for any society. As in the case of Dürrenmatt's Kohler, Wörle's game-playing exposes the contingent and, very often, purely formal nature of the values which capitalist society offers to its members, yet the obsessive nature of Wörle's games also shows the extent to which he is a victim of the same needs which he reviles in the 'Knechte'. In this way, Wörle's game-playing may be understood as the product of a desire to share in a stable set of values which might give his life meaning and purpose, combined with a disillusioned conviction that capitalist society has no such stability to offer.

Notes

[1] Heinz Ludwig Arnold, 'Vom Ende eines Billiardspielers', *Focus*, 19 March 1993.
[2] Thomas Rietzschel, 'Doch die Verhältnisse, sie sind nicht so', *Die Presse*, 10 July 1993.
[3] Chaim Noll, 'Lieber ein Verbrecher sein als ein Versager', *Die Welt*, 25 March 1993.
[4] David W. Robinson, 'Christoph Hein between ideologies, or, Where do the Knights of the Round Table go after Camelot falls?', *Contemporary Theatre Review*, 4 (1995) 2, 79–85, here 82.
[5] Rietzschel, 'Doch die Verhältnisse'.

[6] Günther Grack, 'Töten, um nicht sterben zu müssen', *Tagesspiegel*, 28 March 1993.

[7] Hein himself claims to have encountered people like Wörle in the West, and considers that his literary figure reflects certain crucial tendencies in capitalist society. See Cornelia Geißler, 'Kennen Sie eigentlich noch Leute, die Bücher lesen?'[Interview with Hein], *Berliner Zeitung*, 1/2 May 1993, and Lutz Hoyer, '"Ich werde als DDR-Schriftsteller in die Grube fahren"' [Interview with Hein], *Freitag*, 28 May 1993.

[8] Peter L. Berger, Brigitte Berger and Hansfried Kellner, *The Homeless Mind: Modernization and Consciousness* (Harmondsworth, Penguin, 1974), 77.

[9] Ibid., 137.

[10] See, for example, Marx and Engels's *Manifest der kommunistischen Partei*, in Karl Marx and Friedrich Engels, *Ausgewählte Werke*, 6 vols (Berlin, Dietz, 1983), I, 415–51, here 419f.: 'Die fortwährende Umwälzung der Produktion, die ununterbrochene Erschütterung aller gesellschaftlichen Zustände, die ewige Unsicherheit und Bewegung zeichnet die Bourgeoisepoche vor allen anderen aus. Alle festen eingerosteten Verhältnisse mit ihrem Gefolge von altehrwürdigen Vorstellungen und Anschauungen werden aufgelöst, alle neugebildeten veralten, ehe sie verknöchern können'. On Marx's understanding of modernity, see also Marshall Berman, *All That is Solid Melts into Air: The Experience of Modernity* (London, Verso, 1983), 87–129.

[11] See Berger et al, *The Homeless Mind*, 124: 'If modernization can be described as a spreading condition of homelessness, then socialism can be understood as the promise of a new home'.

[12] See also Hein's comments in Janice Murray and Mary-Elizabeth O'Brien, 'Interview mit Christoph Hein', *New German Review*, 3 (1987), 53–66 (here 63): 'Erst wenn Unerträgliches benannt wird, wird es wahrhaft unerträglich. Es ist eine Erfahrung, die wir alle haben machen müssen, daß eben nicht der schreckliche, der tödliche Vorgang das Fürchterliche ist, sondern sein Benennen'.

[13] The dinner-party chatter of Horst, the West German academic satirized in *Der fremde Freund*, is described in similar terms: 'Der Professor aus Bochum sprach über die Immanenzkritik der "Ökofreaks". [...] Übergangslos sprach er dann von Sprachverschleuderung und Amerikanismen. Er konnte offenbar über alles reden. Auf mich wirkte er wie eine Comicfigur, die beständig kleine runde Blasen vollspricht und sie dann irgendwohin segeln läßt' (*fF*, 90).

[14] Francis Fukuyama, *The End of History and the Last Man* (New York, The Free Press, 1992), 42. For an assessment of the end of the GDR based on similar premises, see Dieter Wellershof, 'Befreiung und Modernisierungsschub. Zur Revolution in der DDR', *Merkur*, 491 (1990), 70–4.

[15] Heinz Klunker, '"Mut zur eigenen Verantwortung": Ein Gespräch mit Christoph Hein', *Deutschland Archiv*, 7 (1990), 1144–7 (here 1147).

[16] On this point, see Jürgen Habermas, *Der philosophische Diskurs der Moderne* (Frankfurt am Main, Suhrkamp, 1988).

[17] See Friedrich Dürrenmatt, *Der Richter und sein Henker*, in *Gesammelte Werke*, ed. by Franz Josef Götz, 7 vols (Zurich, Diogenes, 1988), IV, 9–117.

[18] David Rock has already noted that the theme of the murder without a motive, which is central to the plot of *Das Napoleon-Spiel*, is to be found in both *Der Richter und sein Henker* and in *Justiz*. See David Rock, 'Christoph Hein und Jurek Becker: Zwei kritische Autoren aus der DDR über die Wende und zum vereinten Deutschland', *German Life and Letters*, 50 (1997), 182–200 (here 191).

[19] *Justiz*, which was published in the West in 1985, appeared under licence to the GDR's 'Volk und Welt' publishing house in 1987. Hein has claimed that the first notes for *Das Napoleon-Spiel* 'stammen etwa von Ende 82', although the final version was written, the author states in one interview, between 1991 and 1992. See Geißler, 'Kennen Sie eigentlich noch Leute, die Bücher lesen?', and Hoyer, '"Ich werde als DDR-Schriftsteller in die Grube fahren"'. Despite Hein's identification of a date for his first thoughts on the book before the appearance of Dürrenmatt's text in either East or West, the similarities between the two works are striking enough to suggest that Hein was aware of Dürrenmatt's novel and possibly adapted elements of it to his own purposes.

[20] Friedrich Dürrenmatt, *Justiz*, in *Gesammelte Werke*, IV, 577–801 (here 765).

[21] Ibid., 600.

[22] Hannes Krauss, 'Steigender Einsatz', *Freitag*, 9 April 1993.

[23] Wörle is particularly scornful, for example, of those 'Knechte' who, in joining a political party, allow themselves to become 'beamtete Rädchen einer gut strukturierten und funktionierenden Bürokratie' (*NS*, 116), abdicating any independence of thought to a higher authority and clinging to their 'Parteibücher' like 'Anhänger einer sektiererischen Heilslehre' (*NS*, 136).

[24] Jean-François Lyotard, *The Postmodern Condition: A Report on Knowledge*, trans. by Geoff Bennington and Brian Massumi (Manchester, Manchester University Press, 1984), 66.

[25] For Lyotard, 'paganism' describes a society which is 'a set of diverse pragmatics' or language games, 'incommunicable to each other', that 'cannot be unified into a unifying metadiscourse'. See Jean-François Lyotard and Jean-Loup Thébaud, *Just Gaming*, trans. by Wlad Godzich (Minneapolis, University of Minnesota Press, 1985), 58.

[26] Ibid., 61.

[27] Frederic Jameson, *The Cultural Turn: Selected Writings on the Postmodern, 1983–1998* (London, Verso, 1998), 60.

8

On Private Utopia and the Possessive Mentality: Christoph Hein's *Randow*

BILL NIVEN

1

Christoph Hein's post-unification play *Randow* was first performed by the 'Sächsisches Staatsschauspiel' in Dresden in December 1994 under the direction of Klaus Dieter Kirst. Hein has had a long association with Kirst and the Dresden State Theatre Company. It was Kirst who staged the first East German performance of *Passage* in 1987 and directed the famous production of *Die Ritter der Tafelrunde* in 1989. Both of these dramas enjoyed considerable success, running for many years in Dresden. *Passage* had been performed 45 times by May 1992, while *Die Ritter der Tafelrunde* was performed for the seventy-fifth time the day before the première of *Randow*.[1] Not surprisingly, then, *Randow* was awaited with a great sense of anticipation. To whet the appetite of potential theatre-goers, the Aufbau Verlag distributed the book edition of *Randow* to bookshops prior to the première, while, at the 'Sächsisches Staatsschauspiel' itself, an exhibition on Hein first performances in Dresden was opened by theatre manager Dieter Görne. Hein attended a press conference beforehand to answer questions on the play, and was in the audience for the première. The stage was set, it seemed, for another successful collaboration between author and company.

The impact of the play, however, was modest. According to reviews, the audience showed interest and applauded with a degree of enthusiasm, but not with real conviction. Some kinder reviewers suggested that expectations had simply been too high. Others found fault with Kirst's production, which was seen as tame, and with stage-designer Peter Schubert's cloth-covered set. The majority of reviewers took issue with *Randow* itself. Not that anyone doubted Hein had written a drama highly critical of post-unification developments in eastern Germany. He had certainly lived up to his reputation of being a very precise observer of contemporary trends. Set on the German–Polish border, the action spans a wide range of issues such as asylum-seekers, racism, renascent nationalism, the continuing influence of former SED and Stasi stalwarts, dubious West–East cooperation, property speculation, and the abuse of 'Rückgabe vor Entschädigung' (restitution before compensation) to the benefit of a conservative west German interest group. Yet this very range was perceived as problematic. Hein had simply packed in too much. 'Viel Stroh, wenig Ertrag', wrote one critic laconically,[2] while the multiplicity of themes reminded another of the saga of the Ewing family in *Dallas*.[3] A further criticism was that the themes, themselves everyday, even banal, had been overstated and treated superficially rather than woven into a deep dramatic structure. Hein was accused of writing 'Journalistendeutsch'.[4] Given that many of the characters were identified with one or more of the topical themes, they came across to reviewers as wooden or 'holzschnittartig' – 'Figurenklischees', as one critic put it.[5] Given, moreover, that the play's perspective was hardly one of sympathy for things west German, reviewers upbraided Hein either for instrumentalizing the 'Anti-Wessi-Komplex' or even for trading in PDS propaganda.[6] *Randow*, a reviewer in the influential *Die Deutsche Bühne* wrote, proved one thing: 'den Sturz des Künstlers aus der Exklusivität in die prosaische Normalität'.[7] Hein, it seemed to many, had lost his touch. Gone was the between-the-lines subtlety of his earlier drama, replaced by a blunt explicitness best left to the newspapers. Critics were also irritated by what they felt to be the lack of humour in the play – which, after all, was billed as 'Eine Komödie'.

The objections are not indefensible. The force of Hein's earlier plays had much to do with a lack of journalistic freedom. Would the social and political criticism implied in *Cromwell*, *Ah Q* and particularly *Die Ritter der Tafelrunde* have seemed so daring had there been a domestic press to complain about conditions in the GDR? Thanks to unification the press throughout Germany is now free to pass critical comment. Topicalizing themes such as *Wessi* interference and shady property deals is therefore hardly adventurous. Moreover, because Hein indeed approaches these and other issues at a realistic level, *Randow* lacks the mythical dimension and the metaphorical force of his earlier drama. *Die Ritter der Tafelrunde* was about the GDR, and yet it was about so much more. The multivalence of the frame of reference constituted the play's aesthetic force. Hein, typically, has said that it would be wrong to interpret *Randow* within an 'Ost-West-Optik'.[8] But it would be hard not to. If Kirst's production was literal, then this was surely because of the nature of the dramatic material. And yet there seems to be an injustice, indeed arrogance in dismissing Hein's realism as banal and clichéd. Perhaps the west German press, from whose newspapers most of the above quotations have been taken, is not as free as it thinks. A glance at the east German weekly *Freitag*, one of whose general editors is Hein himself, reveals a more differentiated opinion. *Freitag*'s reviewer points out that, while *Die Ritter der Tafelrunde* was about the quest for the Grail, *Randow* is about trying to find one's feet in the everyday world. 'Keine Gralssuche, sondern Alltagsproblematik in einer Übergangsgesellschaft'.[9] The leading Swiss daily *Neue Zürcher Zeitung* sees in the dramatic personae something 'alltäglich und monströs zugleich' and points out that, whereas Hein's earlier plays and prose demonstrated how closely the fate of the individual was tied to state power, in *Randow* the figures are tied to quite another power, namely 'das überall gültige Recht des Stärkeren'.[10] The focus on the everyday must, then, be seen in the overall literary context of Hein's work, and, given the (albeit critical) utopian preoccupation of that work, within the context of the historical transition from socialism to capitalism.

The two dramatic worlds of *Die Ritter der Tafelrunde* and *Randow* are linked. The Arthurian knights' hopes of finding the Grail are fading; the ideal social and political order is further from their reach than ever. Yet the fragmentation of the original knightly order as a result of this disillusionment also represents a chance for reorientation. Mordret, Artus's son, embodies this chance. His political refusal is not apathy, but a plea for time and space for self-definition. In this he is strikingly similar to Anna Andress in *Randow*. True, she was active during the *Wende*, so was not politically sceptical. Moreover, she was not so much oppressed by doctrinaire idealism in the GDR as by a typical form of female socialization, her personal freedom and artistic creativity hampered by two unsuccessful marriages and an alcoholic second husband (significantly named 'Krappmann'). But like Mordret she feels the need to turn away from politics and society. Living alone on the Polish–German border, she strives to follow her own inner voice; while this process is difficult, it is one she identifies with. The impression is of a woman endeavouring to acquire a sense of inner and artistic freedom.

Randow is thus in a sense a sequel to *Die Ritter der Tafelrunde*. It is a pessimistic sequel. *Die Ritter der Tafelrunde*, in this respect a very GDR play, did not declare utopian ideas to be dead; rather such ideas had got lost somewhere in the growing divide between both state practice and ideology, now characterized by stagnation, ennui, gerontocracy and even repression, and the original humanist ideals. The route to the self taken by Mordret suggests that the utopian will only have a chance if the individual forcibly detaches himself or herself from dictated norms. Dissent is the immediate ideal as it creates a basis for pluralism, dialogue and, ultimately, new consensus. As chance would have it, unification brought with it capitalism and a liberal philosophy based on the rights of the individual. Would not Mordret flourish in such a society? Hein places a Mordret-like character, Anna, into a capitalist context to test the water for the actual chances of individualism – and leaves his audience to conclude that self-definition can be as illusory a prospect under capitalism as it often was under socialism. In *Die Ritter der Tafelrunde*, ageing intolerant knights at least still pursue the Grail; in *Randow*, characters are more interested in pursuing properties, money, game, asylum-seekers, or even Anna herself. In other words, the self-definition of some is predicated on intruding on the rights of others, whose self-definition – witness Anna – thereby becomes impossible. A non-intrusive self-definition such as Anna's is a noble ideal, but the reality is that, under capitalism, the intrusive self is the norm.

Hein, to return to the point of the critical utopian preoccupation of his work, has done what one might have expected him to do: transferred his focus to the West. For years he measured socialism by its own standards and found it wanting; now he does the same with Western liberalism, and finds it equally wanting. In *Die Ritter der Tafelrunde*, the rhetorical evocation of the improving world is exposed as precisely that: rhetoric. In *Randow*, it is the rhetoric of the unlimited possibilities of capitalism that is revealed for what it is: a mask barely concealing a brazen materialism which may benefit the interests of some but certainly limits the possibilities of others. The transition from socialism to capitalism, then, may indeed have liberated the individual from state repression. But it has also meant the slide from hopes of self-definition and equality of chance into the reality of inhibiting and inhibited subjectivity, atomization and helplessness. This is, of course, the danger inherent within the capitalist system: its lack of any truly corporate ideal, in contrast to socialism. The fine balance between individuality and an inherited tradition of transcendent awareness, at the end of *Die Ritter der Tafelrunde*, has given way to banal greed. It is from this perspective that Hein's portrayal of banality in *Randow* must be understood. In capitalist society, the normality of self-interest induces a misguided sense of its triviality. Normalization desensitizes. *Randow* may represent an attempt to *resensitize* by concentrating the dramatic focus on the negative effects such normality has on the individual Anna Andress. When west German reviewers accuse Hein of banality, they reveal that they have not proved receptive to the didactic force of the play, but have un-self-critically demonstrated the very tendency towards trivialization which Hein critically unmasks.

2

The capitalist dream of unlimited possibilities is, then, like the socialist utopia before it, fraught with serious flaws. There are massive restrictions on individual development under capitalism, as there were under socialism. Hein points up negative continuities. This has always been his general agenda. While writing within the GDR, he had investigated issues such as political repression (in the novel *Horns Ende* (1985)), psychological deformity (in the novella *Der fremde Freund* (1982)) and the compromised status of the intellectual (in the novel *Der Tangospieler* (1989)). The society he depicted was hardly liberated, the effects of an unchallenged Stalinist and even National Socialist legacy only too visible. That he should go on pointing out continuities after 1990 is therefore not surprising, but is challenging because now the continuity is between real existing socialism and capitalism. Nor does Hein shirk from drawing quite concrete, if implicit situational parallels. The killing and incineration of two Rumanian asylum-seekers in the play, an event which haunts the dramatic action throughout, is, obviously, a critical comment on post-unification racism and nationalism. But it is also intended both as a criticism of the dehumanizing effects of capitalism, and as a provocative parallel to the killing of east German fugitives at the inner German border. Hein had already referred in an essay of 1991 to the existence of a new wall, this time one of money, designed to keep out foreigners so that the west need not share its wealth.[11] In *Randow*, this 'wall' is in place. Local mayor Voss and Federal Border Protection officer Kowalski, moreover, use the strip immediately in front of the border for hunting. The implication is not just that foreigners are a form of game, but also that the German–Polish border, like the former East German border, is equipped with a death strip. In 1993 the Bundestag changed the asylum laws to make it possible to send asylum-seekers apprehended at the border straight back to the country they had used as a transit land. As a result, many asylum-seekers now seek illegal entry by, among other things, attempting to swim across the treacherous River Oder. Between 1993 and 1995, 37 fugitives died on the German–Polish and German–Czech border, mostly through drowning.[12] There may be no culpability here in any direct sense, but the deaths, arguably, would not have occurred without changes to legislation. The unclarified (and thus generally attributable) killing of fugitives in *Randow* is an explicit expression of the racism and greed which many believed to be behind the changes to the Basic Law, and which is perhaps visible in the tacit acceptance of the many drownings.[13]

If the GDR sought to keep people in for reasons of self-preservation, the FRG keeps them out, more for reasons of protecting vested interests. A further provocative parallel is posited in the play. Anna, effectively, is driven out of her home. Voss wants to get his hands on her house, as does Kowalski, who fancies it for himself and his wife. In both cases, possession of the house would provide an excellent vantage-point from which to keep an eye on game, or on the border, quite apart from the investment potential. A constant series of intrusions into Anna's property and personal space, a series of hardly veiled threats, the killing of the Rumanians and ultimately of her own dog lead to her decision to sell up and leave. Her near-expulsion reminds one strongly of the forced evacuations (known as 'Zwangsaussiedlungen') to which many GDR families living on the German–German border had been subjected in 1952 and 1961. Then, the motive had been the wish to cleanse the border of ideologically suspect individuals and to step up security. Now the motive is more mixed, but basically materialist.

One might argue, then, that an appropriate motto for Hein's play would be, essentially, *plus ça change*. Both state socialism and capitalism can represent mechanisms of protectionism. Not surprisingly, perhaps, those East Germans responsible for helping to enforce these mechanisms in the GDR have no problems shifting loyalties from socialist state ideology to capitalism, or to specious notions of national interest. As if to underpin this, Hein introduces into *Randow* a number of joint ventures. The first of these involves

Kowalski, who, as a member of the West German border guards, once stood at the forefront of the Western defence system, and Voss, who, as an SED mayor, was firmly on the other side of the physical and ideological divide. Now, in their opposition to asylum-seekers and interest in hunting and property, they have a common goal. The second of these ventures involves Herr Paul, a west German property wheeler-dealer in Cologne, and Stadel, a former Stasi employee. This is not only a capitalist–Stalinist joint venture – in which capitalism very much issues the orders (Stadel does Herr Paul's dirty work for him) – it is also a nationalist–Stalinist, indeed National Socialist–Stalinist one. For Herr Paul is not only a convinced nationalist, he also has links to at least one organization with a Nazi past, in whose interests he is trying to reclaim property. Moreover, he spouts Darwinist rhetoric, sympathizes with National Socialist ideals and plays down Nazi crimes. As for Stadel, he, in his Stasi days, spearheaded a group of skinhead toughs who served in his own words as 'eine mobile und zivile Eingreiftruppe' operating 'an vorderster Front' (*Rw*, 37). The post-unification marriage of drawing-room Nazism with the vestiges of militant Stalinism is, then, anticipated by the pre-*Wende* existence of Nazi elements within Stadel's troop itself.

Hein has also subjected the dramatic structure and plot to a process of fusion, and one is justified in wondering whether this convergence is intended as a literary equivalent to the joint ventures at the heart of the play. For the most part, *Randow* consists of two separate, but parallel strands of dramatic action. The main line of action centres on Anna and the Randow valley, the secondary one on Herr Paul, who has property interests not in the Randow, but at Alt Rehse. The strands are linked in general theme, namely that of possession. But they unfold in discrete scenes, and this separateness highlights the differences. Writer and critic Friedrich Dieckmann astutely observes in his critique of *Randow* that the two 'levels', as he calls them, can be defined as 'die der großen und die der kleinen Gier'.[14] While Herr Paul deals in several extensive property deals, Voss and Kowalski focus their acquisitive energies on one property. Herr Paul manipulates from the distance and from the colonializing West, the classic background operator who never gets his *own* hands dirty. While Voss and Kowalski resort to crude threats, Herr Paul appears to do everything by the book, hiding behind a veneer of respectability. Herr Paul, moreover, seems to be working not just for himself, but for his nationalist clients. The difference is one between specific, explicit, unmediated greed, and a more generalized, implicit, mediated greed, masked as commitment to the national interest (thus Herr Paul claims that he and his clients want to build an 'Akademie des Geistes' at Alt Rehse (*Rw*, 41)). In the final scenes, however, the two strands of action unexpectedly converge. Suddenly, everyone is after the same property. Herr Paul succeeds in purchasing Anna's house for a client, thereby certainly frustrating Kowalski and possibly Voss as well. One critic writes in this respect of a joint venture of the dramatic action: 'Am Ende kommt es zu einem *Joint-Venture*: Handlung A wird mit Handlung B verknüpft'.[15] Certainly the link-up of the two strands underpins their interrelatedness: both forms of greed, direct and indirect, are expressions, at opposite ends of a scale of control, of the same social and economic condition. Indeed the existence of Herr Paul is the precondition for the more grasping mentality of a Voss and a Kowalski, because it is Herr Paul who manipulates legal and economic mechanisms such as the 'Treuhand' and 'Rückgabe vor Entschädigung' and thus helps to institutionalize greed. Lust for possession is endemic to the system. But at another level the interweaving of the strands is managed by Hein with considerable ambivalence. Is Voss lying when he insists to Kowalski that he was helpless to prevent the sale? If we assume he is lying, then we must conclude that a new joint venture has been formed, namely between Voss and Herr Paul and Stadel. In this case, Hein's point would be that such ventures, even where they appear as friendships (as in the case of Voss and Kowalski), are subject to instant dissolution when better offers come along. Joint ventures are characterized by a cynically contingent solidarity. If we assume Voss is not lying, then we must conclude, simply, that the business interests of the background manipulators are always going to win out over those of more local operators.

The conclusion of the play sees the takeover of the Randow valley by an exclusive clientele of uncertain identity and intent. All we learn about the new owners is that they intend to build an international 'Kongreß- und Ausbildungszentrum' (*Rw*, 117), but, given their association with the nationalist Herr Paul, the audience assumes the invasion of conservative forces. In line with the play's joint venture agenda, however, Stadel and his former Stasi troupe are given the jobs that are promised along with the purchase.[16] We do not learn of the outcome of Herr Paul's attempt to secure Alt

Rehse for the successor organization to the 'Hartmannbund', a medical organization that had been involved in Nazi crimes.[17] But the chances of nationalist success are good, and here, too, the joint venture operates: it is Stadel who organizes Herr Paul's campaign of repossession in Alt Rehse itself. The linking up of Stalinist stalwarts such as Voss and Stadel with staunchly conservative west Germans such as Kowalski and Herr Paul represents an apparently unproblematic collaboration of reactionary elites. The taste for power and influence bonds these people more strongly than their ideological differences ever divided them. Rather than reunification leading to the demise of Stalinism, it has led to the assimilation of former Stalinists into the power structures of capitalism. The negative face of the socialist utopia lives on, indistinguishable from the negative face of capitalism. The convergence makes it possible for continuities in the grand historical narrative of control and manipulation to operate with the same personnel. Stadel can continue to work for background operators, as he did in the GDR, and to terrorize the population. Voss is a slightly different case, given that the east German inhabitants of the Randow valley have tolerated and perhaps even encouraged his return as mayor despite his compromised past. But the principle of continuity applies to him too. The most alarming facet of Hein's play is undoubtedly the re-emergence of nationalistic and racist interests. These would appear to provide the new ideological and spiritual superstructure in which the acquisitive interests are embedded, now that socialist ideals are out of fashion, and the capitalist West no longer needs to define its identity in terms of anti-socialist jargon and paradigms. Hein has repeatedly stated in essays and interviews that neither West nor East effectively came to terms with National Socialism. His play suggests that a degree of chauvinistic nationalism has survived the Cold War, a dangerous substratum that can now function as an ideological basis for East–West synthesis.

3

Hein's play, however, goes beyond an indictment of the evils of material greed, racism and nationalism. Pressure is brought to bear on Anna not just from Voss and Kowalski, but also from her second husband Krappmann and from her daughter by her first husband, Susanne. Pressure takes in all cases the form of unannounced and stubborn intrusion. The first scene consists of Anna trying in vain to send Voss away. In the third scene, it is Krappmann who descends upon her (his excuse is that his car has broken down). In the fifth scene, Kowalski intrudes, asks Anna to lease him a room, and even makes a pass at her; ironically, it is the arrival of her daughter Susanne, representing another intrusion, which rescues her from Kowalski's unwelcome advances. Intrusion is associated with the proffering of unsolicited advice. Not only Voss and Kowalski warn Anna against the undesirable condition of solitude. The seventh scene is taken up with Susanne telling Anna that living without a man is not good for her, the ninth with Krappmann doing the same. 'Eine junge Frau, nachts, und so einsam', laments Voss (*Rw*, 10). 'Als Frau, so einsam, so dicht an der Grenze', warns Kowalski (*Rw*, 46). 'Das ist kein Haus für eine alleinstehende Frau', states Krappmann baldly (*Rw*, 66). 'Du kannst in einem einsamen Haus nicht ohne einen Mann leben', Susanne tells her mother (*Rw*, 60). Anna's confidence in her ability to live alone is not strong, and it hardly withstands this bombardment. The central point here, of course, is that she is not meant to. Voss and Kowalski want her to move out, Krappmann wants to move in. Susanne, representative of an unpolitical, love-parade generation who interprets her mother's political activities during the *Wende* as a form of degeneration (*Rw*, 61), is unable to accept that Anna appears more emancipated than she herself is. Their motives may be different, but all the characters around Anna instrumentalize age-old prejudices about female dependence on males (whether as sexual mates or physical protectors) to get what they want, while appearing to be concerned for Anna and convinced of the natural inviolability of gender roles. It is significant, too, that they try to satisfy their own needs by engendering needs in Anna. They need her to be dependent.

Viewed from a sociological perspective beyond the immediate bounds of their petty interests, the characters around Anna act to reimpose conformity upon someone who threatens to break out. Anna, striving to become independent of men socially, sexually and professionally, represents a threat to a male-centred society. By feeding Anna's insecurities, the other characters try to strengthen her sense of anxiety and, accordingly, her sense of her own inadequacy and of the need for support. The attempt at reimposition represents a form of control little different in essence to the ideological strait-jacket into which the GDR authorities tried to press their citizens – Hein, again, highlights continuities. Underlying all such forms of control is, perhaps, machismo. As all figures living at the periphery are, Anna is a threat to an established order. Hein's play conveys the impression that the border is not only imaginable, given its status as a geographical, political and social margin, as a fitting symbolic locus for withdrawal and redefinition, but it can also be viewed as a place where awareness of the proximity of otherness and the need to exclude it is particularly high. Just as the Rumanians in the play have to be kept out of Germany, if necessary by means of murder, because they threaten conventional paradigms of ethnic homogeneity, so Anna has to be kept within the confines of male social parameters, if necessary by expelling her from her house and her tentative new identity. Hein has always been sympathetic to the cause of female emancipation, and *Randow* continues a line which one can follow in his literary work from *Der fremde Freund* through to *Die Ritter der Tafelrunde*. That *Randow* is also about male views of the world and the place of others within it is clear enough from the fact that the grabbing mentality is exclusively represented by male characters. And it is clear from the parallelism between male views on dogs and male views on Anna.

Anna's large dog Frosch is a multivalent 'character'. On the most obvious level, as indicated by the affectionately diminutive name, he is her companion (that she is satisfied with canine comfort in her solitude is a damning indictment of the inadequacy, for Anna, of other human beings). On another level, the freedom she allows him – he is often permitted to roam free, and she brings him in at night rather than leaving him out as a guard-dog – enables him to live as she does. His existence mirrors and corroborates her own. On yet another level, raising the issue of his dramatic function, he serves not only as a symbol for Anna, but also as an expression of the same persona. This is particularly evident in the scene where Krappmann, having just sprung a surprise visit on Anna, asks to see Frosch, only to be told by Anna that she has locked him up. She fears that Frosch, who was once very attached to Krappmann, will only suffer from the encounter. That she also fears for herself is clear from the ensuing dialogue. 'Ich könnte ja hier bleiben. Wegen Frosch', Krappmann says. 'Nein, das kannst du nicht. Meinetwegen', answers Anna (*Rw*, 23). It is not hard to see in Anna's locking up of Frosch here both a symbolic expression of her attempt to protect herself against the impact of Krappmann, and a means of securing this protection as it were by transference. But locking him up is also the first step in the curtailment of his and, by extension, her own freedom. When Frosch is killed under mysterious circumstances, this killing results in, indeed almost seems to signify, the termination of her attempt to define a new independent life in the Randow valley. The killing of the two Romanians had deepened her sense of insecurity and is intended in the play as a threatening prefiguration of what might happen to her should she not bow to the wishes of others. But it does not make her leave. It is Frosch's sad end that does.

The association of Anna with Frosch operates at one further level. Whether it be Voss, Kowalski or even Krappmann, the men pursue a dual policy. Firstly, they try to convince Anna that a woman on her own is prey to all sorts of threats against which she cannot defend herself. Secondly, they condemn her for her lax treatment of her dog, which is variously criticized for running free and frightening off the game, not barking when it should, and being a lap-dog rather than a guard-dog. It may be that the male consensus is that she needs protecting and supporting, while the dog needs disciplining. But when it comes down to it, they both, in the eyes of the male world, need the same thing: the firm guiding hand of a man. Frosch is untrained, anathema to hunters like Kowalski and Voss, who vie with one another in extolling the obedience and discipline of their own hunting dogs (*Rw*, 16). They also extol their swiftness and aggressiveness. Essentially, the men's dogs are slaves to the male will and a mirror-image of the male ethos: they are trained to be as grasping (of game, in this case) as the men themselves, the antithesis of Frosch, who has been allowed to develop in the more liberal – and thus liberating – image of Anna. An untrained dog is an unmanned dog; an independent woman is an unmanned woman. Both are transgressions in a male world. In the opening scene of the play, Voss's criticisms of Frosch and warnings of possible threats to his life accompany his suggestion to Anna that she cannot handle life on her own in such a way, that she is invited to understand his references to Frosch as implicit references to her, an implicitness which almost becomes explicit when he warns Anna 'how easily something can happen' if she does not take her dog on the lead (*Rw*, 13).

It is the male dogs who win out, as it is the men. Anna returns to the Randow valley at the end of the play to take one last look and to retrieve remaining belongings from her former house. The house has since been gutted of its contents. All that she can find is Frosch's dog-brush and his dog-bowl. Yet, far from being frustrated by this meagre find, she suggests to Stadel that this was precisely what she had come back for (*Rw*, 119). He fails to comprehend this, but the audience understands the significance of these objects not just as mementoes of a loved dog, but as almost sacred artefacts symbolizing her erstwhile bid for freedom, represented in Frosch. Perhaps such artefacts are the hope of future freedom, not just reminders of the past. She asks Stadel to be allowed to stay a while. He turns down her request with reference to his dogs. 'Vor denen habe selbst ich Respekt' (*Rw*, 118). The Randow valley is now in the control of the meaner male variety of dog, as, indeed, it is in the control of the meaner males, a former Stasi troupe whom Herr Paul compares with young wolves and whom he expects to be lean and hungry (*Rw*, 110).

Randow is an unsolved murder mystery. We never learn who killed the asylum-seekers. This is a deliberate dramatic ploy to spread the possibility of guilt evenly across several of the characters, inviting us to regard their conduct and attitudes critically. *Randow* is also a dogslaughter mystery. Here, too, it could have been anyone. Voss, Kowalski, Krappmann, even Susanne – each stands to benefit from the increased sense of exposure and isolation which Frosch's death inevitably means for Anna. But it may be that Krappmann is the likeliest suspect as far as Frosch is concerned. He took him for a walk just before his murder. In a brief monologue at the end of the ninth scene, Krappmann proclaims *his* sense of affinity with Frosch. 'Ich bin auch nur ein armer Hund, Frosch, ein armer, herrenloser Hund' (*Rw*, 85). He then performs a little bark to underpin this. The equation of 'masterless' with 'worthless' which 'herrenlos' implies is significant: Frosch, having no master, has no right to life. Krappmann is not so much 'herrenlos' as 'frauenlos', but his drifting existence, his dependency on Anna and on alcohol, as well as his attempt to glorify his academic failure as the result of political discrimination rather than his own incompetence, all point to a deep sense of self-disgust, a sense of being 'without manliness', in *this* sense 'herrenlos'. Frosch dies for many reasons. One may be as a substitute for Krappmann's suicide, an act of sacrificial proxy – a possible motive quite apart from Krappmann's envy at Frosch's position at Anna's side.

4

Is there then no substance to the criticisms levelled at Hein's play outlined at the beginning of this chapter? In certain respects, there is some. If Hein bills his play as a comedy, then this is not because it is particularly funny, which it is not (despite occasional comic misinterpretations and touches of bathos), but because the play constantly focuses on rendering transparent the discrepancy between word and meaning. With the exception of Anna, characters often hide their true intentions behind phrases and gestures. *Vis-à-vis* Anna, particularly, self-interest can be expressed as solidarity and concern. The play is at this level a criticism of consumer society, where advertising and packaging delude customers into thinking it is *their* interests that are being catered for. But it is unfortunate that Hein, in the figure of Herr Paul, should have tried to complement this very effective ironic register with a degree of satire. Hein's interesting portrayal of the nexus between nationalism and capitalism threatens at times to lose in force in the same measure as Herr Paul is reduced to an anti-*Wessi* caricature. Equally questionable is the moral relativism in the Herr Paul/Stadel scenes. Stadel is a negative ex-Stasi tough, yet Hein would have it that he is deeply disturbed when he learns of the National Socialist atrocities in which Herr Paul's clients' predecessor organization, the 'Hartmannbund', was implicated. Equipping Stadel with a conscience to throw Herr Paul's consciencelessness into relief and imply that morally disreputable east Germans are less disreputable than morally disreputable west Germans does seem cheap. Moreover, that Herr Paul cynically allows Stadel and the Stasi to be used as a scapegoat in Alt Rehse has the effect of casting the latter, within the context of the plot, in the role of victims.

By and large, though, Hein's play has more to it than the reviews might lead us to believe. It is about far more than 'problems of unification'. The movement from hopes of social utopia to smaller-scale hopes of personal reorientation is marked by failure given the continuity of invasive doctrines and repressive strategies. Where socialism sought to own minds and dispositions, capitalism seeks to possess in more material, yet no less pervasive ways; where socialism imprisoned its citizens, capitalism seeks to exclude the other. At a more profound level, Hein's play is a pessimistic comment on patriarchal patterns. There is a further level, one of sophisticated metaphor. The border-area in which Anna lives was declared a nature reserve after the *Wende*, opening it up to the local population after generations of exclusive use by Wilhelminian, Hitlerian and then socialist Germany for military purposes. The demilitarization is at the same time a renaturalization, generally indicative, perhaps, of the chances potentiated by the end of the Cold War. The renaturalization of the *border* itself, however, is a specific metaphor for the freeing up of space beyond the centre. After generations of life lived in the centripetal pull of ideologies, the end of communism, division and the immediate nuclear threat would seem to have cleared the way for the tolerance and even encouragement of the creative periphery. But such hopes are soon dashed, for the activities of huntsmen in the nature reserve are a form of remilitarization. And, at the end of the play, the border is reoccupied by an exclusive cartel. The gunshots which threatened the idyll (*Rw*, 27) are now replaced by the soft thuds of hammers as Stadel's men fence off the Randow valley (*Rw*, 116). The closing up of border space implies the reimposition of ideology, in this case, perhaps, a neo-conservative one masking itself as European, very much in the style of Herr Paul himself – a severe statement on the condition of united Germany in its sixth year.

Notes

[1] For an account of the theatrical and critical reception of Hein's *Die Ritter der Tafelrunde*, see Bill Niven, 'A play about socialism? The reception of Christoph Hein's Die Ritter der Tafelrunde', in Arthur Williams, et al (eds.), *'Whose Story?' – Continuities in Contemporary German-language Literature* (Bern, Lang, 1998), 197–218.

[2] Ernst Schumacher, 'Ostwestdeutscher Zerrspiegel', *Berliner Zeitung*, 23 December 1994.

[3] Wolfgang Engler, 'Froschs Ende', *Die Zeit*, 30 December 1994.

[4] Reinhard Wengierek, 'Wenn das Theater der Zeitung nachläuft', *Die Welt*, 23 December 1994.

[5] See, for instance, Hartmut Krug, 'Wessis mit Elan und Ossis ohne Visionen', *Badische Zeitung*, 28 December 1994.

[6] Wengierek, 'Wenn das Theater der Zeitung nachläuft'.

[7] Knut Lennartz, 'Er ist wieder da', *Die Deutsche Bühne*, 2 (1995), 36–7, here 36.

[8] Ibid., 37.

[9] Jörg Magenau, 'Hunger auf Hoffnung', *Freitag*, 6 January 1995.

[10] Stephan Zimmermann, 'Zwischen Angst und Hingabe', *Neue Zürcher Zeitung*, 25 December 1994.

[11] Christoph Hein, 'Eure Freiheit ist unser Auftrag. Ein Brief an (fast alle) Ausländer – wider das Gerede vom Fremdenhaß der Deutschen' (*MJ*, 64–70).

[12] See '37 Flüchtlinge an den Ostgrenzen umgekommen', *Süddeutsche Zeitung*, 9 May 1996.

[13] The fate of some of those fugitives who at least succeeded in reaching Germany and applying for asylum has been equally tragic and perhaps indicative of a certain heartlessness on the part of German bureaucrats. One asylum-seeker – a Kurd – died unnecessarily of cirrhosis of the liver in August 1995 after the authorities in Bremen delayed a life-saving liver transplant (see 'Asylbewerber starb nach Behördenpannen', *Süddeutsche Zeitung*, 18 August 1995). In the same month, a Nigerian with a German wife hanged himself in a prison cell after learning that he was to be expelled (see 'Abschiebehäftling erhängt sich in Zelle', ibid.).

[14] Friedrich Dieckmann, 'Große und kleine Gier', *Frankfurter Allgemeine Zeitung*, 23 December 1994.

[15] Ralph Hammerthaler, 'Ein Zeitstück nach der Wende', *Süddeutsche Zeitung*, 28 December 1994.

[16] The events Hein describes in the Randow valley could be based on a number of wrangles over rights of use, but are most similar perhaps to the drawn-out and continuing dispute over the Colbitz-Letzlinger Heath near Magdeburg, which was used as a military training ground first by the Nazis and then by the Russians. After the Russian military left in June 1994, many local people and environmentalists hoped that the area would be declared an area of natural beauty, for use by tourists and local nature-lovers. But the Defence Ministry in Bonn took over the heath for military training in August 1994. Repeated complaints led in 1997 to a decision by the Defence Ministry to allow a third of the heath to be designated as a nature reserve (see 'Weiter Streit um die Letzlinger Heide', *Frankfurter Allgemeine Zeitung*, 20 June 1992, and 'Verbale Gefechte um einen Truppenübungsplatz', *Süddeutsche Zeitung*, 18 April 1997).

[17] Hein has based this episode on a true case. After unification, Alt Rehse, a small village near Neubrandenburg in Mecklenburg-Vorpommern, became the subject of a bitter and protracted property dispute between the local community and the 'Kassenärztliche Vereinigung' (KV). In 1933, the 'Hartmannbund', an organisation of doctors, bought part of Alt Rehse and founded a medical school there. This school, the 'Führerschule der deutschen Ärzteschaft', was responsible, among other things, for developing bacteriological weapons and for training doctors in 'racial science'. Several doctors trained there later 'applied' what they had learnt in Auschwitz-Birkenau, where one of their tasks was to identify the

'racially worthless', a selection which meant certain death. After 1945, the West German KV became the successor organisation to the 'Hartmannbund' – hence the post-1990 property claim. In 1998, 240 hectares of land in Alt Rehse were transferred to the KV. The issue is not entirely settled, however, as the rights of ownership over a 25 hectare park, together with its country house, have still to be decided on (see 'Halbinsel Wustrow bleibt Streitobjekt', *Süddeutsche Zeitung*, 26 December 1998).

9

'Mehr Freiheit zur Wahrheit': The Fictionalization of Adolescent Experience in Christoph Hein's *Von allem Anfang an*

DENNIS TATE

As Christoph Hein's first major work conceived and written after the collapse of the GDR, *Von allem Anfang an* (1997)[1] was inevitably going to be closely scrutinized to see whether the *Wende* had had any significant impact on his creative priorities or his style of writing. Equally inevitably, Hein was going to be determined in advance to frustrate any expectations his readers might have had that he would now present life in the GDR in a different light simply because the state had ceased to exist and works of literature were no longer subject to censorship. The disappointment expressed by some of the reviewers of his previous novel, *Das Napoleon-Spiel*, when it appeared in 1993, derived at least in part from the fact that it defied classification as a *Wende-Roman*, that eagerly anticipated but strangely elusive phenomenon of the first half of the 1990s. Only later did it become clear that *Das Napoleon-Spiel* had been conceived well before the dramatic events of the autumn of 1989 and that its publication had been significantly delayed, less by the impact of German unification on Hein's creative plans than by his slow recovery in the early 1990s from a near-fatal brain haemorrhage.[2]

Von allem Anfang an also took a long time to come to fruition. It was Hein's main creative preoccupation from the time he finished his play *Randow*, premièred in 1994,[3] and it involved a complete reworking of his original conception. As he confirmed in an interview of November 1998 – 'Ich habe [*Von allem Anfang an*] zerschlagen und die Einzelteile dann neu zusammengesetzt' – his new prose text was subject to the same ruthless process of revision and compression which has characterized all of his fictional work from *Der fremde Freund* onwards.[4] As in the 1980s in the GDR, Hein had no intention of satisfying the expectations of the cultural establishment regarding the kind of work he ought to be producing.

This time, however, his response had to be a more subtle one, since the search for the elusive *Wende-Roman* had now been replaced by a process in which many other authors of the ex-GDR had willingly become involved, the task of providing stocktaking accounts of life in the GDR in autobiographical form. The older generation of GDR authors had led the way in establishing the notion that the collapse of the state to which they had committed themselves called for a personal response, without recourse to the narrative distancing from personal experience which the use of fictional structures allows.[5] The publication of Stefan Heym's *Nachruf*, a classic account of a life of conflict with authority in Nazi Germany, the USA and then the GDR, spanned the *Wende*, with the West German edition of 1988 followed by a more intensely discussed East German reprint in 1990; Hermann Kant, the disgraced ex-president of the GDR Writers' Union, attempted to salvage something of his reputation with his *Abspann* of 1991; Heiner Müller showed such a postmodernist disregard for the niceties of composition that he had his *Krieg ohne Schlacht* (1992) compiled for him from the scripts of a series of interviews; Günter de Bruyn attracted most critical praise, and the largest readership, for his more thorough and self-critical life-story in two parts, *Zwischenbilanz* (1992) and *Vierzig Jahre* (1996), while Günter Kunert added a more embittered tone to these retrospectives with his *Erwachsenenspiele*, which appeared at the same time as Hein's *Von allem Anfang an* in the autumn of 1997.

The assumption behind much of this wave of writing that producing explicit autobiography would, in itself, guarantee greater truthfulness and authenticity than fiction ever could, was not one shared by authors of Hein's generation, whose deeper awareness of modernist culture has left them resistant to absolute distinctions of this kind. In his novel *'Ich'* of 1993, Hein's contemporary Wolfgang Hilbig presented his perspective on the moral confusion of the era of the Stasi files by reducing the 'Ich' of his protagonist to a codename he uses when he works as an 'informeller Mitarbeiter', just one identity among many in the disorientated life he leads. Anyone sharing Hilbig's view of the fragmented self of the contemporary intellectual would have found it impossible to accept the implications of Günter de Bruyn's statement, in his preface to *Zwischenbilanz*, that he was now abandoning fiction, which had made him into a professional liar, in order to dedicate himself to speaking the truth in writing his autobiography: 'Der berufsmäßige

Lügner übt, die Wahrheit zu sagen'.⁶ Or, to take another example from among Hein's near-contemporaries: Klaus Schlesinger may have experimented before unification with an autobiographical chronicle as a means of making sense of the period in his life after he left the GDR in disillusionment (published in 1990 under the title *Fliegender Wechsel. Eine persönliche Chronik*). Yet when it came to confronting the more remote period of his adolescence in the Berlin of the early 1950s (in his work of 1996, *Die Sache mit Randow*), Schlesinger found the fictional framework of a first-person narrator more appropriate to his aim of making sense of his memories.

The fact that *Von allem Anfang an* is ostensibly closer to Hein's personal experience than all of his previous prose-writing nevertheless led to questions being regularly posed in interviews as to whether it was directly autobiographical.⁷ Up until now he had been able to argue persuasively that his works of fiction represented the transformation of a core of first-hand experience into a quite distinctive 'Kunstwirklichkeit' – with the emphasis clearly on the creative challenge of producing convincing portrayals of antipathetic characters like Claudia (*Der fremde Freund*), Spodeck and Kruschkatz (*Horns Ende*), Dallow (*Der Tangospieler*) and Wörle (*Das Napoleon-Spiel*) rather than slightly distanced self-portraits. It now appeared that he had placed himself at the centre of *Von allem Anfang an*, only lightly disguised as the first-person narrator Daniel. But there was no change in his strategy for dealing with this line of questioning from interviewers: he had always claimed that personal experience and memories were an essential point of departure and that all of his works were in some respects autobiographical, but that the creative challenge was to use this stock of subjective material in a precise and meticulous way as the basis for the invention of credible fictional characters.⁸ Rather than seeing the writing of autobiography as a guarantee of authenticity, Hein had relished the freedom fiction gave him to go beyond the limits of autobiographical fact in a modernist 'game' with an autonomous reader.

This understanding of literature as a game, signalled by his choice of titles such as *Der Tangospieler* and *Das Napoleon-Spiel* for earlier works, is a point to which he has regularly returned in the context of *Von allem Anfang an*. In his interview of 1994 with Hyunseon Lee he spoke of his fictional characters collectively as 'spielerische Möglichkeiten, in denen man das eigene Leben auch potenziert und da auch mit dem eigenen Leben zurechtkommt'.[9] In his interview with Marlies Menge marking the appearance of his new novel he insisted that it was 'nicht autobiographischer als "Napoleonspiel"', masking the truth of personal experience, in the same way as he had done in his previous novel, as the best means of getting close to it. In all of his work truth was obscured '[m]it den Masken des Spiels, die mehr Freiheit erlauben. Auch mehr Freiheit zur Wahrheit'.[10] Discussing *Von allem Anfang an* more than a year later in *Der Spiegel* he argued that he had been especially anxious in writing a novel about adolescence to avoid the danger of producing 'ein[en] vergoldete[n] Rückblick' without the necessary distance from his autobiographical experience.[11]

Despite this absolute consistency on Hein's part in his statements about his approach to fiction, he also appears to be providing more scope in *Von allem Anfang an* for readers with a general awareness of his family background and upbringing to read it as if it were also a work of autobiography. If there had been a degree of ambiguity about his earlier novel *Horns Ende* (1985) regarding the relationship between the author and Thomas, the youngest of his five protagonists, then the single protagonist of his new work, Daniel, appears to a greater degree to be identifiable with the author himself.[12] Thomas was clearly a near-contemporary of Hein's, with a broadly similar biography up to the time when *Horns Ende* is set, the summer of 1957, even if it is presented in fairly fragmentary form and differs in some important details (for example, the fact that he is the elder of the two children of the local pharmacist rather than one of the family of six raised by a Lutheran pastor and his wife whom we know Hein to have been).[13] The idea that he might be the author's mouthpiece emerges most strongly from the dialogues between Thomas and the dead Horn at the start of each chapter of *Horns Ende*, in which the now adult Thomas is being urged, in the narrative present of the early 1980s, to take on the moral responsibility for remembering exactly what happened in this bleak period in GDR history and communicating this knowledge to others (by implication, as a means of stimulating some desperately overdue debate about how to rectify past mistakes). Whatever links may exist between Thomas's home town of Bad Guldenburg and Hein's Bad Düben would only have been apparent at this stage to a reader with independent first-hand knowledge of the latter, since Hein has never provided a non-fictionalized portrait of the town he lived in until he was fourteen.

The Fictionalization of Adolescent Experience 121

Von allem Anfang an, read in the light both of *Horns Ende* and of Hein's biography, seems to come even closer to providing an autobiographical framework, evidently underlining the central significance of the 1956–7 period for Hein's personal development by directing the historical focus just a matter of months backwards in time from the setting in *Horns Ende*. Daniel, speaking in the first person, provides a full account of his life in the year between Christmas 1955 and November 1956. Like Hein, he is born in Silesia during the Second World War, the son of a pastor and his wife who are then forced to flee westwards in the face of the advancing Red Army in the last months of the war (*VA*, 31). The rapidly growing family resettles in a small town (not named in the text) in Saxony, where Daniel attends the local primary school. At the end of his eight years of compulsory education,[14] he is prevented on account of his family's Christian beliefs from transferring to the neighbourhood *Oberschule*, which forces his parents to take the illegal step of sending him to a *Gymnasium* in West Berlin to enable him to take his *Abitur*. Daniel's departure from his home town in the autumn of 1958 forms the chronological cut-off point of the text (*VA*, 5–6).

The reader inclined to take Thomas and Daniel as related parts of a 'portrait of the artist' in his early adolescence will be encouraged by the range of topographical details common to both works. Even though Thomas's family background is different, the environment of Bad Guldenberg is reassuringly similar to that of Daniel's anonymous town. Both are spas in decline (*HE*, 32; *VA*, 115), with the older core of the town around the market square, including the 'Marienkirche' and the few unexciting shops and offices, augmented recently by a fire-station (*HE*, 41, 131, 312; *VA*, 106–8 – in the latter, the primary school and the manse are located here as well). A postwar housing estate, the 'Siedlung', has been built on the outskirts (*HE*, 196; *VA*, 53–4), and is a cause of social tension. The main sources of excitement for an adolescent boy are the 'Bleicherwiese' beside the square, where the gypsies set up their annual camp in *Horns Ende* (*HE*, 6) and where the visiting troupe of acrobats, the Veltronis, perform in *Von allem Anfang an* (*VA*, 106), and the 'Anger', where a 'Rummelplatz' is located at certain times of the year (*HE*, 307; *VA*, 23). Traditional sources of employment like the 'Molkerei' have been augmented by a new factory, for which the new housing estate provides the workforce (*HE*, 34, 181; *VA*, 57, 170–1). A site of minor historical significance just outside the town is provided in the earlier novel by the castle and its museum, and more peripherally in the recent one by the old monastery and its roofless 'Refektorium' (*HE*, 74–5; *VA*, 115). Further afield, the *Oberschule* is located in both works a short railway journey away in the *Kreisstadt*, called Wildenberg in *Horns Ende* (*HE*, 94; *VA*, 188), while Leipzig is in both cases the urban hub of this provincial world (*HE*, 83, 104; *VA*, 37). On the basis of this wide range of similarities, it would be no surprise if Bad Düben were also to contain most of the features described in these two texts.

Yet do these patterns of topographical similarity have any import other than of the most general and negative kind, summed up by Daniel's reference to it as a typical 'langweilige Kleinstadt' (*VA*, 174) or by Thomas's stronger urge to liberate himself 'von dieser Stadt und den schlimmen elf Jahren meines bisherigen Lebens [. . .]. Ich wollte sie vergessen, austilgen, so gründlich, als seien sie nie gewesen' (*HE*, 78)? It certainly would be misguided to use them as the justification for an autobiographical reading, as this would overlook the small but significant discrepancies which Hein has also carefully built into his portraits of Thomas and Daniel, as reminders that his relationship with them is a more complex fictional one.

Age differences, for example, are not just coincidental. Thomas reminds us at the end of *Horns Ende* that he is just twelve years old in September 1957, when he has to come to terms with the suicide of the man who meant much more to him than anyone else in this provincial backwater (*HE*, 309). As well as having a different family background to Hein, Thomas is thus more than a year younger than the author, who was born in April 1944. Daniel, in contrast, is an important shade older than Hein, already aged two when the family fled from Silesia at the beginning of 1945 (*VA*, 31 and 137) and progressing from the seventh to the eighth grade in school over the months of 1956 covered in detail in *Von allem Anfang an*.[15] Even though, as already indicated, his family appears to be directly modelled on Hein's, a closer comparison of the available information suggests that some differences have been deliberately introduced – for example, Daniel is the second oldest of seven children (*VA*, 12, 66–7), while the author is the third oldest of six – to serve as a warning against any blurring of the distinctions between fact and fiction. And as all of the characters outside the family with whom Daniel comes into close contact during this period of his life – his 'Nenntante' Magdalena, his holiday friends Jochen and Pille, the acrobat Kade, his first girlfriend Mareike, his school classmates Bernd and Lucie, and his German teacher Frau Kaczmarek – all disappear from his life from the time he moves to West Berlin, there are no other continuities outside his fictional framework which might be compared with biographical facts. The main focus of *Von allem Anfang an* is, in any case, on the private experience of the onset of puberty, and the reader's confidence in the authenticity of Daniel's account will derive from the coherence and credibility of the text rather than external biographical considerations. The post-unification desire to read it as a source of information about the GDR of the middle 1950s or for the clues it may provide to the GDR's subsequent downfall should thus rapidly give way to a proper consideration of its literary value, allowing the possibility of placing it in the broader German cultural context which stretches back a century to classical accounts of adolescence such as Frank Wedekind's *Frühlings Erwachen* and Robert Musil's *Die Verwirrungen des Zöglings Törless*.[16]

Hein's narrative structure underlines the gulf which separates *Von allem Anfang an* from other literary attempts at post-unification moralizing or political point-scoring. In a key passage covering just two paragraphs in the middle of the first of his nine chapters, his narrator, the first-person voice of the present-day Daniel, sets out his aims. The emphasis is immediately on the difficulties of remembering exactly what he experienced some forty years ago, when all of the stories he wants to tell are full of gaps, the result of what he graphically describes as 'ein regelrechter Mottenfraß' (*VA*, 10). All the older members of his family, including his Aunt Magdalena, who figures prominently in this first chapter, are either dead already or close to death, so he is rapidly running out of witnesses able to comment on his version of events. This may, however, not be a major problem, since his intention is to recount what he went through on the threshold of puberty, directly as he experienced it and without the benefit of hindsight:

[ich] werde versuchen, die Lücken zu füllen mit dem, was ich erlebt, und mit dem, was ich gesehen, aber nicht verstanden habe. Mit dem, was ich gehört habe, aber was mir nicht erzählt wurde. Und mit dem, was vor meinen Augen geschah und was ich dennoch nicht sah. Damals. (*VA*, 10–11)

This reconstruction requires a degree of fictionalization, as the narrator readily admits, although he is anxious to reassure readers that all the additional material he is using to produce coherent stories also forms part of his store of authentic images and phrases from this period in his life:

> Ich versuche, die Geschichten zu vervollständigen, sie mit den Bruchstücken der Erinnerung anzufüllen, mit Bildern, die sich mir einprägten, mit Sätzen, die aus dem dunkel schimmernden Meer des Vergessenseins dann und wann aufsteigen und ins Bewusstsein dringen. (*VA*, 11)

He fully admits that this is a painful process, as many of these fragments of memory have 'schartige Kanten, die in mir etwas aufreißen' (*VA*, 11), but has evidently convinced himself that this is a task he needs to undertake without further delay.

Having defined his narrative approach in this clear-cut way, the present-day Daniel virtually disappears from sight. Only on a few other occasions in the text does he step back to a similar degree from his re-creation of the younger Daniel's experience, reflecting further on what he has just described, but not from the standpoint of certainty and wisdom which novels structured in this retrospective way often seek to provide. The narrator admits that there are issues which still puzzle him and cannot be resolved, such as the reasons for his mother's unhappiness in her married life and the intense jealousy which alienated her from her husband during her pregnancy at this time, which caused the young Daniel considerable anxiety. In a passage beginning 'Ich weiß nicht, warum Mutter so eifersüchtig war' and punctuated with speculative terms like 'vielleicht' and 'ich glaube [nicht]', the present-day Daniel is still searching for clues to support his hypothesis that the family's enforced move from Silesia at the end of the war was particularly traumatic in her case, looking through photo albums and recalling the stories his grandparents told him about her earlier life, but he is painfully aware that he has failed to do her justice in his story (*VA*, 30–2). Elsewhere in the text it is usually just a momentary switch of tense which reminds us of the narrator's present-day situation, whether as a parenthetic comment – 'Ich glaube, es war das einzige Spiel, was sie besaß' (*VA*, 12) – a linking sentence – 'Ich erinnere mich nur an einen einzigen Sonntag, an dem ich [...] den Vormittag nicht in der Kirche verbringen musste' (*VA*, 172) – or brief expressions of regret – 'Ich habe von Kade nie wieder etwas gehört' (*VA*, 131), 'Ich besitze nichts von [Tante Magdalena], nicht einmal ein Foto' (*VA*, 197).

Apart from such occasional brief shifts back to the present-day perspective, the narrative remains firmly focused on the 'damals' of 1956, looking forward only as far as the day when Daniel leaves this provincial backwater for ever for West Berlin, which provides the internal framework for the story. The event on the world stage which allows the narrative to be pinned down historically, the Hungarian uprising and its brutal suppression early in November 1956, only impinges on Daniel's consciousness in the final chapter, 'Glace surprise', describing his first visit to West Berlin. This means that the chronology has to be determined retrospectively, but there are enough interconnecting references to indicate that chapters two to nine are in sequential order, beginning with Christmas 1955, and that Daniel's departure for West Berlin in Chapter One comes nearly two years after his first sight of the city. In this way Hein has succeeded in placing this period of intense change in Daniel's life in a dramatic historical context, yet without suggesting that the development of his thirteen-year-old protagonist is fundamentally affected by such external events. He is, for instance, more interested in the technology which has created the electronic news screen on the Ku'damm than in the grim news it is conveying (*VA*, 183–5).

Hein has also paid close attention to the balance of his narrative between the recreation of places and events, the characterization of the individuals who were important to Daniel at this stage of his life, the dramatization of important moments in these relationships, and the presentation of his often confused thoughts and emotions. Detailed scene-setting is the narrator's way both of putting his memory to the test and creating atmosphere: the meticulous description in Chapter One of Aunt Magdalena's old-fashioned, but fascinating flat above the local bakery makes it clear why Daniel's after-school visits to do his homework there are so stimulating; the exact recreation of the stultifying routine of the family's exchange of Christmas presents shows why it tends to be a time of tension rather than of pleasure (Chapter Two), and so on.

The treatment of the various individuals with whom Daniel comes into contact properly reflects the naïvety of his adolescent perspective: his tendency to hero-worship older lads such as Jochen or Kade, whose lives seem more exciting than his, and the disappointment which inevitably follows when they lose interest in him, is conveyed as it happens without recourse to narrative distancing. But he is also learning rapidly about the ways in which adults can suffer and change behind their façade of authority and control, and this is reflected particularly in his deepening relationship with Aunt Magdalena over the year covered by the text. Her growing willingness to talk to him about her cruel treatment at the hands of her long-dead fiancé (*VA*, 25–7), her unfulfilled fantasies (*VA*, 166–7) or the way she was shocked out of her illusions about the nature of war (*VA*, 194–6) is evidence in itself of the speed at which Daniel is growing up.

The extent to which Hein's narrator is prepared to let a sympathetic character like Magdalena speak for herself in scenes like these, where she is revealing the more dramatic moments in an otherwise uneventful life, provides further evidence of how he is transforming the 'Bruchstücke [. . .] der Erinnerung' referred to in the opening chapter into a work of fiction, rather than restricting himself to the conventions of autobiography. He makes particularly effective use of extended dialogue in letting his readers experience the young Daniel's confusion for themselves, in situations where narrator comment would be completely superfluous. For example: he shows graphically how Daniel tries to disguise his total ignorance of homosexuality after hearing the word 'schwul' for the first time from his streetwise and prejudiced classmate Bernd (*VA*, 47–50). Chapter Eight, 'Die schlummernde Venus', recounts Daniel's encounters with his first girlfriend Mareike predominantly in dialogue, leaving it up to readers to think their own amused (and probably sympathetic) thoughts as they follow his progress from initial embarrassment to resourcefully trying to persuade her to dance naked for him (especially *VA*, 158–61). More subtly, Daniel's grandfather's blow-by-blow account of how he has been dismissed from his post as manager of an agricultural estate in Sachsen-Anhalt for refusing to join the SED is presented almost entirely in reported speech. The couple of phrases left in direct speech convey the narrator's bitter sense of irony, both that this is alleged to be the beginning of a new era – 'Jetzt ist eine neue Zeit' – and that his devoutly Protestant grandfather is being dismissed by a Party secretary who declares regretfully, unaware that he is using Luther's most famous expression of dissent, 'Ich kann nicht anders' (*VA*, 77–9).

However important narrative devices like these are in varying the pace and intensity of Daniel's story, the main co-ordinating element in *Von allem Anfang an* is provided by the narrator's portrayal of his subjective thoughts and feelings on the threshold of puberty. His Christian upbringing may have given him a sense of morality, but it has not provided him with a basis for understanding the nature of relationships or his own sexuality. It is his struggle to come to terms with the two latter issues, largely in isolation, which forms the main focus of the nine stories. In Chapter Two, the new tension in his parents' relationship releases deep anxieties that they are about to get divorced, and we see him desperately trying to find out what is going on behind the adult façade of silence, as he pieces together whatever information he can extract from his aunt, his older brother and his grandparents about the causes of his mother's jealousy. In the process he risks using the word 'schwanger' for the first time in a question (*VA*, 33), and begins to grasp that there may be a link between his mother's emotional volatility and her sixth pregnancy. In Chapter Three, after his encounter with Bernd and his discovery that the visiting science lecturer from Leipzig is 'schwul', he is frustrated by the inadequacy of the alternative explanations he winkles out of his father and his German teacher, which refer to homosexuality first as an unfortunate 'Krankheit', then as some kind to threat to 'hygiene' in the school (*VA*, 54, 58). In three of the next four chapters, Daniel rapidly has to come to terms with the onset of puberty and with the nature of heterosexual relationships. (The fact that he has already been an eager assistant to his older friend Sebastian in producing copies of nude photographs for illicit circulation in the town has, of course, not helped in the slightest to prepare him.) On holiday at his grandparents' home he is allowed by his older friend Jochen to watch him and his girlfriend Pille making love at the edge of the forbidden *Russensee*. Daniel's first sight both of a naked female body and of an erect penis causes the arousal which leads to his own first ejaculation. A couple of weeks later, back in his home town he is – more accidentally this time – witness to another sexual encounter, between his friend Kade from the visiting troupe of acrobats and his geography teacher, Frau Blüthgen. Now it is more of an embarrassment – the sight of a teacher's naked bottom in decidedly unromantic surroundings – and a potential threat to the grade average in his final year of primary school which will be crucial to his hopes of being accepted later by the *Gymnasium* in

West Berlin. Then he takes his first independent steps in the direction of sexual experience when the opportunity occurs with Mareike during a schools' drama festival in Dresden, stimulated both by his success there as an actor and by the sight of classical nudes such as Giorgione's 'Schlummernde Venus' during their outing to the city's famous art-gallery. Dramatic irony dictates, however, that the aspiring young lovers are interrupted before their determination is put to the test, probably to Daniel's great relief. As a contrast, both Chapter Nine and the frameworking Chapter One throw light on his harmlessly romantic yearning for his classmate Lucie, undimmed even by her exposure of his illicit visit in November 1956 to West Berlin, which leads to Daniel being humiliated in class for having fallen prey to 'feindliche Propaganda' about the nature of the Hungarian uprising (*VA*, 192).

These scenes, recounted with a self-deprecating honesty and willingness to confront taboos still surrounding aspects of male sexual development, have given *Von allem Anfang an* a special significance for many male readers, according to Hein himself:

> Nach Lesungen [. . .] kommen auffällig häufig Männer zu mir, um von Erfahrungen aus ihrer Jugend zu berichten – das habe ich vorher so nie erlebt. Es gibt viele Bücher, die Frauen zu reden bringen, dieses scheint eines zu sein, daß Männer zum Reden bringt – auch ältere darunter, für die das offenbar ganz ungewohnt war.[17]

The key to this accessibility may be the success with which Hein depicts the emotional vulnerability of a male adolescent – the ignorance of sexuality alongside the fear of exposing that ignorance to his peers, the isolation from any obvious source of advice and support, the ease with which embarrassment occurs, the fear of appearing physically inadequate – while showing his determination to overcome this vulnerability by the flawed process of independent learning which has already been described. While much of this may be specific to his generation, there is little which can be attributed exclusively to the GDR context, which further underlines why the assessment of Hein's text should not be expected to rest primarily on the information it provides on the GDR of the middle 1950s.

Von allem Anfang an does nevertheless have a political dimension. From the perspective of a thirteen-year-old, it is the nature of the GDR education system which is bound to be highlighted, and particularly the way in which it discriminates against children who do not participate in extra-curricular 'gesellschaftliche Tätigkeiten' (*VA*, 144) such as the activities of the *Thälmannpioniere* (*VA*, 191), the junior branch of the *Freie Deutsche Jugend*. As a Christian whose parents will not permit him to join, Daniel knows well before he finishes primary school that he will face the same judgement as his older brother David – being seen as capable of achieving 'das Bildungsziel einer sozialistischen Oberschule' but not its ideological 'Erziehungsziel' (*VA*, 173). In his exposed position he learns to avoid suffering unnecessary 'Ärger' (*VA*, 192) by keeping quiet about relatively harmless undesirable influences like Aunt Magdalena's boardgame 'Krieg zur See' (*VA*, 13) or a 'westlicher Kalender' marking the wrong holidays and including anti-communist jokes (*VA*, 36). Periods of heavy indoctrination appear, however, as in the aftermath of the Hungarian uprising (*VA*, 192), to be the exception rather than the norm.

The other political issue which impinges directly on his consciousness is the enforced collectivization of land and the way in which efficient estate-managers like his grandfather are discarded because they refuse to go through the motions of joining the SED, only to be replaced by incompetent *apparatchiks* (*VA*, 77–80, 141). To Daniel these are 'die Bestimmer' (*VA*, 81), who wield power in an arbitrary and unaccountable way. It seems no coincidence that the two occasions when Daniel describes himself as being 'verwirrt' – since the publication of Musil's *Die Verwirrungen des Zöglings Törless* a key term in any portrayal of adolescent turmoil – come after his emotional confusion has been intensified by the impact of politics on his life, after the sexually fascinating Pille has suggested she might join the Party which has just treated his grandfather so shabbily (*VA*, 99) and after he has had his visit to West Berlin exposed by the more ethereal Lucie (*VA*, 193).

This falls well short of a damning criticism of the 1950s GDR. At school Daniel is given the grade 1 marks he deserves, which will help him to gain entry to the *Gymnasium* in West Berlin; his interest in the stage (which he obviously shares with the author) is stimulated by his teacher, Frau Kaczmarek, and his involvement in the schools' drama festival in Dresden may be the first step on a career path; his father is not afraid to take on the school authorities when he feels Daniel is being unjustly treated. The Christian community may be discriminated against in the education world, but appears otherwise able to operate openly: the 'Marienkirche' is tolerated in the centre of town, its youth organization; the *Junge Gemeinde* (persecuted in 1952-3, as readers of Uwe Johnson's novel *Ingrid Babendererde* will be aware) continues to exist (*VA*, 170); it is even possible (a mildly sectarian point, perhaps) for a devout Catholic like Lucie to become the leading light in the *Thälmannpioniere*. The Russian occupation forces are only mentioned once, in relation to the young soldier who was apparently crippled by standing on a mine in what is now known as the 'Russensee'. Crossing the still open border between the GDR and West Berlin remains relatively straightforward, even if a pastor has to go against his principles and lie to avoid difficulties (*VA*, 177-8). Although the title of Hein's text may initially appear to evoke phrases such as 'von allem Anfang an zum Scheitern verurteilt', the GDR does not yet appear to be a hopeless case, from the perspective of the young Daniel at least. Nevertheless, as a compliant member of the Warsaw Pact, it is certainly in a state of developmental crisis of its own in the autumn of 1956, which may be one reason why Hein has placed Daniel's private turmoil against the public backdrop of Eastern European events in a slightly contrived way.[18]

In one of his interviews following the publication of *Von allem Anfang an*, Hein insisted on the continuing need to look back on the GDR as coolly as possible, in pursuit of the goal of 'Genauigkeit ohne Zorn und Eifer'. 'Irgendwann', he added, 'werden wir auch die letzte fürchterliche Wahrheit über die DDR erfahren: Sie war ein ganz gewöhnlicher deutscher Staat'.[19] Seen in this light, his latest text seems to underline the sheer mediocrity of the GDR as a state to grow up in, its failure to offer anything better than previous German states had done, despite all its claims to the contrary. The features of this society which stick in Daniel's mind more than GDR-specific problems with education or land collectivization are its continuities with the German past – the intolerant treatment of outsiders (whether the homosexual scientist or Daniel's grandfather as an 'Umsiedler'), the use of bureaucratic regulations, set out here in a communal 'Hausordnung', to restrict personal growth, justified by the declared need 'uns vor uns selber zu beschützen' (*VA*, 165), the propagandistic use of notions such as dying heroically for one's fatherland which, as Aunt Magdalena reminds Daniel, should have been discredited once and for all after the carnage of the First World War (*VA*, 194-6), and so on. This may be Hein's way of countering the tendency of the 1990s to demonize the GDR as a failed communist state without adequate regard to the historical context from which it emerged. Surprisingly for an author who is regularly described as a 'Chronist ohne Botschaft',[20] Hein appears to be offering his readers a message in the title of this otherwise cautious retrospective. The advice to which it refers comes from Aunt Magdalena, not to Daniel but to his younger sister Dorle, after she has complained that their family's life has changed for the worse since her grandparents moved in. Magdalena's enigmatic response is: 'Dem Leben muss man von allem Anfang an ins Gesicht sehen' (*VA*, 140). She interprets her maxim oddly. First she encourages Dorle to look for the positive advantages of change (the family now being together all year round) rather than focusing solely on the tensions the move has caused. She then adds that it is sometimes necessary in life to make do with second-best – 'manchmal muss man sich im Leben mit dem Zweitschönsten zufrieden geben' (*VA*, 140) – accepting that her friendship with Dorle may appear 'das Zweitschönste' compared to Dorle's summer holidays at her grandparents' old home, yet is now a relationship that they will both have more time to develop. Only later does Daniel begin to reflect on Magdalena's maxim, in a state of anxiety after he has learnt that Pille is pregnant and thinks (quite absurdly) he could be the father. For him, 'looking life in the face' makes sense only in relation to the sudden, unexpected sight of Pille's naked body at the *Russensee* and his first, bewildering ejaculation: 'Und ich dachte daran, was Tante Magdalena zu Dorle gesagt hatte, dass man manchmal nicht umhin komme, dem Leben ins Gesicht zu sehen'. The phrase then takes on a further dimension of guilt and self-pity with the thought that he may be responsible for a pregnancy:

[...] dann passierte es halt, dass ein Mädchen ein Kind bekam und man selbst im Schlamassel saß, weil man dem Leben ins Gesicht gesehen hatte, auch wenn man erst zwölf oder dreizehn Jahre alt war. (*VA*, 142)

If 'looking life in the face' only means, as Magdalena suggests, thinking positively and putting up with disappointments, then it is hard to see why Hein is giving it prominence as the unspoken second half of his title. If it means more than this, such as facing up to one's moral responsibilities in life, as the phrase might suggest to someone older than the thirteen-year-old Daniel, then it is the reader's task to define what that meaning is. And whether a moral commitment of this kind could ever realistically be taken on 'from the very beginning' is extremely questionable from the perspective of a text which takes such an honest look at the often bewildering transition into puberty. Seen in this light, Hein's choice of title may be another aspect of his literary 'game' with his readers, another instance of his refusal to insert clear-cut messages into his creative work, drawing a clear dividing-line between it and his public life as an intellectual, where he has consistently displayed the sense of moral responsibility which has earned him the respect of his fellow writers across the old German ideological divide and has led, in the autumn of 1998, to him being elected the first president of the reunited writers' association PEN.

Von allem Anfang an, then, is much more than the lightly disguised autobiography it appears to be at first sight, and a work less damning of the 1950s GDR than might be expected in the first major post-unification project of an author whose educational progress and subsequent literary career were both seriously disrupted by the SED regime. It is, in contrast, a compellingly authentic portrayal of the 'Verwirrungen' of early adolescence, placed in a carefully recreated socio-political context but presented in explicitly fictional terms. The striking absence of the simplified ideological stocktaking (whether for or against the GDR) which had such a distorting effect on the work of ex-GDR authors in the first half of the 1990s makes *Von allem Anfang an* in a refreshing sense a *Nach-Wende-Roman*, setting the tone for the more measured reassessment of life in the GDR which can only properly begin as the turbulence of the years of transition begins to subside.

Notes

[1] It is noteworthy that this is one of the first German literary texts to put the controversial 'Rechtschreibreform' of the middle 1990s into practice.

[2] See Hein's interview with Lutz Hoyer, 'Ich werde als DDR-Schriftsteller in die Grube fahren', *Freitag*, 28 May 1993, and the chapter on *Das Napoleon-Spiel* by Phillip McKnight in his monograph *Understanding Christoph Hein* (Columbia SC, University of South Carolina Press, 1995), 113. McKnight seems unclear, however, about when this crisis occurred, dating it as 1990 here, but as 1992 in the chronology at the beginning of the volume (ibid., xv).

[3] See Hein's interview of November 1994 with Hyunseon Lee, in Lee, *Günter de Bruyn – Christoph Hein – Heiner Müller: Drei Interviews* (Siegen, Universität Gesamtschule Siegen, 1996), 32–53, here 35.

[4] See Hein's interview with Martin Doerry and Volker Hage, '"Ich vermisse die alte BRD"', *Der Spiegel*, 9 November 1998, 277–81, here 278. For a similar reference to his reworking of *Der fremde Freund*, see his interview with Frauke Meyer-Gosau, 'Ich bin der Leser, für den ich schreibe' (*TuK*, 81–91, here 83–5).

[5] Hein's comments to Hyunseon Lee on the wave of autobiographies of the early 1990s suggest that he saw this as the expression of a particular need of the older generation for personal stocktaking and not something which authors of his generation aspired to (Lee, *Drei Interviews*, 39).

[6] Günter de Bruyn, *Zwischenbilanz. Eine Jugend in Berlin* (Frankfurt am Main, Fischer, 1992), 7. De Bruyn has continued to employ this simplified contrast since, for example, in his historical study of the genre, *Das erzählte Ich. Über Wahrheit und Dichtung in der Autobiographie* (Frankfurt am Main, Fischer, 1995), which inverts the title of Goethe's *Dichtung und Wahrheit* in order to highlight what he sees as the special quality of the genre.

[7] Teasingly, perhaps, for the first time in his career Hein provides no genre specification on the title page of one of his publications.

[8] Ibid., 51.

[9] Interview with Lee, *Drei Interviews*, 46.

[10] 'Nur die Masken erlauben Freiheit: Marlies Menge unterwegs mit Christoph Hein', *Die Zeit*, 29 August 1997.

[11] Interview with Doerry and Hage, '"Ich vermisse die alte BRD"', 278.

[12] See Hein's biographical comments in 'Über mich' (*MJ*, 240–3), and as reported by Marlies Menge in her article for *Die Zeit*, or the more detailed biographical overview provided by McKnight, *Understanding Christoph Hein*, xiii–xvi.

[13] See McKnight, *Understanding Christoph Hein*, xiii.

[14] It was only in the late 1950s that the better-known 'allgemeinbildende polytechnische Oberschule', offering ten years' compulsory education, was introduced in the GDR. See Bundesministerium für Gesamtdeutsche Fragen (ed.), *A bis Z. Ein Taschen- und Nachschlagebuch über den anderen Teil Deutschlands* (Bonn, Deutscher Bundes-Verlag, 1969), 177.

[15] This age difference creates an odd gap in the text regarding Daniel's school situation between the autumn of 1956 – when it is already clear that he will not be allowed to progress from the eighth grade of the *Grundschule*, which he has just entered, to the *Oberschule* – and the autumn of 1958, when he is about to join his elder brother, two years after the latter has started school in West Berlin. What he has done in the school year 1957–8 remains a mystery.

[16] These comparative points of reference are suggested in some of the reviews of *Von allem Anfang an*, such as those by Fritz J. Raddatz (*Die Zeit*, 19 September 1997) or by Gregor Dotzauer (*Der Spiegel* supplement *Bücher '97*). For a digest of reviews see *Fachdienst Germanistik*, 11 (1997), 16.

[17] Interview with Martin Doerry and Volker Hage, '"Ich vermisse die alte BRD"', 278.

[18] Hein's rather cocksure statement of 1992 – 'Ich nehme [...] für mich in Anspruch, [...] elfmal das Ende der DDR beschrieben zu haben' (in an interview with Peter von Becker and Michael Merschmeier, 'Warum ich in der DDR geblieben bin', *Theater Heute*, 4 (1992), 31–6, here 32) – comes to mind in relation to *Von allem Anfang an* and its 1956 context, since the issues of national autonomy within communism highlighted by the Hungarian uprising were never successfully addressed thereafter. This could thus be counted as a twelfth description of the sickness of GDR communism which led to its eventual death, even if it was not yet necessarily a terminal condition.

[19] See 'Der Kürbis, die Mauer und ein Gärtner in Berlin', *Mitteldeutsche Zeitung*, 7 October 1997. I am grateful to Simon Bevan for drawing my attention to these comments.

[20] Underlined by the title of the volume edited by Klaus Hammer, *Chronist ohne Botschaft. Christoph Hein. Ein Arbeitsbuch* (Berlin, Aufbau, 1992).

10

Bibliography

DAVID CLARKE AND BILL NIVEN

CONTENTS
1. **Primary Literature**
1.a Prose works
1.b Drama
1.c Essays, speeches and articles (anthologies)
1.d Essays, speeches and articles (in chronological order)
1.e Interviews and discussions
1.f Edited volumes
1.g Miscellaneous

Works are listed chronologically.

2. **Secondary Literature (1992–1999)**
2.a General studies
2.a.a Books and monographs
2.a.b Articles
2.b Monographs and articles on individual works
2.c Miscellaneous

Books and articles are listed alphabetically, by author's name.

Editors' note: The following provides a comprehensive list of published texts by Christoph Hein, as well as a secondary bibliography covering the years 1992–1999. For secondary material on Hein published prior to 1992, readers should consult the bibliography by Heinz-Peter Preußer and Klaus Hammer (CB, 268–309). Secondary literature from before this date is included where not listed by Preußer/Hammer. Reviews are followed by [R]. All abbreviations, unless otherwise stated, are the same as in the rest of the current volume.

Primary literature

1.a Prose Works

1. *Einladung zum Lever Bourgeois* (Berlin and Weimar, Aufbau, 1980), includes:
   1.a. 'Einladung zum Lever Bourgeois'. First published in *Programmheft der Volksbühne am Luxemburgplatz*, Berlin (1974/1975 season).
   1.b. 'Aus einem Album Berliner Stadtansichten', includes:
   1.b.a. 'Die Witwe eines Maurers'. First published in *Protokolle* (1980), 3, 82.
   1.b.b. 'Friederike, Martha, Hilde'. First published in *Litfaß* (1980/1981), 5, 4–14, and reprinted in *Deutsch als Fremdsprache*, 21 (1984), Sonderheft, 44–5.
   1.b.c. 'Die Familiengruft'. Reprinted in *Tintenfisch*, 22 (1983), 57–60.
   1.b.d. 'Charlottenburger Chaussee, 11. August'.
   1.b.e. 'Nachtfahrt und früher Morgen'.
   1.b.f. 'Frank, eine Kindheit mit Vätern'.
   1.b.g. 'Der Sohn'. NB this story is not included in the first West German edition of *Einladung zum Lever Bourgeois*, which appeared under the title *Nachtfahrt und früher Morgen. Prosa* (Hamburg, Hoffmann und Campe, 1982).
   1.c. 'Leb wohl, mein Freund, es ist schwer zu sterben'. Reprinted in Hagen Bartusch and Ute Scheffler (eds.), *Die zweite Beschreibung meiner Freunde. DDR-Prosa der 70er und 80er Jahre* (Halle and Leipzig, Mitteldeutscher Verlag, 1989), 109–17; Claudia Schlottmann (ed.), *'Liebst du mich?': Geschichten von der Liebe* (Frankfurt am Main, Luchterhand, 1990), 58–66; Ingrid Gründer (ed.), *'Die erste Liebe ist immer die letzte': Liebesgeschichten* (Hamburg and Zurich, Luchterhand, 1992), 261–8.
   1.d. 'Der neuere (glücklichere) Kohlhaas'.
   1.e. 'Die russischen Briefe des Jägers Johann Seifert'.
2. *Der fremde Freund. Novelle* (Berlin and Weimar, Aufbau, 1982). Excerpts published in *neue deutsche literatur*, 30 (1982), 6, 18–32. First published in West Germany as *Drachenblut. Novelle* (Darmstadt and Neuwied, Luchterhand, 1983), and reprinted as a series in *Tagesspiegel*, 3 June–28 July 1984.
3. *Das Wildpferd unterm Kachelofen. Schöne Geschichten von Jakob Borg und seinen Freunden*, illustrated by Manfred Bofinger (Berlin, Altberliner Verlag, 1984). First published in West Germany as *Das Wildpferd unterm Kachelofen. Ein schönes dickes Buch von Jakob Borg und seinen Freunden*, illustrated by Susanne Rotraut Berner (Weinheim and Basle, Beltz & Gelberg, 1984).
4. *Horns Ende. Roman* (Berlin and Weimar, Aufbau, 1985). First West German edition: *Horns Ende. Roman* (Darmstadt and Neuwied, Luchterhand, 1985). Excerpts published in *Tintenfisch* 25 (1986), 114–21.

5. *Der Tangospieler. Erzählung* (Berlin and Weimar, Aufbau, 1989). First West German edition published as *Der Tangospieler. Roman* (Frankfurt am Main, Luchterhand, 1989).
6. *Bridge freezes before Roadway. Erzählung* (Berlin, Berliner Handpresse, 1990). Extract published in Stiftung Preußische Seehandlung (ed.), *Der Berliner Literaturpreis* 1992 (Berlin, Mathias Gatza, 1992), 35–52.
7. 'No Sea Route to India', *Time* (New York), 25 June 1990. German version first published as 'Kein Seeweg nach Indien', *Freitag*, 30 November 1990. Reprinted in *TDB*, 13–19; Bundesministerium für Bildung, Wissenschaft, Forschung und Technologie (ed.), *Von Abraham bis Zwerenz* (Bonn, Cornelsen, 1995), 661–6.
8. *Das Napoleon-Spiel. Ein Roman* (Berlin, Aufbau, 1993). Extract published as 'Der Spieler', *neue deutsche literatur*, 41 (1993), 3, 8–34.
9. *Exekution eines Kalbes und andere Erzählungen* (Berlin, Aufbau, 1994), includes:
9.a. 'Exekution eines Kalbes'.
9.b. 'Ein sächsischer Tartüff'.
9.c. 'Der eine hauet Silber, der andere rotes Gold'.
9.d. 'Der Name'.
9.e. 'Der Krüppel'.
9.f. 'Zur Frage der Gesetze'. First published in *neue deutsche literatur*, 42 (1994), 1, 90–2.
9.g. 'Jelängerjelieber Vergißnichtmein'.
9.h. 'Unverhofftes Wiedersehen'.
9.i. 'Die Krücke'.
9.j. 'Moses Tod'.
9.k. 'Matzeln'. First published as *Matzeln* (Berlin, Berliner Handpresse, 1991) with 6 colour illustrations by Ingrid Jörg. Reprinted in *Freibeuter*, 53 (1992), 119–23.
9.l. 'Die Vergewaltigung'. First published in *Neues Deutschland*, 2/3 December 1989. Reprinted in *Freitag*, 14 January 1994; Bundesministerium für Bildung, Wissenschaft, Forschung und Technologie (ed.), *Von Abraham bis Zwerenz* (Bonn, Cornelsen, 1995), 666–70. Also published as *Die Vergewaltigung*, with 6 original engravings by Dieter Tucholke (Leipzig, Faber & Faber, 1991).
9.m. 'Ein Exil'.
9.n. 'Eine Frage der Macht'.
9.o. 'Auf den Brücken friert es zuerst'. First published as *Bridge freezes before Roadway* (see 6 above).
9.p. 'Ein älterer Herr, federleicht'. First published in *neue deutsche literatur*, 40 (1992), 3, 32–8.
10. *Von allem Anfang an* (Berlin, Aufbau, 1997). Extracts published as 'Flüssige Luft', *neue deutsche literatur*, 45 (1997), 4, 5–20, and 'Schöne Bescherung', *Badische Zeitung*, 24 December 1997.

1.b Drama

1. *Cromwell und andere Stücke* (Berlin and Weimar, Aufbau, 1981), includes:
1.a. *Cromwell. Ein Schauspiel.* First published in *Theater der Zeit*, 33 (1978), 7, 52–64.
1.b. *Lassalle fragte Herrn Herbert nach Sonja. Die Szene ein Salon. Schauspiel in drei Akten.*
1.c. *Schlötel oder Was solls. Eine Komödie.*
1.d. *Der Neue Menoza oder Geschichte des kumbanischen Prinzen Tandi. Komödie nach Jakob Michael Reinhold Lenz.*
2. *Die wahre Geschichte des Ah Q. Stücke und Essays* (Darmstadt and Neuwied, Luchterhand, 1984). Referred to hereafter as *Ah Q*. Includes 1.b and:
2.a. *Die wahre Geschichte des Ah Q (Zwischen Hund und Wolf). Nach Lu Xun.* First published in *Theater der Zeit*, 38 (1983), 10, 57–64.
3. *Schlötel oder Was solls. Stücke und Essays* (Darmstadt and Neuwied, Luchterhand, 1986) (referred to hereafter as *Sch*), includes 1.a and 1.c.
4. *Passage. Ein Kammerspiel in drei Akten* (Darmstadt, Luchterhand Theater, 1988). First published in *Theater der Zeit*, 42 (1987), 5, 54–64.
5. *Die wahre Geschichte des Ah Q/Passage* (Berlin, Henschel, 1988), includes 2.a and 4.
6. *Die Ritter der Tafelrunde. Eine Komödie* (Frankfurt, Luchterhand, 1989). First published in *Sinn und Form*, 41 (1989), 4, 786–829. Reprinted in *Theater der Zeit*, 44 (1989), 7, 55–64; *Theater heute* (1989), 7, 27–35.
7. *Die Ritter der Tafelrunde und andere Stücke* (Berlin and Weimar, Aufbau, 1990), includes 4, 5, 6 and:
7.a. *Brittanicus. Tragödie von Jean Racine,* translation by C.H.
8. *Randow. Eine Komödie* (Berlin, Aufbau, 1994).
9. *Bruch. In Acht und Bann. Zaungäste. Himmel auf Erden. Stücke* (Berlin, Aufbau, 1999), includes:
9.a. *Bruch. Schauspiel in vier Akten.* First published in *Theater der Zeit* (1999), 2, 78–96.
9.b. *In Acht und Bann. Komödie in einem Akt.*
9.c. *Zaungäste. Lustspiel.*
9.d. *Himmel auf Erden. Lustspiel.*

1.c Essays, speeches and articles (anthologies)

1. *Öffentlich Arbeiten. Essais und Gespräche* (Berlin and Weimar, Aufbau, 1987).
2. *Die fünfte Grundrechenart. Aufsätze und Reden 1987–1990* (Frankfurt am Main, Luchterhand, 1990). Referred to hereafter as *fGr*.
3. *Als Kind habe ich Stalin gesehen. Essais und Reden* (Berlin and Weimar, Aufbau, 1990).
4. *Die Mauern von Jerichow. Essais und Reden* (Berlin, Aufbau Taschenbuch, 1996).

1.d Essays, speeches and articles (in chronological order)

1. 'Besson ou le manque de gout', *Cahiers Théâtre Louvain*, 35/36 (1978). Reprinted as 'Besson oder der Mangel an Geschmack', *Öa*, 108–15.
2. 'Anmerkungen zu *Lassalle fragt Herrn Herbert nach Sonja. Die Szene ein Salon*', *Programmheft zur Uraufführung am Düsseldorfer Schauspielhaus* (1980). Reprinted in *Ah Q*, 76–80; *Öa*, 29–33.
3. 'Anmerkungen zu *Cromwell*', *Programmheft zur Uraufführung am Theater der Stadt Cottbus* (1980). Reprinted in *Sch*, 173–6; *Öa*, 116–19.
4. 'Waldbruder Lenz. Über Sprache, Poesie und Herrschaft', *Connaissance de la RDA*, 13 (1981). Reprinted in *Ah Q*, 136–60; *Literatur Konkret*, 9 (1984/1985), 67–73; *Öa*, 70–96; Jakob Michael Reinhold Lenz, *Briefe zu Werthers Leiden. Mit einem Essai von Christoph Hein* (Frankfurt am Main and Leipzig, Insel Verlag, 1992), 79–111.
5. 'Lorbeerwald und Kartoffelacker. Vorlesung über einen Satz Heinrich Heines', given at the Friedrich-Schiller-Universität in Jena (9 December 1981). First published in *Ah Q*, 165–87. Reprinted in *Öa*, 5–28.
6. 'Öffentlich arbeiten', contribution to a discussion at a conference of the Berlin branch of the GDR Writers' Union (3 June 1982). First published in *Ah Q*, 161–4. Reprinted in *Tintenfisch* 24 (1985), 42–4; *Öa*, 34–8.
7. 'Über Friedrich Dieckmann', speech given in honour of Friedrich Dieckmann on the occasion of Dieckmann's receipt of the Heinrich Mann Prize, awarded by the Academy of Arts (1983). First published in *Mitteilungen der Akademie der Künste der DDR (Berlin)*, 21 (1983), 4, 7–9. Reprinted in *neue deutsche literatur*, 31 (1983), 7, 159–64; *Öa*, 57–65.
8. 'Massa Sloterdijk und der linke Kolonialismus', *Literatur Konkret* (Hamburg, 1983). Reprinted as 'Linker Kolonialismus oder der Wille zum Feuilleton' in *Sch*, 183–200; *Öa*, 135–53.
9. 'Worüber man nicht reden kann, davon kann die Kunst ein Lied singen. Zu einem Satz von Anna Seghers', speech given in De Balie, Amsterdam (28 October 1985). First published in *Connaissance de la RDA*, 22 (1986), 61–70. Reprinted in *Öa*, 43–56; *MJ*, 165–78.
10. 'Zwei Sätze zu Thomas Mann', contribution to 'Aufbau-Autoren lesen Aufbau-Autoren' in the Theater im Palast, Berlin (24 September 1985). First published in *Öa*, 66–9. Reprinted in *MJ*, 211–14.
11. 'Sprache und Rhythmus', *Programmheft zur Aufführung von 'Die wahre Geschichte des Ah Q' am Düsseldorfer Schauspielhaus* (1985). Reprinted in *Öa*, 39–42.
12. 'Maelzel's Chess Player goes To Hollywood. Das Verschwinden des künstlerischen Produzenten im Zeitalter der technischen Reproduzierbarkeit. Brief an Phillip McKnight' (March 1986). First published in *Freibeuter*, 31 (1987), 63–71, and *Freibeuter*, 32 (1987), 11–19. Reprinted in *Öa*, 165–194; *fGr*, 9–33; *MJ*, 119–149.

13. 'Brief an M. ♂., Regisseur der westdeutschen EA von *Schlötel oder Was solls*', *Programmheft des Staatstheaters Kassel* (1986). Reprinted in *Öa*, 130–4.
14. 'Die Welt ist kleiner geworden: Zum internationalen Friedensforum "Berlin – ein Ort für den Frieden"', forum organized by the GDR Writers' Union (May 1987). First published in *fGr*, 101–3. Reprinted in *AK*, 73–6.
15. 'Die Zensur ist überlebt, nutzlos, paradox, menschen- und volksfeindlich, ungesetzlich und strafbar. Rede auf dem X. Schriftstellerkongreß der DDR', Berlin (November 1987). First published in *Die Zeit*, 4 December 1987. Reprinted as part of 'Arbeitsgruppe IV. Literatur und Wirklichkeit', in *X. Schriftstellerkongreß der Deutschen Demokratischen Republik* (Berlin and Weimar, Aufbau, 1988), 224–305; *fGr*, 104–27; *AK*, 77–104.
16. 'Des Menschen Auge hat's nicht gehört. Von der Magie und den Magiern', in John Erpenbeck (ed.), *Windvogeldreieck. Schriftsteller über Wissenschaften und Wissenschaftler* (Berlin, Der Morgen, 1987), 11–34. Reprinted in Christoph Hein (ed.), *Johann Wallbergen: Sammlung natürlicher Zauberkünste* (Leipzig, Kiepenheuer, 1988); *fGr*, 34–56; *AK*, 7–33.
17. 'Ein deutscher Molière. Zur "Bargfelder Ausgabe" der Werke Arno Schmidts', *Literatur Konkret*, 13 (October 1988). Reprinted in *fGr*, 74–88; *AK*, 54–70.
18. 'Elmar Faber und Christoph Hein: Literatur & Publikum. Ein Briefwechsel', *Sinn und Form*, 40 (1988), 3, 672–8.
19. 'Ein bißchen laut. Zum 100. Geburtstag von Kurt Tucholsky', speech given in the Deutsches Theater in Berlin (7 January 1989). First published in *fGr*, 230–41. Reprinted in *AK*, 251–64; Irmgard Ackermann and Klaus Hubner (eds.), *Tucholsky heute: Rückblick und Ausblick* (Munich, iudicium, 1991), 13–21; *MJ*, 215–28.
20. 'Biographie Leo Löwenthal', *Exil* (Maintal), 9 (1989), 2, 78.
21. 'Die Zeit, die nicht vergehen kann oder Das Dilemma des Chronisten. Gedanken zum Historikerstreit anläßlich zweier deutscher 40-Jahrestage', speech given at the Folkwangschule, Essen (29 May 1989). First published in *Blätter für deutsche und internationale Politik*, 35 (1990). Reprinted in *fGr*, 128–54; *AK*, 105–36; Christoph Hein, Ulrich Schreiber, Autorengruppe (eds.), *Kunst als Opposition* (Essen, Die Blaue Eule, 1990), 9–42; *MJ*, 9–40.
22. 'I saw Stalin once', *Zeit-Magazin*, 11 August 1989. Reprinted as 'Als Kind habe ich Stalin gesehen', in *fGr*, 155–9; *AK*, 137–41; *MJ*, 41–5.
23. 'Ein stilles, vergessenes Opfer. Dank für den Stefan-Andres-Preis', speech given at Schweich (near Trier), 9 September 1989, in *AK*, 227–9.
24. 'Die fünfte Grundrechenart. Rede im Ost-Berliner Schriftstellerverband, 14. September 1989'. First published in *Die Zeit*, 6 October 1989. Reprinted in *fGr*, 163–72; *AK*, 145–58; Michael Naumann

(ed.), *Die Geschichte ist offen. DDR 1990: Hoffnung auf eine neue Republik. Schriftsteller aus der DDR über die Zukunftschancen ihres Landes* (Hamburg, Rowohlt, 1990), 59–70. Also reprinted as 'Gutgemeint ist das Gegenteil von wahr. Für Gustav Just', in *Sonntag*, 5 November 1989.

25. 'Öffentliche Erklärung. Vorgetragen bei einer Lesung im "Berliner Ensemble"', 15. Oktober 1989'. First published in *fGr*, 173–4. Reprinted in *AK*, 157–8.

26. 'Ein Berliner Traum im October 1989, der bereits im August 1968 von deutschen Panzern auf dem Wenzelsplatz überrollt wurde. Zur Podiumsdiskussion "DDR – wie ich sie träume", 24. Oktober 1989', Haus der Jungen Talente, Berlin. First published in *fGr*, 182–3. Reprinted in *AK*, 167–8.

27. 'Der Dialog reicht nicht aus. Ansprache in der Erlöserkirche, 28. Oktober 1989'. First published in *fGr*, 184–8. Reprinted in *AK*, 169–74.

28. 'Der Apfelwein der Madame de Guermantes. Betrachtungen über Poetik-Vorlesungen', speech given at the University of Leipzig (31 October 1989). First published as 'Der Most der Herzogin von Guermantes', *Liber Nr.2* (supplement of *Frankfurter Allgemeine Zeitung*), 15 December 1989. Reprinted in *Sinn und Form*, 42 (1990), 3, 631–5; *fGr*, 89–97; *AK*, 217–26; *MJ*, 198–208.

29. 'Der alte Mann und die Straße. Ansprache auf dem Alexanderplatz, 4. November 1989'. First published in *fGr*, 194–6. Reprinted in *AK*, 175–7.

30. 'Brief an den Rowohlt-Verlag, Reinbek' (20 November 1989). First published in *fGr*, 210. Reprinted in *AK*, 199–200.

31. 'Erklärung von Christoph Hein vom 29.11.89', in Daniela Dahn and Fritz-Jochen Kopka (eds.), *...und diese verdammte Ohnmacht. Report der Untersuchungskommission zu den Ereignissen vom 7. und 8. Oktober 1989 in Berlin* (Berlin, BasisDruck, 1991), 327–8.

32. '"...und andere". Für Gustav Just', speech given during a concert in the East Berlin 'Schauspielhaus' commemorating the victims of Stalinist persecution in the GDR, 10 December 1989. First published in *Frankfurter Rundschau*, 15 December 1989. Reprinted in *Sonntag*, 7 January 1990; Gustav Just, *Zeuge in eigener Sache* (Berlin, Der Morgen, 1990; Frankfurt am Main, Luchterhand, 1990); *fGr*, 213–9; *AK*, 230–9.

33. 'Achtung Abgründe. Laudatio für Max Frisch anläßlich der Verleihung des Heinrich-Heine-Preises', Düsseldorf (13 December 1989). First published in *fGr*, 220–9. Reprinted in *AK*, 240–50; *Heine Jahrbuch*, 30 (1991), 234–40.

34. 'East Berlin Diary', *The New York Times Magazine*, 17 December 1989. Reprinted as 'Brief an Sara, New York'. First published in *fGr*, 197–209. Reprinted in *AK*, 184–98.

35. 'Leserpost oder ein Buch mit sieben Siegeln. Für Christa Wolf', in Angela Drescher (ed.), *Christa Wolf. Ein Arbeitsbuch. Zum 60. Geburtstag der Autorin* (Berlin and Weimar, Aufbau, 1989; Frankfurt am Main,

Luchterhand, 1990). Reprinted in Walter Jens, Hans Mayer, Christoph Hein, Klara Obermüller, *Christa Wolf zum sechzigsten Geburtstag am 18. März 1989* (Frankfurt am Main, Luchterhand, 1989), 21–41; *fGr*, 57–73; *AK*, 34–53; *MJ*, 179–98.
36. 'Christoph Hein zu Günther Grass: "Nachdenken über Deutschland"', *Die Weltbühne*, 6 March 1990, 295–8. Reprinted as 'Über Günther Grass', in Dietmar Keller (ed.), *Nachdenken über Deutschland 1: Reden* (Berlin, Verlag der Nation, 1990), 9–13.
37. 'Unbelehrbar sein, das ist eine Pflicht des Intellektuellen', acceptance speech for the Erich Fried Prize (6 May 1990), *Frankfurter Rundschau*, 25 May 1990. Reprinted as 'Unbelehrbar – Erich Fried. Rede zur Verleihung des Erich-Fried-Preises am 6. Mai 1990 in Wien', in *Freibeuter*, 44 (1990); *TDB*, 20-34; Alexander Bormann (ed.), *Die Schriftsteller und die Restauration* (Darmstadt, Häusser, 1991) [=*Internationale Erich-Fried Gesellschaft Jahrbuch*, 1 (1991)], 17–28; *MJ*, 46–53. Also reprinted as 'Die Geschichte liebt die Ironie', *Der Morgen*, 23/24 June 1990.
38. 'Über die Möglichkeit eines Lehrstuhls für Poetik', in Christoph Hein, Ulrich Schreiber, Autorengruppe, *Kunst als Opposition: Beiträge zu Musik, Theater, Tanz* (Essen, Die Blaue Eule, 1990), 88–92.
39. 'Kein Krieg ist heilig, kein Krieg ist gerecht', *Berliner Zeitung*, 13 February 1991. Reprinted as 'Adresse aller Berliner Theater vom 13.2.1991', in *"Ich will reden von der Angst meines Herzens." Autorinnen und Autoren zum Golfkrieg* (Frankfurt am Main, Luchterhand, 1991), 52–3.
40. 'Erinnerung an eine Zeit', in Daniela Dahn and Fritz-Jochen Kopka (eds.), *...und diese verdammte Ohnmacht. Report der Untersuchungskommission zu den Ereignissen vom 7. und 8. Oktober 1989 in Berlin* (Berlin, BasisDruck, 1991), 9–13. Reprinted as 'Vorwort zum Bericht der Untersuchungskommission', *TuK*, 69–73.
41. 'A World Turning Point', *TuK*, 3–5.
42. 'Nicht reif. Asyl, Einheit und die Macht der Medien', *Frankfurter Allgemeine Zeitung*, 24 October 1991.
43. 'Wir dürfen dem Ungeist keinen Raum geben', open letter to Joachim Gauck, *Frankfurter Rundschau*, 13 December 1991.
44. 'Wir haben Angst zu verarmen', *Der Spiegel*, 9 December 1991, 75–81. Reprinted as 'Eure Freiheit ist unser Auftrag. Ein Brief an (fast alle) Ausländer – wider das Gerede vom Fremdenhaß der Deutschen', in *CB*, 51–5; *MJ*, 64–70. Also reprinted as 'Wir kennen die Welt', *Deutsches Allgemeines Sonntagsblatt*, 4 September 1992.
45. 'Die Mauern von Jerichow. Ansichtskarte einer deutschen Kleinstadt, leicht retuschiert. Dresdner Rede' (9 February 1992). First published as 'Ansichtskarte einer deutschen Kleinstadt, leicht retuschiert', *neue deutsche literatur*, (1992), 4. Reprinted in *MJ*, 71–100. Extracts printed as 'Die Mauern von Jerichow', *Freitag*, 14 February 1992; 'Achten wir auf den Nachtfrost', *Süddeutsche Zeitung am Wochenende*, 7/8 March 1992;

'Der Name der Anpassung', *Badische Zeitung*, 5 May 1992. Extract also reprinted in Franz Josef Görtz et al, *Deutsche Literatur 1992. Jahresüberblick* (Stuttgart, Reclam, 1993), 32.
46. 'Schöne Jahrhundertblicke. Rede eines Stellvertreters für Hans Mayer zum 85.', March 1992, *MJ*, 229–36.
47. 'Zur 3. Bitterfelder Konferenz am 2./3. Mai 1992', *MJ*, 149–51.
48. 'Unhaltbare Zustände als Status quo. Rede zur Verleihung des Ludwig-Mühlheims-Preises' (2 June 1992), *MJ*, 101–5.
49. 'Über mich. Rede bei der Aufnahme in die Deutsche Akademie für Sprache und Dichtung, Darmstadt' (October 1992). First published in *Jahrbuch der Deutschen Akademie für Sprache und Dichtung*, 1992, 145–7. Reprinted in *MJ*, 240–3.
50. 'Gruß an Grass', *Freitag*, 16 October 1992.
51. 'Abstand, Distanz, Nähe', lecture at Keio University, Tokyo (May 1994), *MJ*, 106–12.
52. 'Prägungen. Eröffnungsrede der Frankfurter Buchmesse 1994'. First published in *Freitag* (*Literatur-Extra zur Frankfurter Buchmesse 1994*), 7 October 1994. Reprinted in *MJ*, 152–61. Extract published as 'Über die Schädlichkeit der Literatur und des Lesens', *Frankfurter Rundschau*, 6 October 1994.
53. 'Deutscher Tag. Ein Nachschlag', *Freitag*, 12 May 1995. Reprinted as 'Deutscher Tag. Zum 8 Mai 1995' in *MJ*, 113–6.
54. 'Der Besserossi', *Theater Heute*, (1995), 11, 36.
55. 'Die erdabgewandte Seite. Ostkarrieren: Vom Aktivisten zum Aktionär', *Freitag*, 17 November 1995.
56. 'Für Heiner Müller', *Freitag*, 12 January 1996. Reprinted as 'Für Heiner Müller zum 9.1.1996' in *MJ*, 237–9.
57. 'Die politische Klasse. Von der Bedrohung der Politiker, die Wähler zu respektieren', *Freitag*, 23 February 1996.
58. '"Ich will gern Friede und Ruhe, aber der Narr will nicht". Über Politik und Intellektuelle', *Freitag*, 8 March 1996.
59. 'Unworte und Bilanzen. Zwischenbemerkung zu einer sprachkritischen Aktion', *Freitag*, 31 May 1996.
60. 'Briefe an die beiden deutschen PEN-Zentren', *Freitag*, 28 June 1996.
61. 'Stephan Hermlin: Homme de lettres', *Freibeuter*, 72 (1997), 145.
62. 'Elfenreigen. Bildersprache in deutschen Nachkriegszimmern', *Freitag*, 7 March 1997.
63. 'Neunzig. Gratulation. Hans Mayers Jahrhundert', *Freitag*, 21 March 1997.
64. 'Ein Landesfriedenspreis für Günther Grass', *Freitag*, 24 October 1997, 1. Reprinted in Volker Hage et al (eds.), *Deutsche Literatur 1997. Jahresüberblick* (Stuttgart, Reclam, 1998), 253–5.
65. 'Arno Schmidt. Flitär? Allerdings! oder Der kahle Mongolenschädel über uns', speech delivered as part of the series 'Die einen über die anderen' at the *Schaubühne*, Berlin (October 1997), *neue deutsche*

Literatur, 46 (1998), 2, 105–30. Extract published as 'Ritter vom Geist? Ritter der Sprache', *Tagesspiegel*, 14 October 1997.
66. 'Demokratie als Belastung', *Tagesspiegel*, 29 April 1998.
67. 'Plädoyer für einen Stalinpreis. Dicke Backen. Über die Bildfälschung einst und heute', *Freitag*, 12 June 1998.
68. '"Ein Territorium des Hasses": Deutsche Schriftsteller äußern sich zum Nato-Bombardement', *Der Spiegel*, 10 April 1999; includes a contribution by Hein, which also appears in 'Junge-Welt-Umfrage: Was sagen die Künstler zum Krieg', *Junge Welt*, 10 April 1999.
69. 'PEN-Zentrum fordert angesichts des Kosovo-Krieges: Schluß mit der Unterhaltung', *Rheinische Post*, 6 May 1999.

1.e Interviews and discussions

1. 'Ein Interview. Christoph Hein antwortet auf Fragen von "Theater der Zeit"', *Theater der Zeit*, 33 (1978), 7, 51–2. Reprinted as 'Ein Interview' in *Öa*, 97–107. Excerpts published as 'Hamlet und der Parteisekretär' in *Sch*, 177–82.
2. Klaus Hammer, 'Gespräch mit Christoph Hein', in Hors Fassel and Klaus Hammer (eds.), *Wissenschaftliche Beiträge der Friedrich-Schiller-Universität Jena. Beiträge zur Literaturgeschichte und -methodologie*, Jena (1982), 198–207. Reprinted as 'Gespräch mit Christoph Hein' in *Öa*, 120–9.
3. Edelmann Gregor, '"Ansonsten würde man ja aufhören zu schreiben..."', *Theater der Zeit*, 38 (1983), 10, 54–6.
4. Hans Brender and Agnes Hüfner, 'Die Intelligenz hat angefangen zu verwalten und aufgehört zu arbeiten. Ein Gespräch', *Deutsche Volkszeitung/die tat*, 9 March 1984. Reprinted in *Öa*, 154–64, and as 'Ich kann mein Publikum nicht belehren' in *TDB*, 68–75.
5. Uwe Hornauer and Hans Norbert Janowski, 'Schreiben gegen die Sterblichkeit', *Evangelische Kommentare*, 2 (1985), 95ff. Reprinted as 'Schreiben als Aufbegehren gegen die Sterblichkeit' in *TDB*, 76–86.
6. Andrea Hurton and Helmut Schneider, 'Der Stil ist der Mensch', *Falter, Wiener Zeitschrift für Kultur und Politik* (2 May–15 May 1985). Reprinted as 'Der Stoff eines Autors ist eben auch der Autor' in *TDB*, 87–94.
7. Bischof, Alois, 'Die Verzweiflung trügt wie die Hoffnung', *Wochenzeitung* (Zurich), 7 June 1985. Reprinted as 'Mut ist keine literarische Kategorie' in *TDB*, 95–100.
8. N. Bary, 'La RDA, la France, l'Europe. Entretien', *Quinzaine littéraire*, 491 (1987), 11–2.
9. Françoise Barthélémy-Toraille, 'Entretien autour de son roman *Horns Ende*', *Connaissance de la RDA*, 25 (1987), 17–20.
10. Grit Hartmann, 'Christoph Hein: "Öffentlichkeit – kein Geschenk". Ein Gespräch', *Börsenblatt für den deutschen Buchhandel* (Leipzig), 154 (1987), 836–8.

11. Janice Murray and Mary-Elizabeth O'Brien, 'Interview mit Christoph Hein', *New German Review* (New York), 3 (1987), 53–66.
12. Krzysztof Jachimczak, 'Gespräch mit Christoph Hein', *Sinn und Form*, 40 (1988), 2, 343–59. Reprinted as 'Wir werden es lernen müssen, mit unserer Vergangenheit zu leben' in *TDB*, 45–67.
13. 'Volker Braun und Christoph Hein in der Diskussion', in Anna Chiarloni, Gemma Sartori, Fabrizio Cambi (eds.), *Die Literatur der DDR. Akten Pisa* (Pisa, Giardini, 1988), 159–68.
14. Hans Jansen, '"Die westdeutsche Literatur ist unpolitisch geworden"', *Westdeutsche Allgemeine Zeitung*, 1 July 1989.
15. Ulrich Schwarz and Hartmut Palmer, 'Die DDR ist nicht China. "Spiegel"-Gespräch', *Der Spiegel*, 23 October 1989. Reprinted in *fGr*, 175–81; *AK*, 159–66.
16. Dieter Krebs, 'Weder das Verbot noch die Genehmigung als Geschenk. Gespräch mit der "Berliner Zeitung"', *Berliner Zeitung*, 4/5 November 1989. Reprinted in *fGr*, 189–93; *AK*, 178–83.
17. Oliver Michalsky, '"Ich finde einen schweren Beginn glänzend"', *National-Zeitung*, 11/12 November 1989.
18. Renate Kruppa, '"Literatur wird wieder Literatur sein können"', *Schweriner Volkszeitung*, 22 November 1989.
19. Frank Schumann, 'Wer heute so laut schreit, soll sagen, was er früher tat. Gespräch mit Christoph Hein', *Junge Welt*, 12 December 1989. Reprinted in *AK*, 208–14.
20. Sigrid Löffler, 'Die Idee des europäischen Hauses ist gestorben', *profil*, 11/12 March 1990. Reprinted as 'Die alten Themen habe ich noch, jetzt kommen neue dazu' in *TDB*, 37–44. Excerpts reprinted as 'Die DDR – auf Knien und mit weißer Flagge in die Einheit', *die tageszeitung*, 17 March 1990.
21. Günter Gaus, 'Christoph Hein: Gespräch vom 14. März 1990', in Günter Gaus (ed.), *Zur Person. Sechs Porträts in Frage und Antwort* (Berlin, Volk und Welt, 1990), 95–114. Reprinted in Günter Gaus, *Deutsche Zwischentöne. Gesprächs-Porträts aus der DDR* (Hamburg, Hoffmann und Campe, 1990), 95–114.
22. Klemens Renolder, '"Arbeit am Nachlaß". Christoph Hein zu einer Fußnote deutscher Geschichte', *Wochenzeitung* (Zurich), 13 July 1990. Reprinted as 'Wird Europa auch zur Bronx? Ein Gespräch mit Christoph Hein', *Wiener Zeitung/Lesezirkel*, 46 (1990).
23. 'Das Geld ist nicht der Gral. Aus einer Diskussion mit Christoph Hein und den Schöpfern des Fernsehfilms "Die Ritter der Tafelrunde" nach der Voraufführung in der Akademie der Künste zu Berlin am 29.9.1990', *CB*, 226–9.
24. Christoph Funke, '"3. Oktober – auch ein Verdienst Christa Wolfs". Der Dramatiker Christoph Hein warnt vor einem vehement erwachenden Chauvinismus in der DDR', *Der Morgen*, 29/30 September 1990.

25. Irmtraud Gutschke, 'Ich bin ein Schreiber von Chroniken', *Neues Deutschland*, 2/3 December 1989. Reprinted in *AK*, 201–7.
26. 'Anschluß auf Knien mit weißer Flagge. Ein Gespräch mit Christoph Hein', in G. Heiß, G. Schmid, O. Rathkolb (eds.), *Österreichs und Deutschlands Größe. Ein schlampiges Verhältnis* (Salzburg, 1990).
27. Frauke Meyer-Gosau, '"ich bin der Leser für den ich schreibe". Ein Gespräch mit Christoph Hein', *TuK*, 81–91.
28. Heinz Klunker, '"Mut zur eigenen Verantwortung": Ein Gespräch mit Christoph Hein', *Deutschland Archiv*, (1990), 7, 1144–7.
29. Hammer, Klaus, '"Dialog ist das Gegenteil von Belehren": Gespräch mit Christoph Hein', *CB*, 11–50.
30. Robert von Hallberg, '16th February 1991', in Von Hallberg, *Literary Intellectuals and the Dissolution of the State: Professionalism and Conformity in the GDR*, trans. by Kenneth J. Northcott (Chicago, The University of Chicago Press, 1996), 200–7.
31. Uwe Kramp, '"Für Intellektuelle kann ein Staat nicht Heimat sein"', *Neues Deutschland*, 1 November 1991.
32. Volker Müller, 'Der Hanseatenweg liegt in Berlin-Mitte', *Berliner Zeitung*, 1/2 February 1992.
33. Ulrich Greiner and Volker Hage, 'Es gibt sie längst, die neue Mauer. Ein Zeit-Gespräch mit Günther Grass und Christoph Hein', *Der Spiegel*, 7 February 1992, 21–2. Reprinted in Franz Josef Görtz et al (eds.), *Deutsche Literatur 1991. Jahresüberblick* (Stuttgart, Reclam, 1992), 260–71.
34. Peter von Becker and Michael Merschmeier, 'Warum ich in der DDR geblieben bin', *Theater Heute*, (1992), 4, 31–6.
35. Peter Teupe and Ulrike Weber, '"Wir sind (k)ein Volk." Interview mit Christoph Hein', *GDR Bulletin*, 18 (1992), 1, 7–13.
36. Detlev Lücke and Stephan Reinecke, 'Der Waschzwang ist da, also muß gewaschen werden', *Freitag*, 29 January 1993.
37. Cornelia Geißler, '"Kennen Sie eigentlich noch Leute, die Bücher lesen?"', *Berliner Zeitung*, 1/2 May 1993.
38. Lutz Hoyer, '"Ich werde als DDR-Schriftsteller in die Grube fahren"', *Freitag*, 28 May 1993.
39. Gansel, Carsten, 'Implosion und Sinndefizit. Gespräch mit Christoph Hein', *Deutschunterricht* (Berlin), 46 (1993), 10, 460–9.
40. Dunja Welke, 'Ich leiste eher Chronistenarbeit', *Neue Zeit*, 26 February 1994, 14.
41. Hyunseon, Lee, *Günter de Bruyn – Christoph Hein – Heiner Müller: Drei Interviews* (Siegen, Universität Gesamtschule Siegen, 1995), 32–53.
42. Andrzej Szczypiorski, Christoph Hein and Detlev Claussen, 'Wie mutig waren die Deutschen?', *Die Zeit*, 13 October 1995.
43. Karin Großmann, '"Mit etwas Rückgrat durch die Zeitläufe kommen". Gespräch mit Christoph Hein vor der Première von *Randow, eine Komödie*', *Sächsische Zeitung*, 17 December 1995.

44. Christian Eger, 'Der Kürbis, die Mauer und ein Gärtner in Berlin', *Mitteldeutsche Zeitung*, 15 October 1997 (Supplement on Frankfurt Bookfair).
45. Conny Lösch, '"Geschichte ist nicht richtig oder falsch. Sie ist." Ein junge-Welt-Gespräch mit Christoph Hein', *Junge Welt*, 18 October 1997.
46. Klaus B. Harms, 'Im Bannkreis der Wahrheit', *Saarbrücker Zeitung*, 18 December 1997.
47. Anonymous, 'Hein: "Durch Prügeln kommt man sich näher"', *Berliner Morgenpost*, 1 November 1998.
48. Michael Bartsch '"Kommt doch zurück!" Christoph Hein über den wiedervereinigten PEN', *Die Welt*, 2 November 1998.
49. Alexander Frisch, 'Stärke zeigen', *Kölner-Stadt-Anzeiger*, 2 November 1998.
50. Joachim Günther, 'Der deutsche PEN – endlich vereint', *Neue Zürcher Zeitung*, 2 November 1998.
51. Fritz-Jochen Kopka, '"Mitleid und Hass trüben den Blick"', *Die Woche*, 6 November 1998, 37.
52. Martin Doerry and Volker Hage, '"Ich vermisse die alte BRD"', *Der Spiegel*, 9 November 1998, 277–81.
53. Ingo Arend and Detlev Lücke, 'Erschöpfung ist eine Produktivkraft', *Freitag*, 13 November 1998.
54. Peter von Becker and Moritz Müller-Wirth, 'Brauchen wir eine Amnestie der DDR-Eliten, Herr Hein?', *Tagesspiegel*, 13 January 1999.
55. Terry Albrecht, '"Ich kenne mehr Ärzte als Könige"', *Theater der Zeit*, (1999), 2, 76–7.

1.f Edited volumes

1. Christoph Hein (ed.), *Johann Wallbergen: Sammlung natürlicher Zauberkünste oder aufrichtige Entdeckung vieler bewährter, lustiger und nützlicher Geheimnisse, insbesondere denen Wein-Negozianten dienende. Nebst einem Anhange von medizinisch sympathetisch-antipathetisch und ergötzenden Kunst-Stücken* (Leipzig and Weimar, Kiepenheuer, 1988).
2. Joachim Walther, Wolf Biermann, Günter de Bruyn, Jürgen Fuchs, Christoph Hein, Günter Kunert, Erich Loest, Hans-Joachim Schädlich, Christa Wolf (eds.), *Protokolle eines Tribunals: Die Ausschlüsse aus dem DDR-Schriftstellerverband 1979* (Reinbek bei Hamburg, Rowohlt, 1991).

1.g Miscellaneous

1. Daniela Dahn and Fritz-Jochen Kopka (eds.), *. . . und diese verdammte Ohnmacht. Report der Untersuchungskommission zu den Ereignissen vom 7. und 8. Oktober 1989 in Berlin* (Berlin, BasisDruck, 1991). The minutes of the nine interview sessions conducted by the commission include questions posed as well as points raised by Hein, who was a commission member.

2. 'Arbeitsgruppe IV. Literatur und Wirklichkeit', in X. *Schriftstellerkongreß der Deutschen Demokratischen Republik* (Berlin and Weimar, Aufbau, 1988), 224–305, contains minutes of the debate on Hein's speech on censorship (see 1.d, 15 above), with contributions by Hein.

2. Secondary literature (1992–1999)

2.a General studies

2.a.a Books and monographs

1. Aizawa, Keiichi, *Der Literat Christoph Hein und die Zeitgeschichte* (Tokyo, Aoyamagakuin University, 1992) [=*Aoyama Business Review*, 17].
2. Albrecht, Terry, *Fremde Blicke: Zeitlichkeit und Rezeptionserfahrung im Werk Christoph Heins* (Bockel, 1998).
3. Dümmel, Karsten, *Identitätsprobleme in der DDR-Literatur der siebziger und achtziger Jahre* (Frankfurt am Main, Lang, 1997).
4. Groth, Joachim-Rüdiger, *Widersprüche: Literatur und Politik in der DDR 1949–1989; Zusammenhänge, Werke, Dokumente*, 2nd edn (Frankfurt am Main, Lang, 1996).
5. Guibert-Yèche, Hélène, *Christoph Hein: L'Oeuvre romanesque des années 80: De la provocation au dialogue* (Bern, Lang, 1998).
6. Hilbk, Andrea, *Von Zirkularbewegungen und kreisenden Utopien: zur Geschichtsdarstellung in der Epik Christoph Heins* (Augsburg, Wißner, 1998).
7. Kiewitz, Christl, *Der stumme Schrei: Krise und Kritik der sozialistischen Intelligenz im Werk Christoph Heins* (Tübingen, Stauffenburg, 1995).
8. Kloetzer, Sylvia, *Mitläufer und Überläufer: Erzählte Ich-Krise in der DDR-Literatur der achtziger Jahre, Christoph Hein und Monika Maron* (Ann Arbor, Michigan, University Microfilms International, 1992).
9. Krol, Maria, *Christoph Heins chronikalische Aufzeichnungen als "Geschichten zur Geschichte"* (Ann Arbor, Michigan, University Microfilms International, 1999).
10. Lueg, Carl Heinrich, *Zeitgenössische Texte im Deutschunterricht der Sekundarstufen I und II: ausgewählte Texte von Christoph Hein* (Aachen, Hauptabt. Erziehung und Schule im Bischöflichen Generalvikariat, 1991).
11. McKnight, Phillip, *Understanding Christoph Hein* (Columbia, University of South Carolina Press, 1995).
12. Peters, Peter, *"Ich Wer ist das": Aspekte der Subjektwerdung in Prosa und Drama der DDR (1976–1989)* (Frankfurt am Main, Lang, 1993).
13. Robinson, David W., *Deconstructing East Germany: Christoph Hein's Literature of Dissent* (Columbia, Camden House, 1999).
14. Schenkel, Michael, *Fortschritts- und Modernitätskritik in der DDR-Literatur: Prosatexte der achtziger Jahre* (Tübingen, Stauffenburg, 1995).

15. Sevin, Dieter, *Textstrategien in DDR-Prosawerken zwischen Bau und Durchbruch der Berliner Mauer* (Heidelberg, Winter, 1994).
16. Wiesemann, Hilary, '"Ohne Hoffnung können wir nicht leben": Atheist Modernism and Religion in the Works of Christoph Hein' (unpublished doctoral thesis, University of Sheffield, 1998).
17. Zekert, Ines, *Poetologie und Prophetie: Christoph Heins Prosa und Dramatik im Kontext seiner Walter-Benjamin-Rezeption* (Frankfurt am Main, Lang, 1993).

2.a.b Articles

1. Andress, Reinhard, 'Christoph Heins Weg durch den Herbst 1989', *CB*, 158–71.
2. Baier, Lothar, 'Höflicher Pessimismus, lustvolle Trauer. Geburtstagsbrief an Christoph Hein zum Fünfzigsten', *Freitag*, 8 April 1994.
3. Bräsel, Sylvia, 'Bilderwelt und Motivik. Anmerkungen zur Prosa von Christoph Hein', in Koreanische Gesellschaft für Germanistik (ed.), *Krisen und Wandlungen der Nachkriegszeit. Zur deutschsprachigen Literatur 1945–1990. Dokumentation der Tagungsbeiträge. Germanistisches Kolloquium in Korea 1993* (Seoul, Koreanische Gesellschaft für Germanistik, 1994), 210–24.
4. Braun, Michael, '"Ein Betroffensein und ein Sichwehren": Zur Schuldfrage im Erzählwerk von Christoph Hein', *Literatur in Wissenschaft und Unterricht*, 26 (1993), 177–92.
5. Dalemans, Jacques J., 'Zwei Frauengestalten bei Christoph Hein: Gertrude Fischlinger in *Horns Ende* and Elke in *Der Tangospieler*', in Michel Vanhelleputte (ed.), *Geschlechtsdifferenz in der Literatur* (Bern, Lang, 1995), 131–68.
6. Diesch, Manfred, 'Bewußtseins-Brechung und Wirklichkeits-Aufnahme: Christoph Hein und Bezüge zur österreichischen Literatur', in Walter Weiss and Hans Höller (eds.), *DDR-Literatur/Österreichische Literatur: ein Dialog im Herbst 1989* (Stuttgart, Heinz, 1992), 99–113.
7. Drescher, Angela, 'Der Christoph Hein Sound', *neue deutsche literatur*, 42 (1994), 4, 164–8.
8. Dwars, Jens-F., 'Nur ein Chronist!? Vom angestrengten Versuch Geschichte(n) zu erzählen in der Prosa Christoph Heins', in Walther Delabar et al (eds.), *Neue Generationen – neues Erzählen. Deutsche Prosa-Literatur der achtziger Jahre* (Opladen, Westdeutscher Verlag, 1993), 165–75.
9. Goltschnigg, Dietmar, 'Die "Dialektik der Revolution" in der Dramatik Heiner Müllers, Volker Brauns und Christoph Heins', *Germanica Wratislaviensia*, 99 (1993), 359–71.
10. Grunenberg, Antonia, '"Geschichte als Entfremdung: Christoph Hein als Autor der DDR', *CB*, 67–83.
11. Hatsumi, Motoi, 'Normativität von Chronik. Uber Christoph Hein', *Doitsu Bungaku*, 95 (1995), 22–32.

12. Hawlicek, Hilde, 'Rede an Christoph Hein', in Alexander Bormann (ed.), *Die Schriftsteller und die Restauration* (Darmstadt, Häusser, 1991) [=*Internationale Erich-Fried-Gesellschaft für Literatur und Sprache: Jahrbuch*, 1 (1991)], 14–16.
13. Hosaka, Kazuo, '"Literatur und Gesellschaft in Deutschland heute" – Ein Kolloquium mit Christoph Hein', *Doitsu Bungaku*, 93 (1994), 219–20.
14. Isenschmid, Andreas, 'Laudatio', in Stiftung Preußische Seehandlung (ed.), *Der Berliner Literaturpreis 1992* (Berlin, Gatzon, 1992), 31–4.
15. Jackman, Graham, '"Unverhofftes Wiedersehen": Narrative Paradigms in Christoph Hein's *Nachtfahrt und früher Morgen* and *Exekution eines Kalbes*', *German Life and Letters*, 51 (1998), 3, 398–414.
16. Janssen-Zimmermann, Antje, '"Subjektive Objektivität": Drei Theatertexte Christoph Heins – eine "Trilogie des Sozialismus"?', in *CB*, 184–94.
17. Krauss, Hannes, 'Schreibend das Sprechen üben oder: "Worüber man nicht reden kann, davon kann die Kunst ein Lied singen" oder: "Als Kind habe ich Stalin gesehen" – Zur Prosa Christoph Heins', *German Monitor*, 29 (1992), 204–14.
18. Lücke, Bärbel, *Horns Ende. Interpretation* (Munich, Oldenbourg, 1994).
19. Meech, Anthony, 'Christoph Hein: "Engagement" in the German Democratic Republic', *Contemporary Theatre Review*, 4 (1995), 2, 71–7.
20. Menge, Marlies, 'Nur die Masken erlauben Freiheit', *Die Zeit*, 29 August 1997.
21. Müller, Gerd, 'Christoph Hein oder: Warum wir mit weniger zufrieden sind', in Herbert Herzmann (ed.), *Literaturkritik und erzählende Praxis: deutschsprachige Erzähler der Gegenwart; Tagungsakten des internationalen Symposiums University College Dublin, 14.–16. Februar 1993* (Tübingen, Stauffenburg, 1995), 41–8.
22. Niven, William J., 'The vanquished self: Christoph Hein's *Drachenblut* and *Der Tangospieler*', *Journal of European Studies*, 22 (1992), 2, 127–41.
23. ——, '"Das Geld ist nicht der Gral": Christoph Hein and the *Wende*', *Modern Language Review*, 90 (1995), 3, 688–706.
24. Pfeiffer, Peter C., 'Tote und Geschichte(n): Christoph Heins *Drachenblut* und *Horns Ende*', *German Studies Review*, 16 (1993), 1, 19–36.
25. Poulain, Elfie, 'La question d'identité du sujet chez Siegfried Lenz et Christoph Hein', *Germanica*, 15 (1995), 63–77.
26. Preußer, Heinz-Peter, and Klaus Hammer, 'Bibliographie. Werke, Inszenierungen, Sekundärliteratur', *CB*, 268–309.
27. Robinson, David W., 'Christoph Hein between ideologies, or, Where do the Knights of the Round Table go when Camelot falls?', *Contemporary Theatre Review*, 4 (1995), 2, 79–85.
28. Rock, David, 'Christoph Hein und Jurek Becker: Zwei kritische Autoren aus der DDR über die Wende und zum vereinten Deutschland', *German Life and Letters*, 50 (1997), 2, 182–200.

29. Saavedrová, Jirina, 'Zur Problematik des Individualstils von Christoph Hein', in *Brünner Beiträge zur Germanistik und Nordistik*, 7 (1991), 41–50.
30. Sändig, Brigitte, 'Zwei oder drei fremde Helden', *Sinn und Form*, 45 (1993), 4, 665–72.
31. Schmidt, Ricarda, 'Erlaubte und unerlaubte Schreibweisen in Honeckers DDR. Christoph Hein und Monika Maron', in Robert Atkins and Martin Kane (eds.), *Retrospect and Review: Aspects of the Literature of the GDR 1976–1990* [= *German Monitor*, 40] (Amsterdam, Rodopi, 1997), 176–96.
32. Schmitt, Evelyne, 'Nécessaire et fragile continuité dans les "chroniques" de Christoph Hein: *Der fremde Freund* et *Horns Ende*', *Allemagne aujourd'hui*, 127 (1994), 48–59.
33. Sevin, Dieter, 'Autoren und die "Wende": Perspektiven zu Christa Wolf und Christoph Hein', *GDR Bulletin*, 18 (1992), 1, 25–8.
34. Shaw, Gisela, 'Christoph Hein: The novelist as dramatist manqué', in Arthur Williams et al (eds.), *Literature on the Threshold: The German Novel in the 1980s* (New York, Berg, 1990), 91–105.
35. Slibar, Neva and Rosanda Volk, 'Ein geistesgegenwärtiger Zeitgenosse am Ende der Zeiten: Sichtverengung und Blickzerstreuung in Christoph Heins Prosatexten', *Acta Neophilologica*, 24 (1991), 77–91.
36. Spies, Bernhard, 'Der Anteil der sozialistischen Utopie an der Beendigung der DDR-Literatur. Am Beispiel Christoph Heins', *The Germanic Review*, 67 (1992), 3, 112–8.
37. ——, 'The end of the socialist German state: The socialist utopia and the writers', *Modern Language Review*, 89 (1994), 2, 393–405.
38. Tiesset, Jean-Luc, 'Christoph Hein: La RDA en négatif?', *Allemagne aujourd'hui*, 130 (1994), 133–40.
39. Wittstock, Uwe, *Von der Stalinallee bis zum Prenzlauer Berg. Wege der DDR-Literatur 1949–1989* (Munich, Piper, 1989), 209–24.

2.b Monographs and articles on individual works

On *Einladung zum Lever Bourgeois*
1. Friedrich, Roy, 'Varianten des Kohlhaas-Motivs in der neueren Erzählliteratur', *Wissenschaftliche Zeitschrift der Brandenburgischen Landeshochschule Potsdam*, 35 (1991), 3, 209–13.
2. Grauert, Wilfried, 'Kollege Racine oder Identitätskonzept für einen sozialistischen Autor. Zu Christoph Heins Erzählung "Einladung zum Lever Bourgeois"', *Zeitschrift für Germanistik*, 5 (1995), 2, 401–10.
3. Marquardt, Joachim, 'Es war einmal ein Land, das hieß DDR oder Wie Kohlhaas zum Staatsbürger ward. Zu Christoph Heins Kleist-Adaption', in *CB*, 56–66.
4. Yèche, Hélène, 'Exemple de mise en scène d'un espace problématique dans la littérature socialiste des années quatre-vingt à travers le récit de Christoph Hein "Voyage de nuit" (1980)', *Allemagne aujourd'hui*, 138 (1996), 111–7.

On *Der fremde Freund*
5. Bauer Pickar, Gertrud, 'Christoph Hein's *Drachenblut*: An internalized novella', in Sabine Cramer (ed.), *Neues zu Altem: Novellen der Vergangenheit und der Gegenwart* (Munich, Fink, 1996), 251–78.
6. Bonner, Withold, 'Ein Mantel des Schweigens. Sprachliche Bilder in Christoph Heins Novelle *Der fremde Freund*', *Der Ginkgobaum*, 11 (1992), 68–80.
7. Braun, Michael, '"in meiner unverletzbaren Hülle werde ich krepieren an Sehnsucht...". Zu den Motiven der Entfremdung und Erinnerung und zur Erzählstruktur von Christoph Heins Novelle *Drachenblut*', in *Studies in Modern and Classical Languages and Literatures* 4 (Winter Park, FL, Rollins College, 1992), 81–7.
8. Bronzweska, Anna, 'Die fremden Freunde: zu strukturellen Gemeinsamkeiten in den Romanen *Der Fremde* von Albert Camus und *Der fremde Freund* von Christoph Hein', in Johanna Jablowska and Erwin Leibfried (eds.), *Fremde und Fremdes in der Literatur* (Frankfurt am Main, Lang, 1996), 213–21.
9. Bulmahn, Heinz, 'Ideology, family policy, production and (re)-education: literary treatment of abortion in the GDR of the early 1980s', *Studies in Twentieth Century Literature*, 21 (1992), 2, 315–35.
10. Dupont, Eric, 'L'image photographique et l'oubli dans la création littéraire: l'exemple de Marguerite Duras et Christoph Hein', *Études Littéraires*, 28 (1995/1996), 3, 35–66.
11. Freund-Spork, Walburga, 'Jeder für sich. Christoph Hein: *Drachenblut* (1982)', in Winfried Freund (ed.), *Deutsche Novellen* (Munich, Fink, 1993), 291–300.
12. Hell, Julia, 'Christoph Hein's *Der fremde Freund/Drachenblut* and the antinomies of writing and "real existing socialism"', *Colloquia Germanica*, 25 (1995), 3/4, 307–37.
13. Jackman, Graham, 'The fear of allegory: Benjaminian elements in Christoph Hein's *The Distant Lover*', *New German Critique*, 66 (1995), 164–92.
14. Kaufmann, Hans, 'Herzloses Pathos: Christoph Hein, *Der fremde Freund*', in Karl Deiritz and Hannes Krauss (eds.), *Verrat an der Kunst? Rückblicke auf die DDR-Literatur* (Berlin, Aufbau Taschenbuch, 1993), 151–6.
15. Robinson, David W., 'Abortion as repression in Christoph Hein's *The Distant Lover*', *New German Critique*, 58 (1993), 65–78.
16. Vancea, Georgeta, *Der narrative Diskurs in Christoph Heins 'Der fremde Freund' (How to Do Thoughts and Persons with Words)* (Uppsala, University of Uppsala, 1993).

On *Das Wildpferd unterm Kachelofen*

17. Osteroth, Reinhard, 'Der gewisse Knick', *Die Zeit*, 2 September 1994 [R].
18. Richter, Karin, '"Die wahren Abenteuer sind im Kopf": Anmerkungen zu Christoph Heins *Das Wildpferd unterm Kachelofen*', in Hans-Heino Ewers (ed.), *Komik im Kinderbuch: Erscheinungsformen des Komischen in der Kinder- und Jugendliteratur* (Weinheim, Juventa, 1992), 135–49.
19. Seidenkuhnel, Kathrin, 'Vergleich der stilistischen Mittel der Figurencharakterisierung in A.A. Milnes *Pu der Bär* und Christoph Heins *Das Wildpferd unterm Kachelofen*', in Angelika Feine and Hans-Joachim Siebert (eds.), *Beiträge zur Text- und Stilanalyse* (Frankfurt am Main, Lang, 1996), 153–63.
20. Yos, Gabriele, 'Reden sie wie du und ich? Gesprächsstilistische Untersuchungen an epischen Texten für junge Leser', in Angelika Feine and Hans-Joachim Siebert (eds.), *Beiträge zur Text- und Stilanalyse* (Frankfurt am Main, Lang, 1996), 181–92.

On *Horns Ende*

21. Albrecht, Terry, 'Die Endphase des zweijährigen Taktierens um die Veröffentlichung des Romans *Horns Ende* von Christoph Hein. Eine Chronik aus dem Jahr 1985/86', *Zeitschrift für Germanistik*, 8 (1998), 1, 131–44.
22. Berger, Christel, 'Nachwort. Entstehungsgeschichte: eine Farce in drei Akten', in Christoph Hein, *Horns Ende* (Leipzig, Faber & Faber [Die DDR-Bibliothek], 1996).
23. Dörfler, Heinz, *Moderne Romane im Unterricht : Modelle und Materialien zu: 'Tauben im Gras' von Wolfgang Koeppen, 'Horns Ende' von Christoph Hein, 'Das Parfum' von Patrick Süskind, 'Kassandra' von Christa Wolf, 'Das Treffen in Telgte' von Günter Grass, 'Brandung' von Martin Walser* (Frankfurt am Main, Scriptor, 1988).
24. Hartmann, Karl-Heinz, 'Erinnerungsarbeit. Hermann Kant, *Der Aufenthalt*. Christa Wolf, *Kindheitsmuster*. Christoph Hein, *Horns Ende*', in Manfred Braunek (ed.), *Der deutsche Roman nach 1945* (Bamberg, Buchner, 1993), 188–202.
25. Hülse, Erich, 'Christoph Hein: *Horns Ende*', in Herbert Kaiser and Gerhard Köpf (eds.), *Erzählen, Erinnern: Deutsche Prosa der Gegenwart. Interpretationen* (Frankfurt am Main, Diesterweg, 1992), 260–84.
26. Klein, Christian, 'L'immobilisation du temps dans le roman *La fin de Horn* de Christoph Hein', *Chroniques allemandes*, 1992, 119–42.
27. Sevin, Dieter, 'Geschichte und Zeitgeschichte in Christoph Heins *Horns Ende*', in Elrud Ibusch and Ferdinand van Ingen (eds.), *Literatur und politische Aktualität* (Amsterdam, Rodopi, 1993), 101–16.
28. Wenzel, Hans-Eckardt, 'Plötzlich öffnet sich Provinz', *Neues Deutschland*, 7 August 1996 [R].

On *Der Tangospieler*

29. Dieckmann, Friedrich, 'Christoph Hein, Thomas Mann und der Tangospieler', *CB*, 153–7.
30. Gerrier, Marie-Geneviève, 'Christoph Hein, *Der Tangospieler*', *Le texte et l'idée*, 7 (1992), 250–2.
31. Hegewald, Wolfgang, 'Begrenzte realistische Reichweiten. Defizitäre Unternehmen: Zu zwei Romanen von Christoph Hein und Monika Maron', in Jörg Drews (ed.), *Vergangene Gegenwart – Gegenwärtige Vergangenheit. Studien, Polemiken und Laudationes zur deutschsprachigen Literatur 1960–1994* (Bielefeld, Aisthesis, 1994), 97–102.
32. Pinkert, Ernst Ulrich, 'À univers kafkaien université kafkaïenne. Le jouer de Tango de Christoph Hein. Trad. par François Genton', *Chroniques allemandes*, 4 (1995), 273–89.

On 'Kein Seeweg nach Indien'

33. Schemme, Wolfgang, 'Die Suche nach einem neuen Utopia: Afrika – Indien oder Oobliadooh?', *Deutschunterricht*, 46 (1993), 10, 450–9.

On *Das Napoleon-Spiel*

34. Anonymous, 'Christoph Hein: *Das Napoleon-Spiel*', *Fachdienst Germanistik*, (1993), 6, 16 [R].
35. Arnold, Heinz Ludwig, 'Vom Ende eines Billardspielers', *Focus*, 19 March 1993 [R].
36. Baier, Lothar, 'Jenseits von Gewinn und Verlust', *Süddeutsche Zeitung*, 31 March 1993, L1–L2 [R].
37. Braun, Michael, 'Das Hein-Spiel: Christoph Heins Blick auf die zynische Vernunft', *Weltbühne*, 18 (1993), 557–9 [R].
38. Baumgart, Reinhard, 'Die Welt – ein Billardtisch', *Die Zeit*, 2 April 1993 [R].
39. Böhmel Fichera, Ulrike, 'Der Sieger: Christoph Heins *Das Napoleon-Spiel* (1993)', *Literatur für Leser*, (1995), 3, 130–6.
40. Böttiger, Helmut, 'Das Amoralische hat Hochkonjunktur', *Frankfurter Rundschau*, 3 April 1993 [R].
41. Cosentino, Christine, '"Die Gegensätze Übergänge": Ostdeutsche Autoren Anfang der neunziger Jahre', *The Germanic Review*, 69 (1994), 4, 146–55.
42. Dopatka, Dietlinde, 'Christoph Hein: *Das Napoleon-Spiel*', *Deutschunterricht*, 46 (1993), 10, 500–2 [R].
43. Ebel, Martin, 'Mord aus Langeweile', *Badische Zeitung*, 30 March 1993, 4 [R].
44. Fries, Fritz Rudolf, 'Das Feldherren-Syndrom', *neue deutsche literatur*, 41 (1993), 5, 137–9 [R].
45. Grack, Günther, 'Töten um nicht sterben zu müssen', *Tagesspiegel*, 28 March 1993 [R].
46. Grawe, Christian, 'Christoph Hein. *Das Napoleon-Spiel*', *World Literature Today*, 68 (1994), 3, 555–6 [R].

47. Grumbach, Detlef, 'Gruppenbild mit Mörder', *Deutsches Allgemeines Sonntagsblatt*, 9 April 1993 [R].
48. Hage, Volker, 'Glückliche Knechte', *Der Spiegel*, (1993), 15, 235–7. Reprinted in Franz Josef Görtz et al (eds.), *Deutsche Literatur 1993. Jahresüberblick* (Stuttgart, Reclam, 1994), 141–5 [R].
49. Hieber, Jochen, '*Das Napoleon-Spiel*: Ein Roman von Christoph Hein als Vorabdruck in der F.A.Z', *Frankfurter Allgemeine Zeitung*, 23 February 1993 [R].
50. Jansen, Hans, 'Der Mord des Billardspielers', *Westdeutsche Allgemeine Zeitung*, 26 June 1993 [R].
51. Kopka, Fritz-Jochen, 'Reicher Irrer: Christoph Heins Nachwende-Buch hat sich die Kritik sich anders vorgestellt', *Wochenpost*, 29 April 1993, 26 [R].
52. Krause, Tilman, 'Verfechter der Vielfalt', *Tagesspiegel*, 9 September 1997 [R].
53. Krauss, Hannes, 'Steigender Einsatz', *Freitag*, 9 April 1993 [R].
54. Kübler, Gunhild, 'Mord aus Langeweile', *Neue Zürcher Zeitung*, 8 June 1993 [R].
55. Leitner, Gerald, 'Buchtip', *Die Presse*, 7 June 1993 [R].
56. Miscke, Roland, 'Aufbruch zu neuen Ufern', *Saarbrücker Zeitung*, 24 April 1993 [R].
57. ——, 'Heftige Leidenschaft für das Risiko', *Mainzer Allgemeine Zeitung*, 24 April 1993 [R].
58. Nödelchen, Peter, 'Das Leben ist wie ein langes Match am Billardtisch', *Westfälische Rundschau*, 13 October 1993 [R].
59. Noll, Chaim, 'Lieber ein Verbrecher sein als ein Versager', *Die Welt*, 25 March 1993 [R].
60. Reich-Ranicki, Marcel, 'Der Billiardmörder', *Frankfurter Allgemeine Zeitung*, 10 April 1993 [R].
61. Rietzschel, Thomas, 'Doch die Verhältnisse, sie sind nicht so', *Die Presse*, 10 July 1993 [R].
62. Scheller, Wolf, 'Im Jammertal der Langeweile', *Handelsblatt*, 2/3 July 1993 [R].
63. Schmidt, Ricarda, '"The gender of thought": Recollection, imagination, and eroticism in fictional conceptions of East and West German identity', in Arthur Williams et al (eds.), *'Whose Story?' – Continuities in Contemporary German-language Literature* (Bern, Lang, 1998), 219–47.
64. Tate, Dennis, 'Trapped in the past? The identity problems of East German writers since the *Wende*', in H. J. Hahn (ed.), *Germany in the 1990s* [=*German Monitor*, 34] (Amsterdam, Rodopi, 1995), 1–16.
65. Tuschik, Jamal, 'Manipulation an der Reizschraube', *Rheinischer Merkur*, 9 April 1993 [R].
66. Vedofsky, Jürgen, 'Ein Roman ohne Effet', *Stuttgarter Zeitung*, 8 April 1993 [R].

On *Exekution eines Kalbes*
67. Borman, Alexander von, 'Christoph Hein: *Exekution eines Kalbes*', *Deutsche Bücher*, (1994), 2, 110–1 [R].
68. Doerry, Martin, 'Ein Leben mit der Lüge', *Der Spiegel*, 28 February 1994. Reprinted in Franz Josef Görtz et al (eds.), *Deutsche Literatur 1994. Jahresüberblick* (Stuttgart, Reclam, 1995), 159–63 [R].
69. Faber, Elmar, 'Nachwort', in Hein, *Die Vergewaltigung* (Leipzig, Faber & Faber, 1991).
70. Gutschke, Irmtraud, 'Die leidigen Gegebenheiten', *Neues Deutschland*, 15 March 1994 [R].
71. Gwosc, Detlev, 'Christoph Hein: *Exekution eines Kalbes*', *Deutsche Bücher* (1995), 1, 32–3 [R].
72. Isenschmid, Andreas, 'Nachrichten vom beschädigten Leben', *Die Zeit*, 18 March 1994 [R].
73. Leistner, Bernd, 'Heins neuer Prosaband', *neue deutsche literatur*, 42 (1994), 2, 155–8 [R].
74. Matt-Albrecht, Beatrice von, 'Spröd und meisterlich: Christoph Heins Erzählband *Exekution eines Kalbes*', *Neue Zürcher Zeitung*, 10 February 1994 [R].
75. Musik, Alexander, 'Gefangene des falschen Lebens', *die tageszeitung*, 20 May 1996 [R].
76. Reid, J. H., 'Christoph Hein, *Exekution eines Kalbes und andere Erzählungen*', in Philip Brady and Ian Wallace (eds.), *Prenzlauer Berg: Bohemia in the East?* (Amsterdam, Rodopi, 1995) [=*German Monitor*, 35], 142–3 [R].
77. Saab, Karim, 'Überschätzt und überfordert', *Märkische Allgemeine*, 28 January 1994. Reprinted in Franz Josef Görtz et al (eds.), *Deutsche Literatur 1994. Jahresüberblick* (Stuttgart, Reclam, 1995), 155–9 [R].
78. Seibt, Gustav, 'Krach in der Mastrinderbrigade', *Frankfurter Allgemeine Zeitung*, 19 February 1994 [R].
79. Zehl Romero, Christiane, 'In the shadow of the rainbow: On Christoph Hein's *Exekution eines Kalbes* and Christa Wolf's *Auf dem Weg nach Tabou*', in Margy Gerber and Roger Woods (eds.), *Changing Identities in East Germany: Selected Papers from the 19th and 20th New Hampshire Symposia* (Lanham, University Press of America, 1996), 63–86.

On *Von allem Anfang an*
80. Anonymous, 'Leuchtschrift am Kudamm', *Der Spiegel*, 25 August 1997, 178 [R].
81. ——, 'Christoph Hein: *Von allem Anfang an*', *Fachdienst Germanistik* (1997), 11, 16–17 [R].
82. Baier, Lothar, 'Nackte Brüste und die Partei der Bestimmer', *die tageszeitung*, 15 October 1997. Reprinted in Volker Hage et al (eds.), *Deutsche Literatur 1997. Jahresüberblick* (Stuttgart, Reclam, 1998), 134–7 [R].

83. Böttiger, Helmut, 'Die Aktualität der fünfziger Jahre', *Frankfurter Rundschau*, 20 December 1997 [R].
84. Drawert, Kurt, 'Von allem Anfang an – von allem Ende her', *Die Weltwoche*, 27 November 1997 [R].
85. Engler, Jürgen, 'Einladung zum Tee', *Neue Promenade*, 3 (1997), 3 [R].
86. Franke, Konrad, 'In Muttis warmem Zwischenreich', *Die Woche*, 26 September 1997, 43 [R].
87. Görner, Rüdiger, 'Lukas und die Artisten', *Die Presse*, 20 September 1997, 4 [R].
88. Grus, 'Protestantismus und Speiseeis', *Frankfurter Rundschau*, 8 December 1997 [R].
89. Gutschke, Irmtraud, 'Die grünen Augen des Evangelisten Lukas', *Neues Deutschland*, 2 September 1997 [R].
90. Hammer, Klaus, 'Wahrheit ohne Lüge', *neue deutsche literatur*, 45 (1997), 5, 168–70 [R].
91. Jacobs, Peter, 'Von der Bindungslosigkeit der Artistengruppe', *Die Welt*, 2 September 1997 [R].
92. Krushe, Friedemann, 'Meergrüner Erlöserblick', *Das Sonntagsblatt*, 17 October 1997 [R].
93. Langner, Beatrix, 'Kleine Schnitte in der Haut', *Beilage der Süddeutschen Zeitung*, 15 October 1997 [R].
94. Leipprand, Eva, 'Auf der Schwelle', *Stuttgarter Zeitung*, 15 October 1997 [R].
95. Matt, Peter von, 'Fort mit der Taschenguillotine', *Frankfurter Allgemeine Zeitung*, 14 October 1997 [R].
96. Muscheid, Michael, 'Über den Fall der Mauer hinaus', *Westdeutsche Allgemeine Zeitung*, 13 December 1997 [R].
97. Oberembt, Gert, 'Die Jahre vor der Mauer', *Rheinischer Merkur*, 5 September 1997 [R].
98. Opitz, Michael, 'Formen des Beginnens', *Freitag*, 10 October 1997, 'Literatur' [R].
99. Raddatz, Frtiz J., 'Besonnte Vergangenheit. Christoph Heins wenig nette Märchen', *Die Zeit*, 19 September 1997 [R].
100. Reinacher, Pia, 'Zurück im Revier der Kindheit', *Tagesanzeiger*, 13 October 1997 [R].
101. Scheller, Wolf, 'Mehltau des spießigen Alltags', *Rheinische Post*, 22 November 1997 [R].
102. ——, 'Die DDR der frühen Jahre', *Kölner-Stadt-Anzeiger*, 2 December 1997, 'Buchbeilage' [R].
103. Speicher, Stephan, 'Als man sich auf alles einrichtete, als man sich gegen alles wappnete', *Berliner Zeitung*, 20/21 September 1997 [R].
104. Steinert, Hajo, 'Nachrichten aus der DDR-Provinz', *Focus*, 10 November 1997, 190–1 [R].
105. Weinreich, Irma, 'Von allem Anfang an', *General-Anzeiger*, 25/26 October 1997 [R].

On *Der neue Menoza*
106. Berens, Cornelia, '"Das gegenwärtige Theater ist Schreibanlaß für Prosa"'. Christoph Hein und J.M.R. Lenz – vom Theater zur Prosa und zurück', in Inge Stephan and Hans-Gerd Winter (eds.), *'Unaufhörlich Lenz gelesen...': Studien zum Leben und Werk von J.M.R. Lenz* (Stuttgart, Metzler, 1994), 391–405.
107. Menke, Timm, 'The reception of Lenz in the final years of the German Democratic Republic: Christoph Hein's adaptation of *Der neue Menoza*', in Alan C. Leidner and Helga S. Madland (eds.), *The Space to Act: The Theater of J.M.R. Lenz* (Columbia, Camden House, 1993), 150–61.

On *Die wahre Geschichte des Ah Q*
108. Hoefert, Sigfrid, 'Zum China-Bild in der DDR-Literatur: Volker Braun, Christoph Hein und Stephan Hermlin', in Adrian Hsia and Sigfrid Hoefert (eds.), *Fernöstliche Brückenschläge* (Bern, Lang, 1992), 189–98.
109. Iwabuchi, Tatsuji, 'Die Dramatisierung der "wahren Geschichte des Ah Q" von Lu Xun in Deutschland und Japan', *Zeitschrift für Germanistik*, 5 (1995), 5, 391–5.

On *Passage*
110. Böhmel Fichera, Ulrike, 'Geschichte findet in der Jetztzeit statt – Exilerlebnis in Christoph Heins Kammerspiel *Passage*', in Dieter Sevin (ed.), *Resonanz des Exils: Gelungene und mißlungene Rezeption deutschsprachiger Exilautoren* (Amsterdam, Rodopi, 1992), 313–25.
111. Cambi, Fabrizio, 'Benjamins *Passagen-Werk* und das Kammerspiel *Passage* von Christoph Hein: ein Beispiel von Wirklichkeitserfindung und Zeitgeschichte', *Jura Soyfer*, 2 (1994), 7–9.

On *Die Ritter der Tafelrunde*
112. Baudrier, Andree Jeanne, 'Deux representations de Lancelot', in Danielle Buschinger and Michel Fink (eds.), *Lancelot-Lanzelet hier et aujourd'hui* (Greifswald, Reineke, 1995), 1–5.
113. Fichte, Jörg O., 'The treatment of Arthur and his court in contemporary German drama', in Piero Boitani and Anna Torti (eds.), *Mediaevalitas: Reading the Middle Ages* (Cambridge, Brewer, 1996), 153–69.
114. Joschko, Dirk, 'Christoph Heins *Die Ritter der Tafelrunde* oder: Grals-Suche zwichen Auf- und Abbruch', in Irene Burg et al (eds.), *Mittelalter-Rezeption IV: Medien, Politik, Ideologie, Ökonomie* (Göppingen, Kümmerle, 1991), 525–41.
115. Krohn, Rüdiger, 'Der "gefährliche Stuhl". Wandlungen des Mythos in den Artus-Stücken von Tankred Dorst und Christoph Hein', in

Krohn (ed.), *Materialien und Beiträge zur Mittelalter-Rezeption* (Göppingen, Kümmerle, 1992), 232–50.
116. Maas, Paul, 'Gral und Tafelsrunde bei Christoph Hein und Adolf Muschg', *Germanistik Luxembourg*, 13 (1998), 117–29.
117. McClintick, Christopher, 'Reimagining Parzifal: contemporary forms of a quest for ontological and cultural meaning', in Jorg Roche and Thomas Salumets (eds.), *Germanics under Construction: Intercultural and Interdisciplinary Prospects* (Munich, iudicium, 1996), 143–56.
118. McKnight, Phillip, 'Iphigenia, King Arthur and the East German state after unification', *Contemporary Theatre Review*, 4 (1995), 2, 197–206.
119. Müller, Ulrich, 'Gral '89: Mittelalter, moderne Hermetik und die neue Politik der Perestroika. Zu den Parzifal/Gral-Dramen von Peter Handke und Christoph Hein', in Irene Burg et al (eds.), *Mittelalter-Rezeption IV: Medien, Politik, Ideologie, Ökonomie* (Göppingen, Kümmerle, 1991), 495–520.
120. Niven, Bill, 'A play about socialism? The reception of Christoph Hein's *Die Ritter der Tafelrunde*', in Arthur Williams et al (eds.), *'Whose Story?' – Continuities in Contemporary German-language Literature* (Bern, Lang, 1998), 197–218.
121. Onderdekinden, Sjaak, 'Ritter von der traurigen Gestalt: Christoph Heins "Tafelrunde"', in *"Der muoz min süezer worte jehen": liber amoricum für Norbert Vorrwinden* (Amsterdam, Rodopi, 1997), 175–91.
122. Raitz, Walter, 'Grals Ende? Zur Rezeption des Parzival/Gral-Stoffes bei Tankred Dorst, Christoph Hein, Peter Handke und Adolf Muschg', in Silvia Bovenschen et al (eds.), *Der fremdgewordene Text. Festschrift für Helmut Brackert zum 65. Geburtstag* (Berlin, de Gruyter, 1997), 320–33.
123. Schoffrey, Andreas, 'Die Ritter der Tafelrunde oder der Weg ist das Ziel: Christoph Hein und die Rezeption des mittelalterlichen Stoffs', in Ulrich Müller and Kathleen Verduin (eds.), *Gesammelte Vorträge des V. Salzburger Symposiums (Burg Kaprun 1990) = Papers from the Fifth Annual General Conference on Medievalism 1990* (Göppingen, Kümmerle, 1996), 493–510.
124. Stillmark, Hans-Christian, 'Gebrochene und verworfene Utopien: Christoph Heins *Die Ritter der Tafelrunde* und Tankred Dorsts *Merlin*', *Mitteilungen des Deutschen Germanistenverbandes*, 45 (1998), 1/2, 84–93.

On *Randow*

125. Block, Simona, 'Der Schrecken nach der Wende', *Westfälische Rundschau*, 23 December 1994.
126. ———, '"Es war einmal wieder Zeit"', *General-Anzeiger*, 29 December 1994.
127. Dieckmann, Friedrich, 'Große und kleine Gier', *Frankfurter Allgemeine Zeitung*, 23 December 1994 [R].
128. Engler, Wolfgang, 'Froschs Ende', *Die Zeit*, 30 December 1994 [R].

129. Hammerschmidt, Ulrich, 'Im deutschen Seelengrund', *Theater heute*, (1995), 2, 15 [R].
130. Hammerthaler, Ralph, 'Ein Zeitstück nach der Wende', *Süddeutsche Zeitung*, 28 December 1998 [R].
131. Kaiser, Christoph, 'Heins deutscher Alltag', *Ruhr Nachrichten*, 23 December 1994 [R].
132. Klunker, Heinz, 'Gegenwart hat Zukunft', *Deutsches Allgemeines Sonntagsblatt*, 23 December 1994 [R].
133. Kranz, Dieter, 'West-Waidmann auf Ost-Pirsch', *Frankfurter Rundschau*, 30 December 1994 [R].
134. Krug, Hartmut, 'Wessis mit Elan und Ossis ohne Visionen', *Badische Zeitung*, 28 December 1994 [R].
135. Lennartz, Knut, 'Er ist wieder da', *Die Deutsche Bühne*, 2 (1995), 36–7 [R].
136. Magenau, Jörg, 'Hunger auf Hoffnung', *Freitag*, 6 January 1995 [R].
137. Platzeck, Wolfgang, 'Bilder aus Deutschland', *Westdeutsche Allgemeine Zeitung*, 31 May 1995 [R].
138. Schuhmacher, 'Ostwestdeutscher Zerrspiegel', *Berliner Zeitung*, 23 December 1994 [R].
139. Schulze-Reimpell, Werner, 'Jagdszenen aus dem Oderbruch', *Rheinischer Merkur*, 30 December 1994 [R].
140. ——, 'Jagdszenen aus dem Osten', *Stuttgarter Zeitung*, 30 December 1994 [R].
141. Schulz-Ojala, Jan, 'Biederfrau und die Brandstifter', *Tagesspiegel*, 23 December 1994 [R].
142. Walther, Peter, 'Mutter heißt jetzt Mum', *die tageszeitung*, 15/16 April 1995 [R].
143. Wehdeking, Volker, *Die deutsche Einheit und die Schriftsteller: Literarische Verarbeitung der Wende seit 1989* (Stuttgart, Kohlhammer, 1995), 147–66.
144. Wengiereck, Reinhardt, 'Wenn das Theater der Zeitung nachläuft', *Die Welt*, 23 December 1994 [R].
145. Zimmermann, Stephan, 'Zwischen Angst und Hingabe', *Neue Zürcher Zeitung* (Fernausgabe), 25/26 December 1994 [R]

On *Bruch*
146. Berke, Bernd, 'Christoph Heins *Bruch*: Der Chirurg als Schatten seiner selbst', *Westfälische Rundschau*, 3 March 1999 [R].
147. Bohnet, Anne, 'Von Genialität bis Krankheit', *Rheinische Post*, 26 February 1999 [R].
148. Deuter, Ulrich, 'Die Tragikomödie der Senilität', *Tages-Anzeiger*, 1 March 1999 [R].
149. ——, 'Verbeult vom Leben', *Tagesspiegel*, 1 March 1999 [R].
150. ——, 'Beulen von der Wirklichkeit', *Stuttgarter Zeitung*, 4 March 1999 [R].

151. Friedrich, Detlev, 'Ärzte für Könige', *Berliner Zeitung*, 2 March 1999 [R].
152. Hartmann, Rainer, 'Dem alten Chirurgen zittern die Hände', *Kölner Stadt-Anzeiger*, 2 March 1999 [R].
153. Heine, Matthias, 'Dr. Sauerbruch bittet zur letzten Operation', *Die Welt*, 1 March 1999 [R].
154. ——, 'Hausbackene Schlichtheit ist das falsche Rezept', *Saarbrücker Zeitung*, 23 March 1999.
155. Jansen, Hans, 'Aus der Zeit gefallen', *Westdeutsche Allgemeine Zeitung*, 2 March 1999 [R].
156. Kill, Reinhard, 'Wenn die Klinik den Chef nicht ruft', *Rheinische Post*, 1 March 1999 [R].
157. Krumbholz, Martin, 'Tragödie eines lächerlichen Mannes', *Theater heute* (1999), 4, 50–2 [R].
158. Löhndorf, Marion, 'Leben in der Illusion des alten Glanzes', *General-Anzeiger*, 2 March 1999 [R].
159. ——, 'Sinnbilder der Stagnation', *Neuer Zürcher Zeitung*, 2 March 1999, 34 [R].
160. Rossmann, Andreas, 'Chef ist, wer über die Anredeform verfügt', *Frankfurter Allgemeine Zeitung*, 1 March 1999 [R].
161. Schreiber, 'Saure Kutteln', *Frankfurter Rundschau*, 2 March 1999 [R].
162. ——, 'Bruchlandung', *Handelsblatt*, 5/6 March 1999 [R].
163. Schulze-Reimpell, Werner, 'Arzt mit Hausverbot', *Rheinischer Merkur*, 5 March 1999 [R].
164. Tiedemann, Kathrin, 'Die Macht der kranken, alten Männer', *Freitag*, 5 March 1999 [R].

On *In Acht und Bann*
165. Delekat, Thomas, 'Triumph des ostdeutschen Theaters', *Die Welt*, 3 May 1999 [R].
166. Friedrich, Detlev, 'Das Politbüro tagt, die BRD liegt im Koma. Zwei Uraufführungen in Weimar, zwei Mauerfallstücke. Resümee: Die Lage ist hoffnungslos', *Berliner Zeitung*, 3 May 1999 [R].
167. Funke, Christoph, 'Goldene Rüstung leer', *Neue Zürcher Zeitung*, 3 May 1999 [R].
168. Grundmann, Ute, 'Trotzige Kinder und röchelnde Patienten', *Rheinische Post*, 4 May 1999 [R].
169. Rossmann, Andreas, 'Siegfried und Sieglinde', *Frankfurter Allgemeine Zeitung*, 3 May 1999 [R].
170. Schulz-Ojala, Jan, 'Kasper im Kartoffelfeld', *Tagesspiegel*, 2 May 1999 [R].
171. Thieringer, Thomas, 'Deutsche Akte mit Siegfried und Sieglinde', *Süddeutsche Zeitung*, 1 May 1999 [R].

On *Öffentlich arbeiten*
172. Fix, Ulla, 'Schriftsteller über Sprache: Sprach- und Kommunikationskultur oder: Mit dem Pfunde wuchern', *Sprachpflege und Sprachkultur: Zeitschrift für Gutes Deutsch* (New York), 39 (1990), 1, 5–8.
173. Jucker, Rolf, 'Zeitgenössische Literatur und die Forderung nach Neuheit. Überlegungen im Ausgang von Christoph Heins Text "Lorbeerwald und Kartoffelacker"', in Herbert Herzmann (ed.), *Literaturkritik und erzählende Praxis: deutschsprachige Erzähler der Gegenwart; Tagungsakten des internationalen Symposiums University College Dublin, 14.–16. Februar 1993* (Tübingen, Stauffenburg, 1995), 49–59.

On *Die fünfte Grundrechenart*
174. Graves, Peter, 'Sorcerers' apprentices', *TLS*, 15–21 June 1990, 131 [R].

On *Die Mauern von Jerichow*
175. Buch, Hans Christoph, 'Offener Brief an Christoph Hein', *die tageszeitung*, 8 January 1992. Extract reprinted in Franz Josef Görtz et al (eds.), *Deutsche Literatur 1992. Jahresüberblick* (Stuttgart, Reclam, 1993), 21–2.
176. Gwosc, Detlev, 'Christoph Hein: *Die Mauern von Jerichow*. Essais und Reden', *Deutsche Bücher* (1997), 1, 26–7 [R].

2.c Miscellaneous
1. AP, 'Vereinigung perfekt', *Westfälische Rundschau*, 31 October 1998.
2. Arend, Ingo, 'Kunststückchen', *Freitag*, 6 November 1998.
3. Bisky, Jens, 'Lieblos begann das Geschäft', *Berliner Zeitung*, 2 November 1998.
4. Dieckmann, Christoph, 'Der Chronist wird König', 5 November 1998, 2.
5. dpa, 'Gaus und Hein werden *Freitag*-Herausgeber', *Tagesspiegel*, 17 March 1992.
6. ——, 'Christoph Hein über Christa Wolf', *Tagesspiegel*, 2 February 1993.
7. ——, 'Hein: "Wolf-Biographie hat radikale Brüche"', *Süddeutsche Zeitung*, 3 February 1993.
8. ——, 'Hein und Christa Wolf zu den Stasi-Vorwürfen', *Saarbrücker Zeitung*, 1 February 1993.
9. ——, 'Christoph Hein Favorit auf den PEN-Vorsitz', *Westfälische Rundschau*, 27 October 1998.
10. ——, '"Da sind alle sehr zufrieden". Christoph Hein erste Wahl für PEN-Präsidentschaft', *General-Anzeiger*, 27 October 1998.
11. ——, '"Das Mißtrauen war auf beiden Seiten". Zusammenschluß der Autorenverbände: Christoph Hein Präsident des geeinten deutschen PEN', *General-Anzeiger*, 31 October 1998.
12. ——, 'Große Mehrheit für Hein', *Ruhr Nachrichten*, 31 October 1998.

Bibliography 163

13. DW, 'Der neue Präsident: Ein gefragter Vermittler', *Die Welt*, 31 October 1998.
14. Eger, Christian, 'Erster Ritter der Pen-Tafelrunde', *Mitteldeutsche Zeitung*, 31 October 1998.
15. Fuchs, Karen, 'Gequälte und Hoffende', *Tagesspiegel*, 1 November 1998.
16. Geissler, Cornelia, 'Die Politik der kleinen Nadelstiche', 14/15 November 1998, 11.
17. Gutschke, Irmtraud, 'Unbeirrbar', *Neues Deutschland*, 31 October 1998.
18. ——, 'Wenn der Sturm sich legt', *Neues Deutschland*, 2 November 1998.
19. Husemann, Ralf, 'Aus der grauen terra incognita: Christoph Hein in der Vortragsreihe "Zur Sache Deutschlands" in Dresden', *Süddeutsche Zeitung*, 11 February 1992.
20. Ignée, Wolfgang, 'Von Mauer und Wende. Das nimmt kein Ende: Christoph Hein liest in Stuttgart', *Stuttgarter Zeitung*, 4 March 1996.
21. jus, 'Plaudern auf Plastiksesseln. Kritisch gesehen: Christoph Hein im Gespräch', *Stuttgarter Zeitung*, 10 August 1996.
22. Magenau, Jörg, 'Von der Oder bis zur Saar', *die tageszeitung*, 2 November 1998.
23. Marschall, Christoph, 'Eine Begegnung mit dem Tod', *Tagesspiegel*, 7 March 1992.
24. Mommert, Wilfried, 'Gefragter und stiller Vermittler', *Der neue Tag*, 31 October 1998.
25. Oehlen, Martin, '"Aufbau" und die "Plus-Auflage" Minus', *Kölner Stadt-Anzeiger*, 12/13 October 1993.
26. Platzeck, Wolfgang, 'Zwischen Ost und West', *Westdeutsche Allgemeine Zeitung*, 31 October 1998.
27. rtr, 'Christoph Hein führt gesamtdeutschen PEN', 31 October 1998.
28. Scheller, Wolf, 'Der PEN in Dresden. Die Probleme sind noch nicht gelöst', *Stuttgarter Zeitung*, 31 October 1998.
29. Schmitz, Helmut, 'Der Widerspenstigen Zähmung', *Frankfurter Rundschau*, 2 November 1998.
30. Schmitz, Sonja, 'Vollbad im Drachenblut', *Rheinische Post*, 22 March 1999.
31. Schröder, Lothar, 'Arbeit für Artus', *Rheinische Post*, 31 October 1998.
32. Schwenger, Hannes, 'Der Mann der Einigung', *Tagesspiegel*, 31 October 1998.
33. Seibt, Gustav, 'Arno Schmidt, ein westdeutscher Befreier', *Berliner Zeitung*, 15 October 1997.
34. Stadler, Siegfried, 'Von der Oder bis zur Saar', *Frankfurter Rundschau*, 2 November 1998.
35. Stolper, Arnim, 'Heins Märchen: Zu einer Äußerung über die Brecht-Rezeption in den Theatern der DDR' (Leserbrief), *Neues Deutschland*, 30 January 1998.
36. Tolksdorf, Stephan, 'Das falsche Gewicht', *Badische Zeitung*, 27 November 1997.

37. Tsp, 'Der Schriftsteller Christoph Hein legt Wert...', *Tagesspiegel*, 26 March 1992.
38. Warnhold, Birgit, 'Das Beschlossene noch einmal beschlossen: Dichter endlich vereint', *Berliner Morgenpost*, 31 October 1998, 3.
39. TK, 'Hein für President', *Die Welt*, 29 October 1998.
40. Wendland, Johannes, 'Die Stunde der Landvermesser', *Deutsches Allgemeines Sonntagsblatt*, 6 November 1998.
41. wsh/dpa, 'Schriftsteller vereint nach 47 Jahren. Christoph Hein wird zum Präsidenten gewählt', 1 November 1998, 37.

Index

Akademie der Künste 10, 12
Als Kind habe ich Stalin gesehen
  12, 43, 58, 62, 65, 82
Angelou, Maya
  I Know why the Caged Bird Sings 74

Basic Law 105
Beckett, Samuel 52
Benjamin, Walter 53–4, 59
  Über den Begriff der Geschichte 54
Besson, Benno 9
Bismarck, Otto von 49
Brecht, Bertolt 41
Bridge Freezes before Roadway 12
Bruch 13
Büchner, Georg 5

Callisto 77
Caspar, Günter 25–6
Commedia dell'arte 51
Cromwell 10, 46–8, 101
Chekhov, Anton 51

Daphne 77
Das Napoleon-Spiel 12, 15, 24, 45–6, 64, 78, 83–4, 90–7, 99, 119–20
Das Wildpferd unterm Kachelofen 11, 85–6
de Bruyn, Günter
  Das erzählte Ich. Über Wahrheit und Dichtung in der Autobiographie 133
  Vierzig Jahre 118
  Zwischenbilanz 118, 133
Der fremde Freund (Drachenblut) 10, 11, 16, 22–3, 43–5, 52, 64, 68–79, 83, 86–7, 98, 104, 110, 117, 119

Der neue Menoza oder Geschichte des Kumbanischen Prinzen Tandi 10
Der Tangospieler 11, 12, 22–3, 44–5, 64, 73, 76–8, 87–8, 104, 119
Dieckmann, Friedrich 106
Die fünfte Grundrechenart 12
Die Geschäfte des Herrn John D. 10
Die Mauern von Jerichow 89–90
Die Ritter der Tafelrunde 11–13, 47, 55–8, 100–4, 110, 114
'Die Vergewaltigung' 62, 65–8, 75–6, 79
Die wahre Geschichte des Ah Q 10–11, 50–3, 66–7, 76, 101
Dürrenmatt, Friedrich
  Der Richter und sein Henker 91, 99
  Justiz 91–3, 97, 99

Einladung zum Lever Bourgeois 10, 66, 74
'Ein sächsischer Tartüff' 76
Engels, Friedrich 98
Exekution eines Kalbes 12, 73

Fallada, Hans 25
Fischer, Samuel 25
Fleißer, Marieluise 1
  Fegefeuer in Ingolstadt 1–2
Fontane, Theodor 3, 6
Freie Deutsche Jugend 129
Fried, Erich 12
Frisch, Max 12

Görne, Dieter 100
Goethe, Johann Wolfgang von 2–3, 5
  Dichtung und Wahrheit 133
Graf, Roland 12

Grams, Wolfgang 7
Gröschner, Annett
  'Maria im Schnee' 64
Gulf War 12

Habermas, Jürgen 90
Hacks, Peter 10
Hardy, Thomas
  Tess of the d'Urbervilles 63, 77
Hartmannbund 108, 115–6
Havel, Vaclàv 11
Hebel, Johann Peter 65
Heimann, Moritz 25
Heine, Heinrich 3, 12
Hemingway, Ernest 15
Hesse, Hermann 95
  Das Glasperlenspiel 91
Hessel, Franz 26
Heym, Stefan
  Nachruf 118
Heyme, Hansgünther 55
Hilbig, Wolfgang
  'Ich' 118
Honecker, Erich 47, 55
Horns Ende 11, 45–6, 64, 67–9, 73–8, 87, 104, 119–22

In Acht und Bann 13

Jameson, Frederic 97
Johnson, Uwe 39
  Ingrid Babendererde 130
Junge Gemeinde 130

Kafka, Franz 15
Kant, Hermann
  Abspann 118
Kesten, Hermann 26
Kirst, Klaus Dieter 55, 100
Kleist, Heinrich von 1–8, 65–6, 90
  Der Prinz von Homburg 1–3
  Die Marquise von O... 63, 65
  Michael Kohlhaas 2–8
Kunert, Günter
  Erwachsenenspiele 118

Lang, Alexander 52
Lassalle fragt Herrn Herbert nach Sonja 10, 48–50
Lenz, Jakob Michael Reinhold 10, 51
Loerke, Oskar 26
Luther, Martin 5, 7–8
Lyotard, Jean-François 96–7, 99

Marx, Karl 49, 98
Mayer, Hans 12
Ministry of Culture (GDR) 9
Modrow, Hans 11
Morgner, Irmtraud 80
Müller, Heiner
  Krieg ohne Schlacht 118
Musil, Robert
  Die Verwirrungen des Zöglings Törless 123, 129

Nabokov, Vladimir 95
  The Defence 91
Nachtfahrt und früher Morgen 10
NATO 13

Öffentlich arbeiten 11, 42, 49, 57, 84, 87–9
Oppenheimer, Robert 20
Ovid 77

Pascal, Blaise 84
Passage 11, 53–5, 84–6, 100
PDS 101
PEN centre 11, 13, 132
Persephone 77
Philomela 74

Racine, Jean
  Britannicus (tr. Hein) 10
Randow 12, 19–20, 58–9, 100–14, 117
Reich, Jens 22
Reich-Ranicki, Marcel 24
Rote-Armee-Fraktion 6

Schengen Agreement 20–1
Schlesinger, Klaus 119
  Die Sache mit Randow 119
  Fliegender Wechsel. Eine persönliche Chronik 119
Schlötel oder Was solls 10, 11
Schriftstellerverband (GDR) 10–12
Schubert, Peter 100
Schweiger, Peter 52
SED 11, 86–7, 90, 101, 106, 126, 129, 132
Siefert, Peter 56–7
Sloterdijk, Peter
  Kritik der zynischen Vernunft 89
Stalin, Josef 47
Stasi 10, 58, 101, 106–8, 112–13, 118
Stötzer-Kachold, Gabriele 80

Tereus 74
Thälmannpioniere 129–30
Tucholsky, Kurt 29
Vom hungrigen Hennecke 10
Von allem Anfang an 13, 14–15, 22–3, 27–40, 64, 74, 78, 117–32
'Waldbruder Lenz' 41
Wedekind, Frank
  Frühlings Erwachen 123
Weiss, Peter 13, 59
Wolf, Christa 82
  Auf dem Weg nach Tabou 80
  Kindheitsmuster 64, 75, 80

Zaungäste 13
Zeus 77
Zweig, Stefan 95
  Schachnovelle 91
Zwischen Hund und Wolf 52